MW01005612

NEW DEAL RUINS

NEW DEAL RUINS

Race, Economic Justice, and
Public Housing Policy

Edward G. Goetz

CORNELL UNIVERSITY PRESS   **ITHACA AND LONDON**

Copyright © 2013 by Cornell University

All rights reserved. Except for brief quotations in a review, this book, or parts
thereof, must not be reproduced in any form without permission in writing from
the publisher. For information, address Cornell University Press, Sage House,
512 East State Street, Ithaca, New York 14850.

First published 2013 by Cornell University Press
First printing, Cornell Paperbacks, 2013
Printed in the United States of America

Library of Congress Cataloging-in-Publication Data

Goetz, Edward G. (Edward Glenn), 1957–
    New Deal ruins : race, economic justice, and public housing policy / Edward
G. Goetz.
        p. cm.
    Includes bibliographical references and index.
    ISBN 978-0-8014-5152-2 (cloth : alk. paper)
    ISBN 978-0-8014-7828-4 (pbk. : alk. paper)
    1. Public housing—Government policy—United States.   2. Housing policy—
United States.   3. Relocation (Housing)—United States.   4. Urban policy—
United States. I. Title.
    HD7288.78.U5G64   2013
    363.5'5610973—dc23   2012038085

Cornell University Press strives to use environmentally responsible suppliers
and materials to the fullest extent possible in the publishing of its books. Such
materials include vegetable-based, low-VOC inks and acid-free papers that are
recycled, totally chlorine-free, or partly composed of nonwood fibers. For further
information, visit our website at www.cornellpress.cornell.edu.

Cloth printing   10 9 8 7 6 5 4 3 2 1
Paperback printing   10 9 8 7 6 5 4 3 2 1

For Susan, Hanne, Mary, and Greta

Contents

Preface   ix

List of Abbreviations   xiii

Introduction: Public Housing and Urban
Planning Orthodoxy   1

1. The Quiet Successes and Loud Failures of Public Housing   24

2. Dismantling Public Housing   48

3. Demolition in Chicago, New Orleans, and Atlanta   75

4. "Negro Removal" Revisited   111

5. The Fate of Displaced Persons and Families   123

6. Effects and Prospects in Revitalized Communities   155

Conclusion: The Future of Public Housing   175

Appendix   191

Notes   195

References   215

Index   235

Preface

I have been researching public housing transformation for close to fifteen years now. The work began broadly as an analysis of policy initiatives being implemented in many cities to deconcentrate poverty that led to publication of *Clearing the Way: Deconcentrating the Poor in Urban America* in 2003. In this current book I focus on only one element of deconcentration policy, the dismantling of old public housing communities and their frequent (but not inevitable) replacement by mixed-income developments. Thus the book has in many ways a more narrowly constructed focus. In other respects, however, the dismantling of public housing has very broad implications and represents a shift in policy that is more notable than that of deconcentration. The radical remaking of public housing is an important watershed moment in American domestic policy. An entire policy landscape and urban landscape are being remade. The dismantling of public housing represents the repudiation of a New Deal policy orientation that saw merit in large-scale government social interventions, and that reflected faith that such interventions could produce positive outcomes. It reverses seventy years of social policy in the United States and reflects a fundamental reorientation of urban social policy. The new urban landscape will reflect the new policy environment that privileges market initiatives and reduces the reach of state intervention. This book attempts to provide some perspective on this epoch-changing initiative.

My study makes use of original data analysis and a synthesis of dozens of other studies of public housing displacement and relocation that have been conducted across the country. The main dataset I have assembled to analyze this question has been created from various sources, including three separate Freedom of Information Act (FOIA) requests made of the Department of Housing and Urban Development (HUD) between 2004 and 2007. These data provide the opportunity to analyze public housing transformation in ways that are completely unique. Large portions of chapters 2 and 4 are based on a quantitative analysis of the HUD demolition data. The more technical matters associated with the quantitative analysis, including the specification of the model and description of variables, are contained in the appendix. In the body of the book I present enough of a description of the analysis to allow all readers to follow the logic of the analysis and to understand the findings.

About five years ago I created a "Google Alert" for myself using the terms "public housing" and "demolition." Each time those terms appear in a searchable document I am notified by e-mail. As a result I have been reading news accounts and opinion pieces related to public housing demolition in cities across the country more or less in real time, as they have occurred. Three things have struck me about what I have been reading over the past years. The first is the sheer volume of articles that have crossed my desktop. It is a rare day when one or two articles do not pop up in my e-mail basket. The movement to dismantle public housing is truly nationwide, and is taking place in communities such as Rome, Georgia, Danville, Illinois, and Waterbury, Connecticut, as well as in Chicago, Atlanta, and Philadelphia. The volume of stories is sometimes difficult to keep up with. Also noticeable about the movement to dismantle public housing is the similarity of the issues being debated from place to place. They include the general optimism of local officials about improving the neighborhoods containing public housing, and the terms used by local officials to describe the housing they intend to demolish. The public housing is often referred to, by officials or by reporters, in terms that suggest it is obsolete, even anachronistic, and often neglected or run-down. In the book I argue that there is a discourse of disaster about public housing in the United States. Typically this discourse emphasizes social pathologies such as crime, violence, family breakdown, and drugs. But the storyline also includes milder references to the obsolescence of public housing and a sense that it is unfit for further habitation in most places. Another issue that surfaces in many accounts of public housing demolition is the concern about the loss of affordable housing in the city that will result. Almost invariably in these accounts, advocates or residents, or sometimes the reporter, will raise the issue of how the loss of these units will affect the availability of low-cost housing locally. Finally, the stories of public housing demolition across the country almost without exception show the mixed responses of residents, some of whom are glad to see the change and many of whom complain about their communities being torn apart. Some will look with anticipation to the day they can move out while others talk about their community as a decent place to live, and one that they will miss. There is often a fear of what lies ahead among those concerned about losing their homes. I have tried to explore these themes and more in this book, drawing from a wide range of examples from cities and towns across the country.

The third characteristic of these online stories of public housing demolition that has struck me is the number of stories that originate in Canada, Australia, and elsewhere. I have often been two-thirds of the way through an article before realizing that I was reading about public housing demolition in an Australian city or a Canadian town. What I know about public housing demolition in those countries is largely limited to the accounts I have come across in this fashion but the similarities with the U.S. situation are striking and deserve greater attention.

I have benefitted greatly by assistance and encouragement of many people along the way. Karen Chapple has helped me think through and develop an understanding of why dispersal programs have produced so few benefits for low-income persons. Janet Smith, Larry Bennett, Derek Hyra, David Imbroscio, and Susan Greenbaum have provided feedback and encouragement on this and other projects. Hoang Ton helped with the data collection for this project and Jeff Matson made the maps. My colleagues at Minnesota, including Yingling Fan and Ryan Allen, provided comments on methods and early findings. Michael Rich made extremely helpful suggestions for the case-study chapter. Bill Wilen steered me to the issues and legal cases related to de facto demolition. Laura Harris and I have tried to organize a group of scholars doing HOPE VI research. The group exists as a loosely connected band of researchers, hoping that at some point something larger than merely the sum of our individual work will emerge. HUD, to date, has not been altogether encouraging of this effort, though they have done nothing to discourage our collaboration.

Portions of the book have appeared in earlier published work. Material on the HOPE VI project in Duluth, Minnesota first appeared in "Better Neighborhoods, Better Outcomes? Explaining Relocation Outcomes in HOPE VI," *Cityscape* 12, 1 (2010): 5–31. I would like to thank the editors for vetting that work. I also thank Taylor and Francis, publishers of *Housing Policy Debate* and *Housing Studies*, for permission to reuse material that appeared in "'You Gotta Move': Advancing the Debate on the Record of Dispersal," co-authored with Karen Chapple, *Housing Policy Debate* 20, 2 (2010): 1–28, and "Desegregation in 3D: Displacement, Dispersal, and Development in American Public Housing," *Housing Studies* 25, 2 (2010): 137–58. Sage Publications kindly granted permission to reuse material from "Gentrification in Black and White: The Racial Impact of Public Housing Demolition in American Cities," *Urban Studies* 48, 8 (2011): 1581–1604. Finally, John Wiley & Sons provided permission to reuse material from "Where Have All the Towers Gone? The Dismantling of Public Housing in U.S. Cities," *Journal of Urban Affairs* 33, 3 (2011): 267–87.

Abbreviations

AHA	Atlanta Housing Authority
CHA	Chicago Housing Authority
CNI	Choice Neighborhoods Initiative
CPPH	Coalition to Protect Public Housing
DCHA	District of Columbia Housing Authority
DHA	Duluth Housing Authority
HANO	Housing Authority of New Orleans
HUD	United States Department of Housing and Urban Development
LIHTC	Low-Income Housing Tax Credit
MROP	Major Reconstruction of Obsolete Projects
MTO	Moving to Opportunity
NAREB	National Association of Real Estate Boards
NCSDPH	National Commission on Severely Distressed Public Housing
NHLP	National Housing Law Project
PFT	Plan for Transformation
PHA	public housing authority
PWA	Public Works Administration
URD	Urban Revitalization Demonstration
USHA	United States Housing Authority

NEW DEAL RUINS

Introduction

PUBLIC HOUSING AND URBAN PLANNING ORTHODOXY

The local housing authority of the future must be a locally focused, opportunity seeking, full service real estate development and holding company, developing and managing the value of its investments for the good of the community.

—Richard C. Gentry, former director of the San Diego Housing Commission

It is a measure of the degree to which public housing is a policy of the past that there is a Museum of Public Housing in Chicago. Furthermore, there is some irony that the museum should be located in that city in particular, for those who ran public housing in Chicago and those who were responsible for it failed miserably. In fact, they failed catastrophically and almost willfully—but that story has been told.[1] The fact is that public housing came to ruin in Chicago. The great New Deal enterprise to provide decent, stable housing for the lower-income and working classes was gradually destroyed through mismanagement, underfunding, poor design, and civic neglect. And so one wonders why, of all places, a museum of public housing would surface there.

Perhaps the intention was to erect an enduring reminder of the dangers of overzealous social engineering or the limits of the welfare state, to enshrine public housing forever as the *Titanic* of American social policy, launched with great hubris but sunk at the cost of so many lives.

On the other hand, Chicago could be seen as the perfect location for such a museum. Deverra Beverly, a lifelong resident of the ABLA public housing project on the West Side of Chicago, and her neighbor, Beatrice Jones, looked around their community in the 1990s and saw the Chicago Housing Authority poised to "transform" public housing in that city by demolishing virtually all of it, scattering the residents, and rebuilding new communities that would mix market-rate housing with a drastically reduced number of public housing units.[2] Beverly and Jones want the museum to commemorate those who lived

1

in Chicago public housing: "We want to leave something so our children or grandchildren will know we were here…that we existed as a community."[3] In that sense, then, no place is more appropriate for the museum than Chicago, for nowhere has the early promise of public housing disappeared so dramatically and so completely. It stands as a memorial to the lives of low-income residents who claimed these places as home, and who created community under the most difficult circumstances.

Although the discourse of disaster dominates discussions of public housing, the reality is that in most places it worked—and still does work. Even the congressional commission formed in the late 1980s to investigate what was called "severely distressed public housing" noted in its 1992 report that "approximately 94 percent of the units are not in such a state; thus, the public housing program continues to provide an important rental housing resource for many low-income families and others."[4] This reality, applying as it does to so much public housing, is at odds with perceptions of the program fueled by popular press accounts of the worst public housing in our largest cities. Indeed, even in those cities, and in those specific projects that have manifestly failed to provide decent and safe housing for its inhabitants, there are contradictory experiences and more complexity than suggested by the disaster narrative. Deverra Beverly lived at the epicenter of public housing dysfunction and yet still celebrates the community that she and others built. Beatrice Harris, another Chicagoan and resident of Wentworth Gardens public housing, told researchers in the 1990s, "This is our community. This is our home.…And I'm telling, ain't nobody puttin' me out.…I love this place, you hear me! I love this place."[5] But public housing residents *are* being put out. More than a quarter million units have been demolished or sold off, some to make way for newer, mixed-income communities, and some simply eliminated. Whether they are defiant like Beatrice Harris, or supportive of the change and anxious for the opportunity to move, residents are being displaced.

The Dismantling of Public Housing

These two narratives, one of catastrophe and the other of quiet success, are stark opposites and they reflect dramatic and fundamental disagreement about the legacy of public housing in the United States. The disagreements about public housing, though, have always been dramatic. Few other social policies pursued by the federal government, and certainly no other housing program, has generated the controversy that has surrounded public housing almost from its beginning. Hailed by progressive reformers and housing advocates, public housing was vociferously attacked by real estate interests and others who called it socialism, and/or claimed it would destroy communities and enflame racial conflict. We are now in a period when the conflicts about public housing are resolving themselves in a nationwide effort to dismantle the program. Demolition is the main means by which the system is being dismantled. Most of the demolition has taken place within the context of the HOPE VI program, which was authorized by Congress in 1992 (and will continue as part of its successor, the Choice Neighborhoods Initiative, or CNI, which began in 2010).[6] Sometimes demolition is accompanied by redevelopment and sometimes not. In addition to demolition, public housing units are being lost through sale and conversion to other uses (a process the Department of Housing and Urban Development calls "disposition"). What demolition (with or without redevelopment) and disposition have in common is a reduction in the stock of public housing. In the following pages I refer to the *dismantling* of the public housing system in the United States to denote these efforts to reduce the public housing stock. Alternatively, I refer to the *transformation* of public housing, and to the *removal* of public housing units. Each of these phrases is meant to identify this overarching trend toward elimination of public housing units (through demolition or disposition) and retrenchment in the provision of public housing for very low income households.

Some may question my characterization of this effort as a *dismantling* of the program. They are likely to point out that many public housing units are rebuilt in the new mixed-income communities that replace the old projects. The new communities are designed in ways that make the subsidized units indistinguishable from the market-rate housing built beside them and thus they offer simply a new way of doing business for public housing. Alternatively, one might point to the fact that despite three decades of unprecedented demolition of public housing, *most* of the stock still remains standing. Thus, the argument might go, references to the death of public housing or to its ruins are hyperbolic at best and misleading at worst.

The evidence for the dismantling interpretation, however, is strong. First, there has been a significant reduction in the number of public housing units across the country. Though advocates of redevelopment position it as the solution to ongoing problems of public housing and as a means of creating stable and decent living environments for the poor, there have been no attempts to use this new model to expand the public housing stock. In fact, the new model is employed almost exclusively to reduce the scope of the program and the number of subsidized, very-low income units. HOPE VI and CNI projects do not increase the number of public housing units within a given city—and rarely have they adhered to even a one-for-one replacement of the demolished public housing. Instead, in most projects there has been a dramatic reduction in the number of public housing units from pre- to post-redevelopment. Nationally, the early projections were that only 60 percent of the public housing units torn down by HOPE VI would be replaced.

HUD and local public housing authorities (PHAs) have also demolished projects outside the confines of HOPE VI and sold units to private and nonprofit entities through the Demolition and Disposition process built into the original public housing legislation. In fact, the elimination of units outside of HOPE VI has now exceeded the number of units demolished by that program. As of August 2012, HUD reports that over 285,000 units have been approved for demolition (including HOPE VI) and more than 250,000 had already been demolished.[7] Thus, the agency has approved demolition of close to 20 percent of the public housing stock nationwide. In some places, the reduction is much greater. In the city of Memphis, Tennessee, local officials gleefully anticipate the elimination of all public housing in that city. At a 2009 ribbon cutting ceremony for a new mixed-income development replacing the old Horn Lake public housing project, Robert Lipscomb, the city's housing director, said, "We're almost there. We have only a few more sites to go before we can eliminate the words 'public housing' from our vocabulary. Wouldn't that be great?"[8] Atlanta, however, has beaten them to the title of first city to demolish all of its family public housing. Las Vegas, Nevada, is eager to follow Atlanta's lead.[9]

A second dimension of the dismantling of public housing is in the shifting of housing assistance to tenant-based forms of subsidy (vouchers), and to the shallow subsidies of the Low-Income Housing Tax Credit (LIHTC) and other affordable housing programs.[10] These changes alter two of the most consequential elements of public housing: the long-term commitment of the subsidy and its depth. The system of permanent affordability and the deep subsidies represented by the public housing program are being exchanged for the short-term contracts of vouchers and the relatively higher income targeting of LIHTC.

Finally, the current efforts to demolish and dispose of public housing are, in all likelihood, a death blow to the program. Public housing—as it was conceived during the New Deal, and as it has operated during the subsequent decades—is no longer seen as a viable policy option for meeting affordable housing needs. Though it was once the centerpiece of national efforts to provide housing for very low income families in the United States, it has been many years since the number of public housing units nationwide has expanded by an appreciable amount. In fact, in the current policy environment public housing is no longer seen even as a resource worth preserving. The units that avoid demolition and continue to operate do so because of the long-term contractual obligations embedded in the way the program works. That is, public housing (like other housing assistance programs) has an afterlife—units remain long after the program has ceased to be an option for future policy and even though policymakers have moved on to new and different ways of meeting affordable housing needs. Thus, the transformation taking place in cities across the country represents a new, neoliberal, post–New Deal policy strategy aimed at ending the welfare state approach to housing assistance embodied by public housing.

This attempt to turn public housing into a museum piece is heralded by many and championed by notable public- and private-sector leaders. Henry Cisneros, first as HUD secretary in the Clinton administration and for years since, has consistently called for demolition of obsolete public housing communities. Private developer Richard Baron has been a leading figure in creating the new mixed-income model that is replacing public housing in many cities, and has been active in disseminating the idea. Peter Calthorpe, a leading urban planner identified with the New Urbanist movement, claims that public housing demolition and redevelopment "diminishes the historic isolation of public housing blocks, creating safe, socially diverse neighborhoods."[11] Noted civil rights attorney Alexander Polikoff, the lead attorney in the landmark *Gautreaux* public housing desegregation case, calls the movement "a hopeful and important step in the direction of deconcentrating poverty."[12]

The initiative to dismantle public housing is, however, misrepresented as an effort to improve the lives of public housing residents. It is, in fact, better understood with reference to three historical dynamics: (1) the centrality of racial issues in defining urban America; (2) the political shift from New Deal social welfare to neoliberal governance strategies; and (3) the economic revitalization of central cities that occurred after the 1990–91 recession. Looming above the entire effort and threatening its viability and undermining its rationale is the sporadic and inconsistent pattern of benefits that ensue for the public housing residents forcibly displaced by the demolition of their communities.

"Useful Work under Government Supervision"

U.S. public housing in the twenty-first century is in many ways a historical artifact. In a physical sense, the earliest public housing buildings from the 1930s and early 1940s are among the best surviving examples of New Deal architecture. These units, the "semi-enclosed courts with walk-up buildings," were frequently well built and have held up well over time. The shift to modernist design themes in the later 1940s and 1950s generally increased the scale of public housing developments and incorporated much more open space for common use and introduced more fresh air and light into urban landscapes that had lacked both. Today, the New Deal designs seem quaint while the modernist projects generate almost universal opprobrium as outdated and socially dysfunctional. Where public housing designers wanted a clear separation between public housing and the slums that often surrounded them, planners now look for developments to seamlessly integrate with the rest of the community. Where New Deal and modernist principles celebrated community and openness through the creation of undifferentiated open space, planners now argue for individual space that clearly demarcates ownership and maintenance responsibilities.

In addition to being widely considered outmoded in a physical sense, public housing *policy* is an artifact of ideas ranging from Keynesianism to the New Deal social welfare state. Large-scale and direct government intervention such as public housing was a product of a political economy that no longer exists, an expanding welfare state underwritten with the surpluses generated by a powerful industrial economy. Politically, public housing's moment was one characterized by a willingness to use the public sector to spread the benefits of prosperity and expand social welfare rights. Conceived of, in part, as a giant public works project, public housing helped put people back to work during the Great Depression. It was then reauthorized and expanded in an era of unprecedented economic prosperity in which surplus state revenues were directed to meeting growing postwar demand for housing and to large-scale renewal efforts to reverse the fortunes of declining central cities.[13] Public housing thus represented a form of government investment in infrastructure that was of benefit to the working class both as a source of jobs and as a source of decent and affordable housing. Each new project was an affirmation of the importance of government investment in contributing to economic and social well-being.

At the dedication of the first completed public housing development in the nation, Techwood Homes in Atlanta, President Franklin Delano Roosevelt said:

> Within sight of us today, there stands a tribute to useful work under Government supervision....Here, at the request of the citizens of Atlanta, we have cleaned out nine square blocks of antiquated squalid dwellings, for years a detriment to this community. Today those hopeless old houses are gone and in their place we see the bright cheerful buildings of the Techwood Housing Project.[14]

His brief talk that day was an elaboration of the idea that government has a necessary and proper role in generating economic activity, contributing to the expansion of employment, and building the nation's infrastructure. Public housing, like the Works Progress Administration (WPA) and other New Deal efforts to propel a lagging economy and put people back to work, reflected an acceptance of the idea that public works were an important and valid economic intervention. Furthermore, it was an intervention aimed at producing benefits for the submerged working class who were suffering as a result of the Great Depression. The fact that housing was an important economic stimulant with considerable ripple effects throughout the economy had been well appreciated even during the Hoover administration that preceded Franklin Delano Roosevelt and the New Deal. Whereas Hoover's political ideology kept him from initiating large-scale public interventions into economic matters, Roosevelt used the deepening crisis of the Depression to justify a series of grand public works projects, including the initiative aimed at clearing the nation's slums and producing new and needed affordable housing for the working class.[15]

Racial Identification and Increasing Economic Marginalization

Over time, as the country climbed out of the Depression, the white working class benefitted from government investment and support for expanded housing choices, including the homeownership initiatives of the Federal Housing Administration (FHA). Rising incomes in the post-Depression era allowed whites to move to new suburban communities being built in metropolitan areas across the country. African Americans, sharing less in the postwar prosperity and having fewer choices in a segregated and discriminatory private housing market, began to see in public housing the best opportunity for decent and affordable living in urban areas. With little demand from whites, the projects became more racially identified over time.[16] Residents with choices moved out voluntarily and those with rising incomes were forced out by program rules. By the 1960s, after little more than twenty years in existence, public housing in the nation's largest cities had become the housing of last resort to an increasingly impoverished and economically marginalized African American population.[17] For fifty years now, the resident profile of public housing has been disproportionately people of color and, in most places, disproportionately black. Though African Americans make up less than 15 percent of the U.S. population, they constituted 48 percent of the residents of public housing nationwide in 2000. In larger cities, two-thirds of public housing residents were black. In some cities, such as Detroit and Washington, D.C., virtually all public housing residents are black.

Although public housing's political support had never been widespread or entirely secure, the shift in its clientele from "the deserving poor" (as represented by the intact families of working, albeit low-income residents) to marginalized single-parent, welfare, and minority families has meant consistent underfunding and a steady disinvestment, both literal and political, from the commitment to provide safe, decent, and affordable housing through public ownership. In too many places the physical stock was allowed to decay, and maintenance was deferred or ignored. As the residents of public housing became more impoverished so, too, did their physical environments. The neglect by public housing managers in some cities and the lack of adequate funding often turned the green open spaces of public housing campuses into hardscrabble dirt, littered with broken glass and debris. Outdoor common areas in the worst projects were dotted with rusting and jagged-edged metal piping, the fossil remnants of swing sets and play areas that had been systematically torn apart and left. The projects were, by the early 1990s, seemingly useful only as a means of evoking memorable metaphors of disaster. Public housing complexes were, according to national leaders, "monuments of hopelessness"[18] and "as close to the approaches to hell" as one could find in America.[19]

Increasingly identified with its growing African American clientele, public housing was stigmatized and became one more wedge driven between working-class whites and African American members of the no longer certain New Deal coalition. The urban riots of the 1960s led to more significant strains between urban blacks and the largely white union movement that had once seen a commonality of interests in public housing. Public housing had thus become another reflection of the racial segregation and unresolved racial conflicts of American cities.

The growing awareness of concentrated poverty perfectly complemented and in time contributed to the narrative of public housing disaster. The no-go zones that had developed in American cities were increasingly depicted in the popular media as contested spaces of urban gangs and wracked by the scourge of crack cocaine and its attendant human fallout. In sum, public housing projects were urban wastelands of violence and predation. In time, scholars made the connection official, demonstrating that public housing complexes built in previous decades were significantly more likely than other communities to become concentrations of poverty in the 1980s.[20] Perceived to a large degree as synonymous, the problems of concentrated poverty and the problems of distressed public housing suggested therefore the same solution: dispersal of the incumbent low-income population coupled with a radical physical redevelopment of the area. Importantly, all of this is being pursued without public or official reference to race and racial segregation in American cities.[21]

Though race may be ignored in the statements made by HUD and PHA officials engaged in the dismantling of public housing, it is nevertheless central to the process. Since 2000, public housing demolition has been aggressively pursued in cities where the public housing population is disproportionately black compared to the rest of the city. The racial targeting of public housing transformation efforts extends even to the project level. Indeed, the displacement of very low income residents through public housing demolition is being disproportionately borne by African American families. The demolition of public housing has systematically targeted projects with higher black occupancy. Thus, as with the urban renewal program of the 1950s and 1960s, one of the main outcomes of public housing demolition has been the forced removal of blacks from their homes.

Neoliberalizing Public Housing

Stagflation and the restructuring of the U.S. economy in the 1970s brought an end to the prolonged period of postwar prosperity and undercut the basis of support for a growing social welfare infrastructure.[22] The neoliberal politics emerging in the 1980s questioned the wisdom and utility of government stimulus efforts and the efficacy of social welfare policy. The persistence of poverty was taken as evidence that "big government" solutions had not worked. Economic dislocations associated with economic restructuring were used as an occasion to scale back regulation and allow the market greater freedom to produce new investment and profit opportunities. The disappearance of public housing is part of this larger dynamic and reflects the failure of the political coalition that supported it and the end of a policy era in which large-scale interventionist policy was a widely legitimized strategy. In perhaps a final irony, some cities used federal stimulus funds authorized in response to the economic crisis of 2007–08, funds that were modeled on the public works initiatives of the New Deal, to demolish public housing.[23]

Neoliberal policy prescriptions are based on the belief that the market is a better way to provide for the social welfare of the population than are redistributive government programs, which, according to the neoliberal model, are antagonistic to growth and prosperity. This core preference for the "discipline of the market" over the alleged excesses and inefficiencies of government has marked many domestic policy reforms since the 1980s. Initiatives begun by U.S. president Ronald Reagan and British prime minister Margaret Thatcher in the 1980s were aimed at reducing the influence and power of organized labor both in the workplace and in national politics, deregulating industry, and downsizing large government initiatives in favor of the market allocation of goods.[24]

The first large-scale strikes against Keynesianism and social welfare-oriented government intervention were jarring. Federal budget cuts in domestic social programs in Reagan's first term reduced subsidized housing program allocations by more than 80 percent over a six-year period. On the labor front, Reagan broke the air traffic controllers strike in 1981 by firing more than eleven thousand union members, setting the stage for a more generalized corporate attack on unions that rolled back workplace gains earned over the previous decades.

Government was reduced by cutting back on revenues through tax cuts and by further deregulation that diminished public control over and participation in the marketplace.

In terms of public housing policy, an entirely new vision of the program was created over a short period of time in the mid-1990s. No longer would public housing communities consist entirely of the poor, they would be mixed-income neighborhoods of low- and middle-income residents. No longer would public housing be configured in large superblocks set off from the neighborhood surrounding it. Instead, it would be reintegrated into the fabric of urban neighborhoods. Similarly, public housing would no longer be set off from the housing market around it but instead connected to it by a mixed-income, mixed-ownership model. The institutional look of barracks housing and the cold and soulless high-rises would give way to a mix of housing types featuring porches and personalized design amenities, making public housing indistinguishable from the market-rate housing within which it was to be embedded. To the designers of these policy changes, all of these improvements required more than tinkering around the edges of existing projects; they necessitated wholesale demolition and redevelopment.

By the time the new model of public housing emerged, disinvestment by HUD and by local housing authorities in the existing stock of public housing was already fairly widespread. PHAs in many cities had simply begun to abandon some of their properties by neglecting to make repairs, allowing units to become and remain vacant, and by not spending repair funds they had received from the federal government, a process that came to be known as de facto demolition. During the 1980s, HUD passively supported these actions and routinely approved the requests for demolition that were the inevitable end result of this process of neglect. In the 1990s though, HUD moved from passive to active on demolition. During Bill Clinton's initial term, Henry Cisneros became the first HUD secretary to advocate openly the demolition of public housing. Some local housing authorities were quick to embrace the change and accelerated their nascent efforts. In Houston, where the housing authority had been trying for years to figure out a way to rid itself of the Allen Parkway Homes, the city's largest public housing project, a HUD grant in 1993 made it happen. Elsewhere, demolitions became opportunities for public celebrations. In Baltimore, the first city nationwide to tear down all of its family high-rise buildings, crowds of people gathered to watch and parades were held to celebrate the first demolitions.[25] In Tucson, the city's housing director and a city councilmember each took a swing at the Connie Chambers public housing complex with a sledgehammer at a celebration complete with mariachi bands and speeches about improving the lives of the poor.[26]

FIGURE 1.   A HOPE VI redevelopment of the Arthur Blumeyer public housing community in St. Louis. Only one of the original four high-rises is left standing in 2004 as the new Renaissance at Grand development is being built in the foreground. Seven years later the city received another grant from HUD to tear down the tower pictured here.

The plan of action for public housing was embodied in a federal program that came to be known as HOPE VI. The effort began with a congressional call in 1989 for a commission to look into the conditions of "severely distressed public housing." As a first step, the National Commission on Severely Distressed Public Housing (NCSDPH) called for an incremental response, a program of rehabilitation and modernization that would allocate millions of dollars toward the repair and renewal of the broken buildings and the broken communities of public housing. This limited approach was abandoned almost immediately, however, in favor of a bolder one—the complete demolition of the old communities and their replacement with entirely new, mixed-income communities. This more aggressive approach emerged within the Clinton administration, and could be viewed as an attempt to "end public housing as we know it," a fitting companion piece to Clinton's effort in the welfare policy arena.

Simultaneously, many public housing authorities reinvented themselves and shed the image of social service agencies providing lifeline support to the very poor. Some have become dynamic real estate developers, building mixed-use, mixed-income developments that have provided affordable low-cost housing only in the context of gentrifying neighborhoods where Starbucks replaced pay-day loan centers, and a revived real estate market was reflected in the shiny windows of Bed, Bath, and Beyond stores, Pottery Barn outlets, and half-million-dollar townhouses. The Chicago Housing Authority (CHA) redid its logo to "CHAnge" to emphasize its new direction. The Atlanta Housing Authority (AHA) privatized most of its internal administrative practices and all of its management operations and "repositioned itself as a diversified real estate company with a public mission and purpose."[27] Renee Glover, head of the AHA and the doyenne of demolition, has become one of the unofficial spokespersons for the movement. The AHA website for many years called Glover a pioneer in the movement to establish "master-planned, mixed-finance, mixed-income residential developments where families of all socio-economic profiles live next to each other in the same amenity-rich community.... In fact, the model Glover created at AHA is now used as *the* redevelopment blueprint by the U.S. Department of Housing and Urban Development."[28] Though officials in Washington, D.C., and other cities might contest it, Glover claims this approach, used across the country, as her own and calls it the "Atlanta model." Glover travels from city to city spreading the word about demolition and redevelopment, and changing the old ways of public housing. Her message is frequently infused with warnings about the dangers of concentrated poverty and the dehumanizing aspects of the old public housing model. "Families were broken or non-existent" she contends of the days of public housing residences in large complexes. "Education was broken. Economic success was unattainable. The threat of crime was a daily, sometimes hourly, reality."[29]

Privatization is one of the central means by which public housing is changing. Some PHAs have sold part of their housing stocks to private developers to convert to market rate or to operate as assisted housing if other subsidies can be found. Management responsibilities are routinely subcontracted to private firms, especially after redevelopment. The AHA's privatization, for example, has left only a skeletal administrative staff for the agency itself. Newly redeveloped mixed-income communities are generally governed by private management companies that impose screening criteria, which disqualify large numbers of previous public housing residents, and work requirements aimed at disciplining the poor.[30] In an extension of the objectives and impulses behind welfare reform, the 1998 public housing reform bill required unemployed public housing residents who were able-bodied to do unpaid community service each month.[31] Some PHAs adopted stricter employment requirements for the residents of their new communities.[32] As the director of the Charlotte, North

Carolina, PHA put it, "public housing should not be a 'safe harbor' for those who 'lack a work ethic.'"[33]

Though the new tenant screening policies reflect neoliberal concerns about the provision of social welfare benefits, they are in some respects a return to policies followed by PHAs in the early years of public housing in the 1930s and 1940s. At that time, public housing in most cities was seen as a resource for the working poor. PHAs deliberately marketed their units to employed households and limited if not completely avoided residency by "welfare families." The New York City Housing Authority is one of the few in the nation that has retained policies over the decades that have continued to target the working poor and has largely avoided turning public housing into housing of last resort for a sub-merged urban underclass.[34] In most other cities, however, the allocation of public housing units soon came to reflect a social welfare orientation that targeted the neediest families, which increasingly meant those on public assistance. In some cases, this was the will of Congress, which changed resident preference policy to favor, at various times, those displaced from the slums cleared to create public housing, previously homeless families, and families paying more than 50 percent of their income on housing.[35]

The new regime of public housing management policies, however, goes beyond the mere reinstatement of original tenant screening standards. In 1996, President Clinton signed an executive order commonly referred to as "One Strike and You're Out" that allowed the eviction of public housing families if anyone in the household was convicted of a crime. This policy, enacted during a period of national moral panic over crime and drugs in U.S. cities, was an extreme form of Congress's "Three Strikes and You're Out" policy that called for severe sentencing rules for third-time offenders. The three-strikes policy itself was the culmination of repeated congressional efforts to "get tough on crime" in urban America, in which each session of Congress tried to outdo the previous one by increasing mandatory sentencing, lengthening sentences for crimes most prevalent in black ghettos, and increasing police and investigative prerogatives in fighting crime.[36] In public housing, the declaration of "federal drug-free zones" in public housing areas allowed the application of stricter federal sentencing rules. This meant the commission of a drug crime on public housing property generated longer sentences for convicted parties than the same offense committed across the street. Although some residents of the most poorly managed public housing welcomed the get-tough approach, public housing residents were in essence being asked to waive some of their civil rights in order to address crime problems that were beyond the management capabilities of PHAs and local police departments.

The core of privatization, however, is the movement of units out of public ownership and control and into the private market. This is being accomplished in several ways. First, there is the sale of public housing units to residents. This was an initiative of the Reagan administration in the early 1980s, mimicking the Right to Buy scheme for British social housing initiated by Prime Minister Thatcher. Sale to tenants has never accounted for much activity in the United States, however. In more recent years, PHAs have sold off stock to developers, sometimes just to make up budgetary shortfalls. The San Diego Housing Commission eliminated its entire stock of public housing by converting it to private (nonprofit) ownership. Though it continues to operate as subsidized housing, there is no longer public ownership or management. In 2010 the Housing Authority of the City of Los Angeles (HACLA) announced plans to dispose of all sixty-eight hundred units in its inventory, converting them to voucher-based housing. The most common form of privatization is the demolition of public units, which are either not replaced in any form or are replaced by Housing Choice Voucher (Section 8) subsidies used by low-income families to rent private-sector housing.

Gentrification and Inner-City Revitalization

Economic changes taking place in American cities in the postrecession period of 1993–95 generated development pressures that also led to the elimination of public housing communities. Neighborhoods in and around downtowns, especially, were subject to significant investment pressures. The dismantling of public housing nicely dovetailed with the opportunity to leverage private-sector investment in inner-city neighborhoods.

In contrast to previous decades, the wave of gentrification that characterized U.S. cities after the 1990s recession was "ambitiously and scrupulously planned" by corporate developers and public officials.[37] This "third wave" of gentrification had more public-sector involvement, took place in cities "further down the urban hierarchy," and transformed neighborhoods more distant from the urban core that had been seen as riskier for private investment in the past.[38] These characteristics are not unrelated, according to Jason Hackworth and Neil Smith. They argue that policy devolution to local governments has made those governments more sensitive to local-source revenue production (such as property and sales taxes) and has therefore heightened the responsiveness of local governments to the benefits of real estate development. The diffusion of gentrification to cities down the urban hierarchy and to more remote and troubled neighborhoods requires a more active and sizable public-sector investment to create the conditions necessary for private capital investment.[39] In the case of public housing redevelopment, the public ownership of the land has long been an impediment to private reinvestment on-site, and the deteriorated physical asset has long impeded private investment in the surrounding community.

The government-initiated demolition and redevelopment of public housing sweeps away both obstacles.

The transformation of large public housing sites, sometimes well over a hundred acres in size, necessitates a leading role for local government for two reasons. First, the PHA must be willing to convert the property to private ownership and thus must be a willing partner in the redevelopment. Second, the size and scale of the projects are such that significant infrastructure investments are necessary to accomplish redevelopment objectives. Such action can sometimes generate a powerful reaction in the private sector as the latent market value of neighborhoods is unleashed once the obstacle of public housing is removed.

As Elvin Wyly and Daniel Hammel have memorably stated, public housing in many American cities had by the 1990s become islands of decay in seas of renewal.[40] Neighborhood changes in the Mission Hill area of Boston, for example, had left the BHA's Mission Main project an isolated enclave of poverty, surrounded by more affluent neighbors.[41] (It was torn down for redevelopment in 1996.) The St. Thomas public housing project in New Orleans sat in the path of revitalization and, as a community of very low income families, soon became isolated in a part of New Orleans, near downtown, that was experiencing upgrading.[42] (St. Thomas was demolished in 2001.) Wyly and Hammel call the Cabrini-Green public housing project in Chicago "the most vivid" example of this phenomenon. Cabrini-Green occupied seventy acres in the middle of the city's gentrifying Near North Side. Its size, however, and the deplorable conditions at the site kept private investment at bay for years. Long identified as a potential site for redevelopment, Cabrini-Green was marked for demolition in 1993 and, though delayed by the lawsuits of residents, it began coming down in 2003. No sooner had the CHA begun clearing the site of public housing residents then developers began building condominiums, which sold for $650,000, and commercial nodes that had been dominated by check-cashing and small-scale convenience stores, quickly converted to shopping areas anchored by upscale coffee shops, home furnishing stores, and franchise clothing stores.

The coupling of public housing demolition with private-sector reinvestment to trigger large-scale neighborhood change quickly became a prominent objective of the HOPE VI program. HUD began to assess possible projects for their potential in leveraging private investment to remake the surrounding residential and commercial environments, and local officials began to use public housing demolition and transformation to achieve much larger urban redevelopment goals. Richard M. Daley of Chicago regarded the transformation of public housing as the city's chief redevelopment strategy during the last ten years of his tenure as mayor. Bruce Katz, one of the architects of HOPE VI, said that "I always thought about HOPE VI as something larger than public housing revitalization. It's one of the premier urban redevelopment efforts of the last 25 years."[43]

As for the extension of gentrification into more remote and riskier neighborhoods, the transformation of Chicago's State Street Corridor of public housing, a twenty-five-block-long corridor of assisted housing that included the Robert Taylor Homes, Stateway Gardens, Wentworth Gardens, and several other projects, stands out. Once among the largest concentrations of public housing in the country, little remains now of the buildings that dominated this part of the city. Much of the area today is marketed by the city of Chicago as "Bronzeville," the historic home of the city's black community, and a place now of renewal and reinvestment. Where the towers once stood are new communities liberally sprinkled with homeownership and market-rate housing. The finishing touch is the renaming so as to end identification of the area with the old projects and to signal to potential residents and investors the beginning of a new era for the neighborhood.[44] Deirdre Pfeiffer argues that this process of altering the discourse about a place through renaming is central to the dynamic of displacement.[45] This conversion of what had been a no-go zone into a "place" with, in the case of Bronzeville, historic importance reflects the dramatic changes that have been induced in the area. The black middle class has reclaimed the area in an example of black gentrification that repeats many of the same demographic changes and tensions of typical gentrification without the racial turnover.[46]

In the Interest of Public Housing Residents

As a policy regime, neoliberalism can take various forms. Although initiated in the 1980s in a manner that did little to disguise its attempt to reduce union power, devalue social welfare objectives, and privilege corporate and market considerations, it is now frequently expressed in more nuanced forms. Contested from the beginning, neoliberalism has evolved into more moderate forms of intervention.[47] "Moderate" neoliberalism is expressed in rhetoric sensitive to place, and sensitive to a broader range of felt needs. Concerns about crime, the desire of homeowners to protect their investments, the desire to protect consumers, even antipoverty objectives are all enlisted to justify neoliberal public policy initiatives.

The dismantling of public housing is a case in point, in so far as the discourse surrounding public housing demolition and redevelopment frequently invokes the interests of the tenants themselves. Though public housing has been stigmatized for decades and though it has been regarded by many as a failure since at least the 1960s, the disaster narrative imagines public housing as much more than simply bad. It is, instead, "soul crushing," the buildings themselves are "monuments to hopelessness," resulting often in "humanitarian disaster."[48] The worst of the nation's public housing may well have deserved those descriptions. Mismanagement, malign neglect, and the overwhelming press of poverty reduced some public housing communities in some cities into war zones of gang conflict, and produced virtually unlivable conditions for the families residing within them. The public-housing-as-disaster narrative, however, portrays the entire program in these terms. In the public imagination of the early 1990s, when the demolition movement was emerging, public housing was equated with the worst forms of urban decay, hopelessness, and marginality in American cities.

The primary victims of these horrific conditions, of course, were the residents themselves. Such dire straits suggested radical remedies, or what Alexander Polikoff calls "radical surgery."[49] The public housing prisons must come down, according to the narrative, and families must be assisted in making good their escape from the environments of misery represented by public housing. The "projects," in this view, need to be replaced by true communities that would attract a mix of residents, some with higher incomes, and a mix of housing options, some for homeowners and those who could pay market rates. The concentration of poverty and the concentration of public housing, it is maintained, must be remade into true opportunity neighborhoods offering the range of resources and amenities available to the middle class.

In this way, then, is it possible for a government official to consider the forced eviction of a very low income family as a means of increasing the housing choice of that family. As a spokesman for the Atlanta Housing Authority said in describing that city's transformation of public housing, "what we want to do is make sure families can make choices about where they want to live. Government bureaucrats are not telling them where to live."[50] Here, one of the most intrusive forms of state power that can be directed against citizens—that is, their forced relocation followed by the demolition of their homes—is presented as the opposite. It is this discourse that stresses the need to free residents from the directives of government that makes it possible to conclude that the best way to improve the lives of those who depend on public housing is to tear that housing down. This narrative makes the dismantling of the public housing system a necessary by-product of efforts to create functioning communities. The loss of units is simply a given; "that was the trade-off," explains noted architect Peter Calthorpe, "fewer public housing units in exchange for communities with more social integration."[51]

The reduction in the size and scope of public housing, and the dispersal of the very low income families, is also seen as a necessity in the effort to redress the unequal spatial distribution of poverty within metropolitan areas. To New

Regionalists who advocate cooperative strategies among local governments to address regional inequities, the concentration of poverty and the unevenness of metropolitan development patterns are both inefficient and inequitable. Spatial inequities in public services such as schools, disparities in access to jobs and in exposure to environmental hazards, and the reproduction of inequality as the result of environmental factors lock in advantages for the affluent and trap the poor in resource-starved communities. The concentration of such housing in core parts of metropolitan areas and its relative absence in developing suburban areas means that the low-income residents of that housing were consigned to inferior environments that are dangerous and hazardous on the one hand and lack opportunities for advancement on the other.[52]

Positioning forced eviction as a progressive approach aimed at increasing the social welfare of the poor limits opposition to this intrusive use of state power, even from those who are its target.[53] Resident opposition to public housing demolition and disposition across the country has been sporadic. In some cases, however, the coercive nature of forced displacement cannot be obscured and the displaced have made their opposition known. The most prominent example of this is post-Katrina New Orleans when public housing residents were not allowed to reinhabit their homes. Chain-link fences kept the tenants from reoccupying the units, and protests outside the buildings and at City Hall resulted in confrontations between police and public housing residents and advocates. Residents have rebelled against the idea of being forcibly removed from their homes in other cities as well. In Chicago they formed the Coalition to Protect Public Housing. Protests have occurred in Atlanta, Seattle, Atlantic City, Minneapolis, and San Francisco as well.[54] In Richmond, Virginia, residents organized themselves into RePHRAME (Residents of Public Housing in Richmond Against Mass Evictions) to demand a set of protections for residents in the redevelopment of public housing in that city. Residents of Los Angeles public housing demonstrated outside the home of HACLA director Rudolf Montiel in 2010 after the agency announced plans to dispose of all of its units.

What is perhaps more remarkable than the demonstrations against public housing demolition, however, is the fact that they do not occur more frequently. Across the country families have been moved out and buildings demolished without any serious incidents of opposition. There are several possible explanations for this. First, many of the demolitions take place after a prolonged period during which the projects are emptied of residents through de facto demolition. As vacancies increase and maintenance and upkeep of the units and the grounds are neglected, more families move out, not to be replaced. The depopulated areas become dangerous as gangs move in or expand their presence by taking over abandoned units. When unlivable conditions have been thus induced the PHA will ask HUD to approve demolition. By that time few residents remain, and those who do have been made to endure such poor living conditions that they are glad to leave.

Second, in cases where redevelopment is to occur (usually through a HOPE VI-funded project), residents are actively recruited to engage in the planning process. They are asked to make contributions to the vision of the community that will replace theirs. They are encouraged in the belief that they will benefit from the redevelopment by being able to move into the new community, though this is, in fact, a relatively rare occurrence. Residents are given a say in the redevelopment planning—allowed to dream about what their community could look like without being told that their odds of actually moving back in are generally less than one in three. Such a process can establish buy-in from the very residents who will lose their housing as a result of the redevelopment.

The third potential reason for an absence of universal opposition to demolition is that some portion of public housing residents welcome the demolition or at least do not mind being forced to move. They may be willing to take their chances in other neighborhoods just to be rid of the situation they currently face. Their quiescence, in this case, is support for the objectives of demolition, or at least their acceptance of the justifications for demolition offered by local officials.

Double Jeopardy

The record in returning displaced families to the completed redevelopments, in those cases where redevelopment takes place at all, is not good. Based on a number of studies, roughly four out of every five families displaced by HOPE VI redevelopments do not return to the site to live. For those displaced by non–HOPE VI demolitions or by the sale of public housing, of course, there is no redeveloped site to which to return. So for the overwhelming majority of low-income families, demolition of public housing *only* means displacement and relocation, typically to other low-income, segregated neighborhoods. Displaced families are given housing vouchers to use in the private market and given modest help to relocate themselves, or they are simply moved into vacant units in other public housing across town. For the most part, these families are moved from one high-poverty, segregated environment into other high-poverty and racially segregated neighborhoods. Despite the expectations of demolition advocates, the families experience only limited, sporadic, and inconsistent benefits from being moved out of their public housing communities. Almost universally they report an increased sense of safety and reductions in visible signs of social disorder compared to the public housing projects from which they moved. But there have been no overall benefits in terms of economic self-sufficiency, physical health, or in a range of educational outcomes studied by researchers. Most of the families, furthermore, report significant disruptions in their networks of social support.

The disappointments in terms of individual benefits are only half of the equation, however. The research shows that public housing demolition and redevelopment have consistently generated significant community-level benefits. Early results show reductions in crime, increases in property values, and increased private-sector investment in neighborhoods after public housing has been torn down. Although one might argue that the disruptions and lack of benefits experienced by public housing residents on the one hand and the demonstrable community improvements often accompanying public housing redevelopment on the other produce a kind of stalemate or balancing of outcomes, this is not really the case. The constituency for the community benefits produced by public housing demolition is much larger than the one for resident benefits. Improvements in health, self-sufficiency, and education predicted for residents would, if they occurred, be experienced only by the residents. The benefits of neighborhood improvement, however, are more widely experienced. Residents of the surrounding community, investors, property owners, public officials, and people who work, learn, or play in the neighborhood all enjoy its renaissance. Prospective new residents and current property owners all derive some benefit from the community impacts. Politically, therefore, the community benefits generated by public housing transformation have outweighed in importance the disappointing results for the public housing residents.

The discourse of disaster that has dominated our understanding of public housing would have us expecting that families welcome the opportunity to escape the prisons of public housing, regardless of whether they are able to return to the redeveloped site. That discourse would lead us to expect residents grateful for the chance to move away, and experiencing significant life-improvements as a result. But the discourse is an oversimplification of life in American public housing. The teenaged author of a book about living in the "projects" of Tucson, Arizona, said of her work:

> The reason I stayed writing the book was because I thought that it was my opportunity to tell people that the projects are not a place where you pass by and get killed. I want all you people to read this book and learn and see how life in the projects was....I lived there. I know that people have said it was a bad place to go. Some people were afraid to even pass through there because they were scared that the people from the projects would assault or kill them. But that was not how it was.[55]

Even in "the worst" public housing, residents construct networks of support, communities of interaction that provide the emotional and material foundations of life. Being wrenched from that community is painful and frightening to the households who suffer considerable disruption in their lives without materially benefitting from their forced displacement. Although policy makers talk of moving residents into neighborhoods of opportunity and delivering them from the evils of public housing, many residents suffer the loss of their social and support networks, and find themselves in nearby ghettos just as segregated and almost as poor as those they were forced to leave.

Indeed, for the occupants of the nation's worst public housing, the events of the past twenty years and the policy changes in place today must be very striking. As residents they were for years mostly ignored while the mismanagement of politicians and administrators turned their communities into nightmares of physical deterioration, social pathology, crime, and violence. For years they endured these conditions, and then when the political environment changed and their communities were finally redeveloped and renewed, they were displaced to different high-poverty neighborhoods to watch the renewal from afar. The failure of public housing, where it did occur, was induced by public policy missteps and bureaucratic and managerial incompetence. Residents were made to pay for these mistakes by being consigned to horrible living conditions for decades. These highly publicized failures are now being used as pretext for a systematic dismantling of the public housing program, facilitating redevelopment opportunities of interest to local officials and developers, while residents are largely shunted aside into other highly segregated and impoverished neighborhoods. Thus, for residents, the entire history is a long and extended application of double jeopardy—first being forced to endure unlivable conditions through the malign neglect of government officials, and then being displaced to other neighborhoods when redevelopment finally occurs.[56]

The Plan of the Book

Chapter 1 provides a history of the public housing program. This, of course, is a book-length topic of its own, so the treatment here must of necessity be abbreviated and focused on those elements most critical to providing a foundation for understanding the current situation. Thus, I lay out the ways in which the early promise and original design for public housing (at least among some of its supporters) was distorted by political, fiscal, and demographic factors at a fairly early date. The discourse of disaster that came to surround public housing is explored, as well as some of the early policy responses to worsening conditions in public housing developments.

Nascent efforts to dismantle public housing emerged in the 1980s. Local housing authorities attempted to divest themselves of the worst of their housing stock by convincing HUD that the projects had become obsolete. Demolition of public housing at that point was unusual and needed to be justified according to rules and standards established by Congress. As the decade progressed, however, HUD acquiesced more and more frequently to the pleadings of local PHAs in this regard. Advocates for residents began to claim that PHAs in some cases were actually creating the conditions for demolition by conscious neglect of properties, a process that came to be known as de facto demolition. In 1992, Congress, in response to a national commission report on public housing, created the HOPE VI program and within a few years demolition was not only commonplace but essentially the cornerstone of federal public housing policy. I explore this recent history in chapter 2 and explain why some cities were aggressive in the dismantling of public housing whereas others were less aggressive. During the 1990s the explanation hinges on the gentrification pressures that some cities were experiencing. Since 2000, race has become more important; in cities where the public housing stock is disproportionately occupied by African Americans (compared to the city population as a whole) the dismantling of public housing has been most rapid. The examination of public housing transformation in America's largest cities is extended in chapter 3 where case studies of Chicago, New Orleans, and Atlanta illustrate the dynamics of public housing transformation within specific political and historical contexts.

In chapter 4 the analysis shifts from the city scale to the project scale and demonstrates again the central role of race in the process of transformation. A comparison of the projects removed in the nation's largest cities with the public housing that so far has been left standing reveals a disparate impact on African American families. This suggests that the effort to date has targeted projects where African Americans reside. Advocates of public housing transformation would argue, however, that such a disparate impact is, in fact, a positive outcome on the grounds that being freed from the terrible conditions in public housing is a benefit to families. Others, however, might stress the injurious nature of forced displacement and argue that the disparate racial impact is an adverse outcome. What to think about the racial targeting of public housing demolition, then, depends to a large extent on the experiences of the displaced. In chapter 5 I present the evidence on this question, reporting both original data and summarizing the body of knowledge that has been produced by dozens of studies across the nation.

The neighborhood impacts of public housing have been frequently invoked to justify the recent policy changes. In some cities the dismantling of public housing has served very specific place-based objectives related to improving the environment for private-sector investment. Patterns of gentrification that are induced by public housing removal are common enough, as is public housing removal that is induced by redevelopment and gentrification plans. Rapid neighborhood change is not, however, an inevitable outcome of public housing transformation. In chapter 6 the neighborhood implications of the dismantling of public housing are examined.

The conclusion provides a summary assessment of current public housing policy and a set of policy recommendations. The dismantling of public housing has much myth and hype associated with it. In the end our judgment of this effort to dismantle public housing and the New Deal policy prescriptions that it embodies should be based on a realistic assessment of the condition and place of public housing in American cities, as well as on a more sober and informed assessment of the impact of that transformation on the residents and communities most directly affected. The abandonment of the New Deal commitment to permanent and direct public-sector provision of affordable housing, if it continues, will have a lasting and significant impact on the safety net available to very low income families.

THE QUIET SUCCESSES AND LOUD FAILURES OF PUBLIC HOUSING

> Even as the image of public housing steadily deteriorates and its few remaining supporters speak in softer tones, tenants keep clamoring to get in....We have, in short, a paradox: Nobody likes public housing except the people who live there and those who want to get in.
>
> —Alvin Rabushka and William Weissert, *Caseworkers or Police? How Tenants See Public Housing*

The story of American public housing is one of quiet successes drowned out by loud failures. Fundamentally shaped by two bruising legislative battles, the program that emerged was importantly compromised in ways that significantly constrained its implementation. The program was limited to serving very low income households, channeled into the nation's most difficult urban neighborhoods, and forced to conform to rigid cost and financial controls. In some places the program was plagued by mismanagement and neglect. Despite these conditions, public housing has, for the most part and in most places, provided and continues to provide functional, decent, and affordable housing for very low income households. Waiting lists for public housing are long wherever it exists, filled with families who are ill-served by the private market. Studies find that the residents of public housing value it highly, and that they have built communities of mutual support that are important in helping them meet daily needs. Even in projects wracked by crime and overwhelmed by deteriorating physical conditions, residents have built communities and relationships that they value. Where public housing has not worked, the failures often have been spectacular and have generated horrific stories of substandard conditions and community dysfunction. Since the 1970s, reports of unlivable conditions in the worst projects have become the most common type of news report about public housing; during the 1990s such reports helped generate visions of a more generalized urban dystopia.[1]

Origins

Public housing in the United States has its origins in two separate reform movements active in the early decades of the twentieth century. The Progressive movement's concerns with urban slum eradication identified publicly owned and
operated housing as a means of improving living conditions for poor families.
The focus of this movement was the debilitating and dangerous conditions in
America's most disadvantaged slums. The environment there was seen as detrimental to the poor and especially to children forced to grow up amid the squalor
and disease of the slum, but also to adults whose morals, health, and initiative
were all thought to be in peril due to the poor living conditions they were forced
to suffer. In particular, slum reformers pointed to heavy overcrowding, the lack
of proper sanitation, poor ventilation, and the lack of natural light, as elements
of the foul environment forced upon low-income families.[2]

As a result, the efforts of slum clearance advocates focused on upgrading the
physical environment of ghetto neighborhoods. This approach reflected a strong
sense of environmental determinism—that the physical conditions within which
people live have great influence over their behavior and life chances. The nation's
first housing codes, established in large cities in the first decade of the twentieth century, were the earliest attempts to regulate the private housing market to
improve conditions in the urban slums. Support within the slum clearance movement for government-run housing that reflected more enlightened urban design
was a logical extension of these efforts. These reformers felt that direct government intervention in the form of publicly funded and operated housing was the
only viable long-term strategy for dealing with the failures of the private market
in slum neighborhoods. Public housing for those in the Progressive movement
was therefore meant to both eliminate the adverse conditions of the slum and to
provide much-needed affordable and decent housing for the neediest.

Operating at the same time was a group of housing reformers advocating for
government-operated housing from a different perspective. As embodied in the
work and words of Catherine Bauer, this vision of public housing, which came
to be known as the Modern Housing movement, followed a European idea that
supported a nonmarket sector of housing to provide decent and stable accommodations for the working class. There were important differences between
this model and the one espoused by the Progressives. The modern housing movement saw housing more as a public utility than as a social service initiative. The
housing reformers wished to target the needs of the working class and build a
European-style system of government housing for workers that involved a range
of union-based organizations, cooperatives, and nonprofit housing associations
as well as local governmental agencies. Affordable housing would be established

and run as a type of public utility permanently outside of the profit framework of the private market.[3] The vision of the housing reformers was therefore broader than that of the Progressives: it was not tied to slum clearance, nor was it to be targeted to the neediest.

At the federal level, public housing began during World War I as an emergency response to wartime needs. The construction of these units, however, was not a blanket commitment to a public housing program as Congress ordered that the units be sold after the war ended.[4] Nevertheless, the precedent of federal government involvement in housing production had been established. A tax incentive for developers to build low-cost housing was attempted during the 1920s, but very little activity was generated because investors had more lucrative options.[5] The work of the reformers, however, began to show up in small-scale experimental efforts in the 1930s. Shortly after FDR's election, the Emergency Relief and Reconstruction Act of 1932 authorized the Reconstruction Finance Corporation to make loans to limited-dividend partnerships for the construction of housing for low-income families. One year later the program was shifted to the Public Works Administration (PWA) in the Interior Department. Because of the lack of private sector interest, the program changed in 1934 to one in which the federal government itself built the housing.

The projects created in this early phase of public housing stand apart from most of the housing developed in later years.[6] Early projects were much more likely to be solidly built and well designed. Indeed, as the years wore on, the projects built in the first ten years of the public housing program tended to stand out among the stock of public housing in the cities where such projects existed. In New Orleans, for example, the Iberville and Lafitte projects consisted of three-story red-brick blocks with "detailed brickwork, tile roofs and wrought-iron balustrades representing a level of craft more likely found on an Ivy League campus" than in a government-sponsored public works development.[7] In Atlanta's Techwood Homes, the very first public housing project completed in the country, each doorway had a canopy, and the buildings were solid and trimmed in stone. The campus design of early projects was intentionally open, providing common spaces, landscaping, and play areas for children, and replacing dark, crowded slums with open and airy conditions, the light symbolizing the moral uplift provided by the place.[8] Outhwaite Homes in Cleveland, built in 1935, was similarly built of solid material and in an art deco architectural style.[9]

At its inception, local officials hailed public housing as the answer to the problems of urban slums and the residents themselves called it "paradise."[10] Public housing was modern housing in place of dilapidated slum dwellings, modern brick-built apartment buildings to replace ramshackle wooden shacks that dotted American slums at the time. To city officials, the opening of a new public housing project was an opportunity to speak of "'an expensive and beautiful village' that would 'take boys and girls off the streets into playgrounds.'"[11]

The PWA program generated fifty-eight developments nationwide, producing about twenty-five thousand units of housing. This effort was squelched by the U.S. District Court decision in *United States v. Certain Lands in the City of Louisville* in 1935, which held that the federal government could not use the power of eminent domain for slum clearance.[12] Rather than appeal the decision, the PWA and the Roosevelt administration encouraged state governments to enact enabling legislation so that the states could engage in slum clearance and public housing construction. Advocates pressed on in the effort to establish a large-scale federal program that would operate through state-chartered agencies.

Legislative Battles

Initial legislative efforts in 1935 and 1936 failed. The Progressive reformers and the modern housing advocates backed competing bills, both the Interior Department and the Commerce Department opposed the efforts, and FDR himself was insufficiently interested in passing housing legislation. But the press of economic conditions and the enormous potential for creating employment in the building trades through a program of public housing changed the political prospects of public housing. Roosevelt's New Deal was largely predicated on the idea that public works could be used as a means of generating jobs and reviving industrial output, and with his other New Deal initiatives struggling in an increasingly hostile Congress, Roosevelt put his full support behind public housing legislation in 1937. Senator Robert F. Wagner (D-NY), the program's legislative sponsor that year, sold it as the "next step in the country's economic recovery," another New Deal public works program whose primary benefit would be the employment that it generated.[13]

Congressional supporters were able to attract more votes for a public housing initiative that was simultaneously a program of slum clearance. Congressional defenders made frequent mention of the program's importance in correcting the unsafe and unsanitary living conditions in the nation's poorest urban neighborhoods.[14] The housing itself was seen as an antidote to the crime, disease, and unwholesome living of America's urban slums. This orientation, however, meant that most public housing would be constructed in the declining parts of American cities.

In addition to the slum-clearance orientation, the 1937 legislation incorporated additional features that were important in shaping the ultimate course of the program. Limits were placed on construction costs and on the incomes of tenants, and PHAs were required to enter into a cooperation agreement with local governments before building and operating any housing.[15] Congress also incorporated an "equivalent elimination" clause into the 1937 legislation that mandated that one unit of substandard housing be taken down for every unit of public housing built. Equivalent elimination ensured that the bulk of public housing projects would be located in previous slum areas and be part of clearance efforts. It also was meant to ensure that public housing would not become a competitor to private market provision of housing, but would rather be only a supplement in locations where the market would not function. The noncompete aspect of the program was critically important to the backers of the bill.[16] According to Senator Wagner, "the most important consideration is, that public housing projects should not be brought into competition with private industry....To reach those who are really entitled to public assistance, and to get into the field where private enterprise cannot operate, is the objective of this bill."[17]

The reauthorization of the program in 1949 proved more difficult politically than the initial passage of the program twelve years earlier. By 1949 even the elements of the program that were aimed at ameliorating opposition, the noncompete orientation and the cost and income limits, were insufficient to avoid a full-on assault by the real estate industry. Virtually every private construction and real estate trade association voiced strong opposition to public housing during the legislative battles of the '40s. The National Association of Real Estate Boards (NAREB), the U.S. Chamber of Commerce, the National Association of Home Builders (NAHB), the U.S. Savings and Loan League, the National Apartment Owners Association, and numerous real estate groups, builders, suppliers, and property owners associations throughout the country vehemently fought the program. Though their opposition was not new (they had unsuccessfully fought the 1937 legislation), their heated rhetoric and use of cold war images was. Opposition to communism, which in postwar America had much greater purchase than it had had during the Depression, was enlisted as a strategy to fight public housing. The government production and ownership of housing embedded in the public housing model was, according to critics, the first step toward a socialist economy. Representative George A. Dondero of Michigan called it "the first fatal step toward national socialism...and the first real imitation of the Russian ideology of government [to] have gained a foothold on the shores of freedom."[18] The charge of socialism was to stick with the program for many years. Senator Harry Byrd (D-VA) "complained of the 'stench of gross inefficiency and Russian communism' which hovered over the projects."[19] In 1952 Congress even required public housing tenants to take an oath of loyalty before taking up residence, fearing that the socialist nature of public housing would make it a natural place for the emergence of Communist Party cells.

The real estate lobby went beyond ideological strategies to invoke the specter of high taxes and racial integration. It paid for advertisements and billboards that read: "Can you afford to pay somebody else's rent?"[20] In the South the lobby appealed to fears that public housing might end residential segregation. "Public housing means the end of racial segregation in Savannah!" screamed the headline of one billboard.[21] The extreme tactics of the opponents set the tone for congressional debate. The floor fight over public housing in the House of Representatives was long and bitter, and even punctuated by a fistfight.[22] About the opposition to public housing that was mounted during the legislative fights of the later 1940s, President Harry S. Truman remarked, "I do not recall ever having witnessed a more deliberate campaign of misrepresentation and distortion."[23]

Though opponents were strong and active, anticommunist hysteria had not yet peaked in the United States in the mid to late 1940s. With Truman's upset victory in 1948 and a huge ninety-two-seat majority for Democrats in the House and a twelve-seat majority in the Senate, proponents were able to get the program through Congress in 1949, but only after it had been made part of a larger program of urban renewal. Though slum clearance always had been an important part of public housing, the 1949 Housing Act reversed the formula and made public housing one element of a much larger and comprehensive strategy of urban clearance and renewal. Housing advocates accepted this arrangement, feeling that tying the program to the urban renewal program would gain greater acceptance for their program.[24] Congressional votes on the bill in 1949 show that support for public housing alone was quite slim. A final motion in the House of Representatives to delete public housing from the urban renewal legislation was defeated by a mere five votes.[25]

Operating within Constraints

The public housing program that emerged from these legislative battles thus took on a particular look, one calculated to appease critics as much as accomplish the goals of its supporters.[26] The charge of public housing—to provide decent, safe, and affordable housing to very low income families in the context of urban decline—is under any circumstances a difficult one. The specific features forced upon it by its opponents have had the effect of making the job even more difficult.

Decentralized Authority and Implementation

Although the funding for the program came from the federal government, it placed authority for program implementation squarely at the local level.

Localities were to create public housing authorities (PHAs) for the purpose of receiving federal subsidies to construct and operate public housing. The choice of whether to participate in the program was a local one, as was the decision about where to locate public housing once a PHA was up and running. This feature of the program created one of the ironies of public housing—that it was more effectively fought by its opponents after its passage than before. In addition to pressuring Congress to limit construction authorizations, the real estate lobby relied on its strong network of local chapters to take up the fight against public housing. In 1950, shortly after the 1949 reauthorization of public housing, Calvin Snyder of NAREB said that "the fight has just begun. The authorization of the gigantic multibillion dollar program has been issued by Congress. The completion of the program is another thing."[27] In order for the public housing program to be implemented state laws had to be amended to allow for such activity and local governments had to make formal requests to establish PHAs. In addition, cooperation agreements were required between the PHAs and local governments.

In California, Texas, and elsewhere, opponents passed laws at the state level requiring public referenda before local governments could participate in public housing. Even where referenda were not required, opponents were able to raise the issue in such a way as to force public decisions on whether or not a city would participate in the program. In many cities, political careers were created or came to an end over the issue of public housing. Local real estate interests in Los Angeles, led by the *Los Angeles Times*, responded to the prospect of public housing in that city with a strong campaign against the local PHA, including accusations of communism aimed at the staff. With a *Times* reporter in the city council chambers giving thumbs-up or thumbs-down signals to council members regarding the way they should vote, the council reversed its initial support of public housing. The *Times* ran an opposition candidate for mayor in 1953 who defeated the incumbent and succeeded in reducing the public housing commitment by half.[28] More than forty municipalities nationwide voted against the program by 1952, while twenty others endorsed the program. Most of the defeats came in smaller cities.[29]

Few suburban communities were interested in public housing at all. PHAs were typically chartered at the municipal scale and thus had authorization to build only in the central city. Other PHAs that were incorporated at the county level nevertheless focused their work in (and sometimes limited it to) the inner city. As a result, public housing has been concentrated in central cities, with few suburban areas building significant amounts. When policies to encourage elderly residents emerged during the 1950s and 1960s, the spatial concentration of public housing in inner cities was reduced. Suburban and nonmetropolitan jurisdictions proved to be much more receptive to elderly residents than to low-income families.

Local Control over Siting

Local implementation meant control over where public housing projects were built. Specifically, city councils and mayors had influence over the siting of public housing projects as each project required a "cooperation agreement" between the PHA and the local council. In many cities, including Chicago, Detroit, Baltimore, and Washington, D.C., city councils quickly took control of the siting process, and inserted local political concerns directly into the process of determining where public housing projects would be placed.[30] This led to a distinct pattern of spatial segregation of projects, and further isolated public housing units from the mainstream market, and public housing residents from the rest of the community. Within central cities public housing tended to be placed in poorer, more rundown neighborhoods, and neighborhoods with high concentrations of minority households.[31] Part of this had to do with congressional directives that public housing be tied to urban renewal. But a good deal of the spatial pattern of public housing was the result of the desire of local leaders to concentrate it in poor and minority neighborhoods, or on otherwise unwanted parcels.[32] Public housing projects were often located in otherwise unattractive locations. The Dallas Housing Authority, for example, located a public housing project across the street and downwind from a lead smelting plant. The plant spewed as much as 269 tons of lead dust into the air annually during periods of peak production and directly into the apartments and play areas of public housing residents for twenty-five years.[33]

When white and middle-class communities resisted the placement of public housing in their midst, local elected officials steered the projects into black slums.[34] There is evidence that the siting options available to PHAs would probably have been limited even without the direct involvement of city councils in siting decisions. In Chicago, white backlash in the form of mobs and riots erupted after the CHA opened public housing adjacent to a white neighborhood. The event significantly altered the agency's subsequent location strategies.[35] Philadelphia and Detroit also saw significant and violent response among whites to the prospect of their communities playing host to public housing.[36]

Two other factors contributed to the marked tendency for PHAs to place public housing in black slums. First, the alternative—building public housing on vacant land—was seen by some as direct competition with private real estate developers. The thinking was that PHAs should restrict their efforts to neighborhoods (such as the black slums) in which private developers would not operate.[37]

Second, there was an objectively large need for more and better housing in the black communities of American cities. So concentrating public housing in those communities not only avoided the visceral response of white constituents, but it could also be said to be addressing one of the central needs of the black community. Under these circumstances, "housing officials took the safest and quickest road—providing more black housing opportunities in black neighborhoods."[38]

By the 1980s, the cumulative impact of the slum clearance objectives of public housing, local discretion over whether or not to participate in the program, and local siting authority was a pattern of pronounced spatial concentration of public housing units within central cities of metropolitan areas, and in high-poverty, racially segregated neighborhoods within those central cities.

Cost-Containment and the Fiscal Model for Public Housing

From the outset, the public housing program was constrained by significant pressures to limit costs. The 1937 bill contained an absolute limit on construction costs of $5,000 per unit through an amendment to the original legislation by Senator Harry Byrd of Virginia. For his part, Byrd saw the cost limits as a means of restraining government spending. Though some of the earliest public housing developments were able to achieve distinctive and pleasant architectural and design outcomes, for the most part cost containment led to shortcuts, the use of inferior materials, and regrettable design decisions. This was especially the case when federal officials at the U.S. Housing Authority (USHA, the federal agency in charge of the program) decided to pressure local authorities to reduce costs even beyond the niggardly federal guidelines in a misguided attempt to demonstrate to program opponents that public housing could be cost-efficient.[39] The imposition of these cost limits ensured that while public housing might initially be better than the slum conditions it replaced, it "would never grace the landscape and bring pleasure to the eye."[40]

Indeed, supporters felt that the cost-containment elements of the program essentially guaranteed a poor physical standard for public housing. Almost immediately, public housing was criticized for its "unnecessarily barracks-like and monotonous" look.[41] Internally, the units bore the marks of countless cost compromises; elevators stopped on every other floor, closets were built without doors, apartments had cement floors and cinder-block walls. Many of these design "innovations" were recommended by the federal oversight agency as means of keeping costs down. The USHA advocated for placing public housing on "superblocks" that interrupted the local street grid and set the projects apart from their surrounding communities. This was seen as both a positive design objective (so as to keep the public housing separate from the slum that surrounded it) and as a means of keeping costs down.[42] Ultimately, PHAs turned to high-rise construction as the most cost-effective approach; in some cases it was the only way to build significant amounts of public housing within the cost guidelines imposed by USHA. The modernist design approach was "trimmed to minimalist designs under the pressures of density and cost considerations, resulting in a readily identifiable 'government housing' aesthetic."[43] The result was often high-rises that were particularly sterile and unwelcoming. Even public housing advocate Catherine Bauer called them "gray fortresses that loomed menacingly over the cityscape."[44]

Cost-containment pressures extended to the fiscal model that was adopted by Congress for the public housing program. Initially, the federal government subsidy was in the form of construction capital to build the developments. The capital debt was retired through annual contributions from the federal government to the PHA. This method of financing in effect extended federal government control over local projects. Through the annual contribution contracts (ACC), the USHA and later HUD exerted influence in the design and operation of public housing. One local public housing administrator said that despite the nominally decentralized nature of public housing, "running a local housing authority was akin to being an East German business manager" dealing with a highly centralized, top-down system of authority and administration.[45]

The shortcuts taken during construction and design to minimize upfront costs had the ultimate effect of contributing to higher operating costs down the road. The shortcuts in materials and design led to more rapid decline of the structures. The poor site design and lack of defensible space increased security and maintenance problems at the buildings.[46] The impersonal architecture and the large number of children in the projects sometimes led to accelerated wear and tear. Residents who cared about the maintenance of common spaces often organized themselves but could not keep up with the deterioration of those spaces.

The projects themselves were required to cover operating expenses out of rent collections. Cash reserves for public housing buildings were limited and until 1968 there was no allowance for capital replacement reserves, which meant it was extremely difficult for PHAs to replace building systems that had aged and deteriorated. Because public housing, as government-owned property, was exempt from local property taxes, PHAs were required to pay a fee in-lieu of taxes to local governments equal to 10 percent of project income. Cash surpluses beyond the allowable limits for reserves were paid back to the federal government to offset the annual contributions and pay down the capital debt.

Even given the inadequacies of the program's design, local PHAs were able to operate the program successfully for the first twenty-five years. But inflation and inner-city demographic changes combined to transform public housing from a way station for the temporarily poor into more permanent accommodations for low-income families. Without operating subsidies for the first twenty-five years of the program many PHAs found themselves in serious fiscal straits by the 1960s. When operating subsidies from the federal government were first introduced ($10 monthly for elderly residents in 1961 and then for all residents in 1964), these were made available only to PHAs with low reserves, in effect punishing the more efficient operations. Rising costs led PHAs to increase rents. As inflation drove construction and maintenance costs higher, Congress and the PHAs were adopting tenant selection guidelines that resulted in an ever-more impoverished resident base. By the end of the 1960s, operating costs and in-lieu tax payments were greater than revenues for many PHAs.[47] The squeeze on public housing residents became so extreme that in some projects residents were paying in excess of 60 percent of their income on rent. An Urban Institute study in twenty-three major cities found that 80 percent of the cost increases between 1965 and 1968 were due to price inflation.[48] With trend lines in costs and revenues moving in opposite directions, PHAs across the nation approached fiscal crisis. By 1968, one half of the largest PHAs in the nation had a deficit.[49]

A well-publicized rent strike by public housing residents in St. Louis brought the issue to a head. Congress responded with the Brooke Amendment, which limited public housing rents to 25 percent of tenants' incomes. This immediately eliminated the rent burden of public housing residents but just as quickly shifted the financial crisis onto the PHAs by severely restricting income. Congress attempted to make up for the revenue crisis they had initiated by providing operating subsidies to PHAs, but that legislation did not pass until 1970 and regular payments to PHAs did not arrive until 1972.[50] In the interim PHAs sank into further financial crisis.

There was awareness at the time that the cost constraints imposed on the program were warping the results. The stultifying architecture and site design, forced by cost considerations that overrode all others, was remarked upon at the time. Some strong proponents of public housing, including Catherine Bauer and other original supporters of the program, were openly disillusioned as early as 1957. Officials who built public housing high-rises, with some exceptions, understood they were misguided but kept building them.[51] The planners did not feel good about high-rises, and the residents knew firsthand the difficulties of high-rise living. "We live stacked on top of one another with no elbow room," said one resident quoted by a Chicago newspaper, "danger is all around. There's little privacy or peace and no quiet. And the world looks on all of us as project rats, living on a reservation like untouchables."[52] Residents rejected the Pruitt-Igoe high-rises in St. Louis almost from the beginning, pushing vacancy rates above acceptable levels after only a couple of years of operation. The project was 16 percent vacant before five years had elapsed, and two-thirds empty before it was fifteen years old. The sense that cost-containment considerations were leading to suboptimal outcomes was palpable in some places. Bradford Hunt describes the history of Chicago public housing as a slow-moving train wreck in which all participants could see the impending crash, but no one could or would do anything to prevent it.[53]

Tenant Selection

Tenant selection was always a contentious issue for public housing advocates and administrators. Tension existed from the very beginning with slum reformers favoring an approach that reserved public housing for the neediest and avoided competition with the private sector in all cases. Their model of public housing was to be reserved for physical locations the private sector would not venture into and for socioeconomic groups the market would not serve. The Modern Housing advocates on the other hand favored an approach that targeted the working class more broadly. With the adoption of the slum clearance model advocated by the Progressives, the controversy was settled in favor of a program that would focus on very low income families.

In the beginning, PHAs adopted policies that reserved units for the working poor. Initially, PHAs across the country were selective in filling public housing units, often making judgments not only about the ability of the family to pay rent but also about their moral character and their suitability as residents of the new communities being created.[54] Most families residing in public housing in the early years were two-parent households in which one was employed. Welfare recipients and single mothers were generally avoided in the tenant selection process. In fact, as Lawrence Vale puts it, "'eligible' did not necessarily mean 'acceptable'" in public housing.[55] Initially, then, public housing was exclusive, and the early projects were considered "a little heaven for poor people"[56] and in places such as Boston became a patronage benefit that politicians handed out to friends and constituents.[57] In New York City, where the influence of the European model of modern housing was greatest, the selectivity of the local housing authority persisted longer than in other cities.[58]

But over time the face and nature of poverty in the United States began to shift and with it the profile of public housing residents. As Vale argues, "the mandate to serve low-income applicants was in perpetual conflict with the desirability of retaining a stable base of fiscally and socially responsible tenants."[59] Congress was strict about limiting eligibility for public housing to those with low incomes. Reflecting the concern that public housing not compete, and that it clearly be set aside for the poor, the program provided for a 20 percent income gap between those who qualified for public housing and the minimum income necessary to compete in local housing markets. Some congressional supporters expected the private sector to "build down" to the income level of public housing and thus fill the unmet housing needs of people whose incomes fell in the 20 percent gap.[60]

Those who were able to improve their earnings over time lost their eligibility for public housing and were required to leave. This put PHAs in the position of having to evict their highest income tenants, a step they took with varying degrees of enthusiasm. In 1940 the Chicago Housing Authority reduced rents to more precisely target lower-income families and as a result made one quarter of their existing tenants ineligible for further occupancy. All of these tenants were evicted; all were white. CHA repeated this step shortly after World War II ended. In fact, once the Depression ended and families who had been temporarily submerged by the economic conditions began to increase incomes in a reviving economy, the clientele for public housing began to shift to the chronic poor. As more working class families had choices in postwar America they moved out of public housing and into the private market. Gradually during the 1940s the face of public housing began to change.

The advocates of public housing recognized this trend early on. They had warned against public housing becoming "welfare housing," thinking that the shift would make the projects themselves more difficult to manage, and strip the program of its political constituency. Housing reformer Edith Elmer Wood argued against the growing practice of setting rents according to the income of tenants (preferring to attract tenants with incomes sufficient to pay rents that were set at levels that would support building maintenance and operations).[61] But when demand for public housing among working families began to wane, and when waiting lists began to be dominated by families without employment-based income, many PHAs changed policies, effectively reducing their own revenue stream and serving a lower-income clientele.

The racial character of public housing also changed early on. Although most PHAs enforced segregation within their housing stock, maintaining separate buildings for white and black tenants, enough of the early projects had been built in white slum areas (or on vacant land) that most residents of public housing were white. But white families always had greater choice in local housing markets than did blacks, given the prevailing patterns of residential segregation and discrimination in American cities of the era. There were, in fact, chronic shortages of decent housing for African Americans in most cities. Thus, most applicants for new public housing projects were black. When Wentworth Gardens in Chicago opened in 1946, thousands of black families showed up to submit applications. The handful of whites who showed up did not stay.[62] It took a strong management approach to maintain a racial mix in the overall tenant profile for large-city PHAs; whites were moving out in response to their own improved fortunes and the expansion of options in the private housing market, while blacks, still confronted with the shackling constraints of segregation in the private market and an acute housing shortage, increased their demand for public housing. The advent of urban renewal in 1949, authorized in the same legislation that renewed the public housing program, generally worsened the housing shortage for blacks by displacing them from their existing housing and demolishing it in favor of new commercial or high-rent development.[63] As more blacks entered public housing, more whites fled, worried about having to share buildings with black families.

Implementation Challenges

Several trends were converging in public housing in major U.S. cities in the 1950s. The income profile of tenants was declining as working families moved out and were increasingly replaced with households whose income was based on public assistance. The racial profile was changing as well given the greater housing choices available to whites and the enduring shortage of housing among blacks. The fiscal profile of public housing was beginning to suffer as costs rose in the postwar economy, but rents—frequently based on the income of tenants—stagnated or declined. Finally, PHAs began resorting to more extreme cost-cutting strategies in the design and construction of new public housing. In the 1950s many cities began building the stark high-rises that in subsequent decades came to symbolize the dehumanizing aspects of the worst public housing. The result of this convergence was the marginalization and stigmatization of public housing. Vale argues that in Boston by the late 1950s, a mere twenty years into the program, public housing was seen as "housing of last resort." Rhonda Williams claims that, by 1962, public housing in Baltimore was seen as a place for "problem families." Chester Hartman wrote in 1963 that public housing in larger U.S. cities had become the "receptacle for the very lowest elements of society."[64]

The trend continued in the '60s as the welfare rights movement gained momentum and many PHAs began to pursue policies to integrate their housing. Whites fled in even greater numbers, and PHA tenant selection began to emphasize families with severe need living on public assistance. As single mothers began to emerge as the fastest-growing segment among the poor, they began to dominate the profile of public housing. By 1966, almost half of all households entering public housing across the country had no employed adult, and half had only a single parent. In large cities, those figures were higher. Very few local housing authorities, the New York City Housing Authority (NYCHA) notably among them, were able to resist the inexorable slide into welfare housing. The NYCHA worked hard to maintain a more diverse income and employment profile among its residents, but it was severely criticized for doing so by local advocates for the poor.[65] Generally, however, the transformation of public housing into a welfare program was complete by the end of the 1960s. In 1968, HUD required PHAs to use a first-come-first-served system for tenant eligibility, eliminating the ability of PHAs to screen tenants on more traditional bases related to ability to pay. In subsequent years, Congress codified this transition by establishing preferences for the neediest.[66] These policies helped to ensure that those in greatest need received public housing, but it also increased the economic, social, and political distance between public housing residents and those in private housing.

The incomes of public housing residents steadily declined in comparison to the trends for society as a whole. Between 1950 and 1970, the median income of public housing residents fell from 64 percent of the national median to 37 percent.[67] By the 1980s, the average income of public housing residents nationally was one-fifth the national average. It was lower than that by 1995.[68]

Mismanagement

On top of the process of physical decline and social transformation, public housing in some major cities was simply badly mismanaged.[69] Public housing was the backwater of local public administration in many cities, reserved for patronage appointments of politically connected individuals with little expertise in running a large and complicated social service and welfare program of the type that public housing had become. In Chicago, for example, the CHA was headed by Charles Swibel, "a slumlord of dubious character" whose appointment gave him responsibility over a real estate empire that he systematically mismanaged to the detriment of hundreds of thousands of low-income residents over a nineteen-year period.[70] Rhonda Williams writes of the nepotism and party cronyism that ruled public housing management in Baltimore.[71] In 1993 the *Baltimore Sun* ran a story describing conditions in Lexington Terrace in which a

> 31-year-old mother of four lives in a mildewed and roach-infested apartment on the sixth floor.... She must bathe by candlelight because of an electrical problem in the bathroom. Water runs without interruption from the spigot in the kitchen because the spigot's valves don't work. Her 5-year-old son ... recently contracted a bacterial infection in his eye from the mildew in the apartment and must undergo minor surgery next week.... Children play on filthy mattresses discarded in the hallways and get skin rashes from bugs and germs.... "This is a living hell," said [one resident]. "You have no cooperation from the management and the maintenance."[72]

The story prompted a visit from the city's mayor, Kurt Schmoke, who apologized to tenants: "I couldn't believe what my eyes were seeing. No wonder you're angry. It looks like a place we forgot."[73]

In Boston, Housing Authority management positions were also used as party patronage, providing secure employment regardless of management experience or interest.[74] Cronyism and the use of public housing jobs as patronage, as seen in Baltimore, Boston, and Chicago, resulted in most PHAs being "grossly overstaffed" and inefficient.[75] A nationwide survey in 1969 found that most PHA commissioners harbored "antagonistic and negative feelings towards public housing families"—the very families they were entrusted with housing.[76] Where outright antagonism was not the cause of unresponsive management, simple incompetence often was.[77]

As Michael Schill argued in 1993, "although there are no systematic nationwide evaluations of PHA management practices, allegations of mismanagement are ubiquitous."[78] HUD began initiatives aimed at improving management as early as the 1960s. During the decade of the '70s alone HUD offered up the Housing Management Improvement Program, the Target Projects Program, and the Public Housing Urban Initiatives Program, all of which were aimed at improving conditions in public housing communities and improving the management capacities and performance of local housing authorities. The programs, however, did not build on each other in any meaningful way, nor did later ones even tend to incorporate the lessons learned from earlier efforts. As Raymond Struyk concluded in his assessment of these programs, "often the initiatives were conceived simply as a method of channeling additional resources to distressed or 'deserving' Authorities."[79]

The tenant management movement that emerged in the 1970s was a direct response to the poor management of public housing projects by PHAs. Residents organized rent strikes in several cities to try to force local authorities to maintain the buildings, replace broken building systems, and make repairs when necessary. There was some feeling, especially among public housing residents, that property management began to fail when the projects turned predominantly black:

> Well when I first moved in it was a country club, okay. Because you had services. See everybody wants to say we became a prison or whatever you want to call it because black people moved in. But you see if they would have gave us the same services as I got when I first moved in here, this place would still be looking good, okay? But what happened was black people moved in and the services were gone.[80]

When building materials and systems began to age, many public housing authorities lacked the resources and the internal capacity to upgrade them. In addition to allowing large systems to fail, minor repairs often took weeks and public housing residents were made to endure substandard living conditions. Developer Richard Baron, who has completed a number of public housing redevelopment projects, notes that "one could argue that the difficulties of traditional public housing were caused largely by a failure of management."[81]

An Exaggerated Discourse of Disaster

The popular image of public housing changed when its demographics changed. Scott Henderson argues that prior to the 1960s national periodicals did not disseminate a negative perception of public housing, frequently depicting projects as important slum-clearance efforts that were improving central city areas.[82] When negative images were attached to public housing they generally focused on what critics claimed was the intrusion of the state into private market processes and creeping socialism. In the 1960s, however, the prevailing discourse about public housing changed. The debate about urban slum clearance vs. socialism gave way to a storyline about public housing that focused on race, welfare dependency, and crime. Several factors contributed to the change, including the increasing presence of African Americans among public housing residents, the emerging dysfunction of some high-rise projects in large cities, and the urban racial unrest of the '60s. The racial changes and tensions occurring in America's largest cities were centrally important in the changing discourse about public housing. As Henderson argues, the shift in perceptions happened "during a period when some of America's largest cities gained black majorities, and as the black civil rights movement entered a more militant and confrontational phase."[83]

Media stories zeroed in on the most dysfunctional high-rise projects, the fantastic failures of public housing, highlighting a largely black population living in dangerous and alienating communities. *Chicago Daily News* coverage of the Robert Taylor Homes in 1965 described the project as

> a hellish way of life....Its own tenants label it a "death trap," a concentration camp, and even, with sardonic self-derision, "the Congo Hilton."...Here live 28,000 people, all of them poor, grappling with violence and vandalism, fear and suspicion, teen-age terror and adult chaos, rage, resentment, official regimenting.[84]

The 1972 demolition of the massive Pruitt-Igoe complex of high-rises in St. Louis provided a lasting image of catastrophic failure that was echoed twenty-five years later by the demolition of other notorious public housing projects across the country. Pruitt-Igoe's demolition produced for it "a symbolic significance unparalleled by any other American public housing project."[85] For years afterward, the fate of Pruitt-Igoe was invoked as emblematic of the public housing experience in America. The project was the subject of over seventy articles in popular and trade periodicals and scholarly works.[86] In the 1980s and 1990s, the storyline of public housing became conflated with a growing moral panic about violent crime and drug use in the nation's urban ghettos. Visions of the "other America" crowded the evening newscasts. Steve Macek offers an example, citing two stories reported on the *CBS Evening News* on consecutive nights in February 1994:

> The story opens with a shot of two men silhouetted against a gritty, downscale city street. "They are there every day" [the] voice-over begins, "outside Chicago's big housing projects, shadowy figures who gather on street corners and stand in doorways, hang out near the playground and sometimes push baby strollers." Meanwhile…we are treated first to a shot of four black men in stocking caps sitting on the stoop of a severe, institutional brick building; this is followed by a shot of black men standing in shadows, a shot—partially obscured by steam rising from the gutter—of a group of men on a street corner, a glimpse of three black men standing in the doorway of a housing project, a shot taken through chain link fencing of some men milling around an outdoor basketball court, and, finally, a quick take of a black man pushing a baby stroller past a desolate vacant lot.[87]

This popular understanding of public housing has led analysts who ought to know better into unfounded generalizations and exaggerations about the state of the nation's public housing stock. The scenario of failure and dysfunction "is a scenario for almost all public housing in the United States," declared Robert Burchell, an urban expert at Rutgers University, in 1987. "There are no more good stories that emerge from public housing. Public housing is viewed nationally as troublesome, difficult to maintain and a blight *in every single one of its locations*" (emphasis added).[88] Richard Baron, head of McCormick Baron Salazar, a real estate development firm that has done many public housing redevelopments, falls into the same trap. Speaking about the Dixie Homes in Memphis and their advanced state of decline, he told the *Memphis Daily News* in 2010 that "all of the public housing in the United States was like these. They were all distressed, all filled with large, low-income families, very marginally managed by local housing authorities."[89]

As Henderson notes, the image of public housing broadcast by the popular media was not wholly inaccurate; hellish conditions existed at many large public housing projects in America's biggest cities. Accidental deaths due to malfunctioning elevators, snipers killing policemen, and gang control of entire projects were a reality in some places. The failures of public housing were appalling, they were highly publicized, and they produced sickening conditions for the low-income families who had little choice but to endure them. These failures became the main element of the public housing storyline that dominated public perception and came to shape public policy in the 1980s and 1990s.

The public-housing-as-disaster scenario was a reality in several large and medium-sized cities and adversely affected the lives of thousands of tenants; it was a real public policy problem. Nevertheless, it presents a narrow and distorted understanding of the public housing experience across the country. Specifically, it (a) suggests a passivity among public housing residents and ignores the active steps taken in city after city by residents who, seeing no help from those nominally responsible for the management of their communities, took it upon themselves to attempt to establish order out of chaos; (b) discounts the value that residents attached to their homes and neighborhoods, and the community they were able to establish even amid desperate conditions; (c) overstates the prevalence of the fundamental breakdown of public housing by ignoring the large majority of projects that operated well, and the large majority of cities and towns in which public housing has been decently managed and provided a much better standard of living for very low income families than was available to them in the private market.

The image of public housing communities wildly out of control, with a tenant base made up of violent criminals on the one hand and passive, cowering victims on the other, does not, in fact, describe the *overwhelming majority* of public housing in the nation. In most cities at most times, public housing provides a better alternative than private-sector housing in poor neighborhoods. One study provides evidence that households in public housing nationwide are less likely to suffer from overcrowding and their children are less likely to have been held back in school than a comparison group of poor families.[90] Even among HOPE VI projects, sites that have presumably met HUD's threshold for dysfunctionality, there are projects that are a far cry from the extreme conditions depicted in the discourse of disaster. For instance, in Portland, Karen Gibson characterizes a demolished project as having been "well designed, racially integrated, and well managed"—facts that many displaced residents recognized and which provided the basis for their attachment to the original project.[91]

The nation's largest PHA, the New York City Housing Authority (NYCHA), has largely avoided the problems seen in Chicago, Philadelphia, and elsewhere. NYCHA has run a very large program of public housing (more than ten times larger than most major cities' public housing stock) quite successfully, providing clean, decent, and safe affordable housing for low-income families. That the vast majority of public housing is in decent condition and that the program "is quietly performing a very tough assignment quite well" is what James Stockard calls "the great secret" of public housing.[92] Though the popular image of public

FIGURE 2.   Cheatham Place, Nashville, Tennessee: the first public housing in the city, built in the 1930s for whites only.

housing is the high-rise, even at the peak of such housing only 27 percent of public housing units were in high-rises, and many of those housed seniors. Instead, about one-third of units nationwide were in garden apartments, 16 percent in other low-rise buildings, and 25 percent were single-family homes.[93] These public housing units do not share the same problems as the run-down, crime-infested, dysfunctional high-rise buildings found in a few of the largest cities in the country. More than 80 percent of the PHAs in the country operate less than five hundred units of public housing, and most of this stock is very functional and provides an essential housing resource for its residents. Seventy-five percent of public housing residents nationwide express satisfaction with their living conditions.[94] In 1999, HUD Secretary Andrew Cuomo told members of the Public Housing Authority Director's Association that "public housing is an overwhelming success in this nation."[95] As one analyst commented, public housing seems unpopular with everybody except those who live there and those who are on waiting lists to get in.[96]

For residents of the worst public housing in American cities, creating order amid the chaos of life in the projects was a formidable task, but residents did not passively acquiesce to the deteriorating conditions around them. On the

FIGURE 3.   Ocean Bay Apartments, formerly known as Edgemere Houses, in Far Rockaway, New York City, built in 1961.

contrary, they went to great lengths to make up for the deficiencies of design, construction, and management that shaped their living environment. Recent scholarship has demonstrated the efforts of public housing residents to build and maintain community, to create order in environments effectively abandoned by management and by city services. Roberta Feldman and Susan Stall have documented more than four decades of grassroots effort by residents of the Wentworth Gardens project on Chicago's South Side to reverse the deterioration of the buildings, the grounds, and the services they were provided by the housing authority.[97] Rhonda Williams studied the efforts of women in Baltimore's public housing to combat the decline of their communities. These activists organized themselves and other residents to fight for better management responsiveness, and when that produced no change they organized rent strikes and forced local authorities to institute resident management systems. Sudhir Venkatesh's study of the Robert Taylor Homes also points to the efforts of public housing residents working to establish livable communities in the face of housing authority indifference and neglect.[98] Each of these studies as well as others describe residents' efforts to construct workable communities within the constraints of poverty, segregation, and discrimination. Ironically, in some of these studies the "discovery" that public housing residents were able to create and nurture their own communities occurred through the recollections of those who had already been forcibly displaced from those communities because of demolition.[99]

Residents in the most troubled public housing were not blind to the conditions in which they lived. Their desire for better conditions is what drove their activism. At the same time, most public housing residents have a different view of their communities than the image of severe crisis and dysfunction described in popular discourse. There has for some time been evidence that "the overwhelming majority of tenants do not accept the tarnished image of public housing."[100] Surveys of residents in St. Louis, Boston, Wilmington, Delaware, and elsewhere showed residents largely satisfied with their housing, while acknowledging the difficulties created by building neglect and poor management. The long waiting lists maintained by most public housing authorities bear witness to the desire of many very low income families to live in public housing (and are equally eloquent in identifying the lack of alternatives in the private sector). A national survey in the mid-1980s found that the average wait for a two-bedroom public housing unit was eighteen months, with twenty-three months the norm for larger units.[101] As Alvin Rabushka and William Weissert noted in 1977:

> Is it not ironical that people should want to move into this housing of last resort? And that people in public housing don't want to leave? Even some tenants who can afford better alternatives in the private housing market don't want to go. Every year public housing authorities have to evict people who exceed the income limitations of the program but who would stay if permitted.[102]

Nevertheless, the discourse of disaster dominated media representations of public housing. By the end of the 1980s, there was a widespread sense among policy makers, city officials, and legislators that public housing in the United States was severely broken, indeed had become, among those less inclined to fix blame on the residents, "a humanitarian disaster."[103] Dysfunctional public housing, furthermore, became part of a larger discourse about system failure in many cities. Reeling from the economic dislocations of the 1970s and '80s, suffering massive job losses, plant closings, and neighborhood deterioration due to economic restructuring, American cities were suffering high levels of crime, violence, and disinvestment. Crack cocaine, which hit city streets in the mid-1980s, was ravishing communities, fueling gang battles for control of turf and control of drug markets. Concentrations of poverty were getting larger and more numerous. At the vortex of this was public housing; it was where "the other America" lived.

Assessing Public Housing

Controversy follows the public housing program everywhere. Public housing was the most hotly debated housing program ever undertaken by the federal government. Controversy continued through the implementation of the program, as questions about the merits of the program and its place in the system of housing assistance shifted to the local level, generating political debates over the role of government in private markets, racial segregation, and the renewal of inner-city ghettos. There is controversy even in the collective assessment of what public housing has meant over the years. There are three schools of thought about public housing. The first regards the program as a failure of government, as a well-meaning but misplaced attempt to tackle social problems through heavy-handed government action that in the end produced as many problems as it addressed.[104] The problems of public housing are, in this scenario, the problems of all large governmental interventions: it was not nimble enough to respond to changing conditions of urban poverty; it produced the wrong incentives for families by shielding them from the discipline of the market; it was subject to too much political manipulation by both local and federal politicians; and it was terribly mismanaged in too many places. Public housing is thus the quintessential example of public intervention gone awry, and further evidence of the inefficiencies of welfare state policies. By the late 1950s, observers argued that public housing was destroying the neighborhoods in which it was located. Even past supporters and those who advocated for it from the beginning were disillusioned with the program's performance.[105] Currently, even some staunch supporters of affordable housing and government-subsidized housing acknowledge what they see as the abject failure of public housing.

The second school of thought places the explanation for public housing failure at the feet of those who designed the program and who compromised it from the beginning. This argument also acknowledges that public housing has been a tremendous failure, but argues that the failure is a reflection of specific design features of the program that crippled it from the beginning.[106] To these analysts, public housing was never given a full chance in the United States; it was designed to fail. Thus, the inability of PHAs to maintain their buildings is due to the impossibly difficult program guidelines created by a Congress unwilling to commit the resources necessary to provide for a workable program. Ultimately, the opponents of public housing, though unable to prevent passage of the program, were able to compromise it to the extent that it would not be successful.[107] This argument is most closely connected with the work of Eugene Meehan, who argued that the opponents of public housing distorted the program during the congressional debates leading to enactment of the 1937 and 1949 bills, and that in order to secure the votes necessary for passage of the bill, public housing advocates made too many compromises, compromises that, in the end, led to the inevitable failure of the program. Specifically, Meehan points to the restrictive fiscal model for the program that led to construction and design shortcuts and pinched administrators during the postconstruction period. Bradford Hunt also argues that fear of political opposition led to overzealous cost-cutting—even beyond congressional guidelines—by the USHA for decades after the program was created, leading to a series of poor decisions about the siting and design of public housing projects in major cities.[108]

In the end, the distinctive elements of these two perspectives blur. According to a third school of thought presented in the previous pages, what is left is an exaggerated focus on the problems of public housing, a somewhat myopic focus on the worst cases without an appreciation for the fact that the conditions that prevailed in Chicago, Atlanta, Philadelphia, and other cities were not universal, and in fact did not characterize the majority of public housing. A more realistic assessment of public housing acknowledges the sometimes spectacular failures of the program, but places those failures alongside the lasting successes of PHAs in New York City, St. Paul, Minnesota, Portland, Oregon, and countless other communities. A more nuanced and full understanding of the public housing story in the United States notes that the design of public housing often set it apart in communities, became identifiable, and contributed to the stigmatization of the communities and its residents. Yet, in the early years, public housing produced notable architecture and archetypal expressions of New Deal design that remained—while they were still standing—historically important representations of that era. Public housing was also certainly diminished in quality by severe cost-cutting pressures. Tenant selection policy contributed to high concentrations of poverty that led to the concentration of social problems in public housing communities.

Mismanagement further impoverished the system in many though not all cities. The program was made to serve the segregationist agenda of local officials during most of the period when new projects were being built. In some places, the combination of these forces led to catastrophic failure. Public housing residents were forced to endure deplorable living conditions made worse by the fact that these were produced through the hand of government, not despite it. But, in most places, even all of these forces together did not lead to disaster. These factors produced difficult but workable housing that was, and continues to be, an extremely important segment of the housing market, providing decent housing for families that are not served well or at all by the private market. Public housing works for hundreds of thousands of people, and waiting lists that have always been long and remain so today provide testament to this fact.

DISMANTLING PUBLIC HOUSING

I am very much opposed to the proliferation of public housing in
Waterbury. It's just another form of welfare to attract the poor to
places where there are no jobs. It hurts everybody, them and us.

—David Corbett, chairman of the Waterbury Housing Authority

Jon Gutzman, executive director of the Saint Paul Public Housing Authority in
Minnesota maintained in 2004 that public housing in that city has helped "liter-
ally thousands of families and individuals [find] a home to stabilize their lives
while they perhaps emigrated to this country, or connected with needed support
services, or obtained an education or a job, or regained their health, or dealt
with a disability."[1] Rick White, the spokesman for the Atlanta Housing Authority,
remarked in 2008 that "his agency determined in the 1990s that 'public housing
is a failed policy, and in many ways an immoral policy.'"[2] The commitment to
public housing on the part of PHA officials, it is fair to say, varies from city to
city. The movement to dismantle the New Deal legacy of public housing is an
uneven one. In cities such as Memphis, Atlanta, Chicago, and New Orleans, housing authorities and local officials are eradicating all or most of the public housing
stock, while in other places, such as New York City, Phoenix, and Saint Paul, little
or no public housing is being lost.

The movement to dismantle public housing began with attempts by some
PHAs during the 1980s to rid themselves of their most troubled projects. In
some cases this took the form of allowing projects to deteriorate and depopulate,
resulting in what resident advocates called de facto demolition. Since the 1990s,
the effort to dismantle became more widespread. Though demolition accounts
for most of the units removed, the sale and disposition of public housing has
also contributed to the reduction of units nationwide. The patterns of removal

across the nation's largest cities suggest that race and gentrification pressures are important in determining the aggressiveness with which cities pursue the transformation of public housing.

Early Demolition of Public Housing

Significant expansion of the public housing stock essentially ended in the 1970s. President Richard Nixon put a moratorium on new federal housing efforts in 1973, halting the expansion of older programs such as public housing. The demolition of the Pruitt-Igoe complex in St. Louis in 1972 was a stunning visual symbol of the problems that many high-rise public housing projects were facing. Congress passed Section 8 of the 1974 Housing and Community Development Act, creating a program of household-based housing allowances, and HUD began shifting its emphasis away from subsidizing "hard units" to subsidizing families directly and allowing them to shop their Section 8 certificates throughout the local housing market.

By the 1980s, the public housing program was generating only a few thousand new units each year and had been eclipsed by the Section 8 program as the lead effort of the federal government in affordable housing. Local governments and the federal government began to look to nonprofit development corporations for the bulk of the new affordable housing units built. There was little innovation in public housing. Most PHAs simply continued to manage and operate their housing; some tried unsuccessfully to cope with the increased pressures of extreme poverty among their own residents and in the communities surrounding public housing projects.

Noticeable efforts by HUD and local housing authorities to disinvest in their public housing stock began during the 1980s.[3] Concentrated poverty was on the increase in American cities. Crack cocaine hit the streets in 1985, adding an additional element of chaos to the lives of America's poorest ghettos and increasing the stakes for gangs vying to control illicit drug markets in the forgotten corners of U.S. cities. It was in this environment that PHAs first began to shed public housing units. It began as a dribble of units demolished or sold, usually a few units here or there, rarely an entire development. Very few of the units taken out, initially, were in high-rise developments. There was no announced program of disinvestment, nor any coordinated effort on the part of HUD to subsidize or incentivize the removal of units. Congress, while not expanding public housing, was still interested in protecting and preserving it. In most cases, the initiative for removing units came from local housing authorities looking for ways to rid themselves of the most troublesome of their housing stock, and they found HUD willing to allow it.

Demolition or sale of public housing units by local housing authorities requires the approval of HUD. The rules and procedures for the demolition of public housing are laid out in Section 18 of the 1937 Housing Act.[4] The Act stipulates that the secretary of HUD can approve an application for demolition of public housing only if (a) the project or a section of the project is obsolete, and (b) the local PHA has consulted with residents in developing the proposal to demolish it. Furthermore, the Act requires that, should demolition occur, all tenants displaced would be "given relocation assistance to other decent, safe, sanitary and affordable housing." In 1969, Congress amended the 1937 Housing Act to require a one-for-one replacement of public units that were demolished or sold. The one-for-one requirement was first inserted as a legislative amendment to the public housing program because Congress was concerned about the loss of low-cost units due to urban renewal. In fact, the journey from "equivalent elimination" (a requirement in the original public housing program that required one unit of slum housing to be taken down for every unit of public housing constructed) to one-for-one replacement was testament to how the fortunes of public housing and slum clearance had changed over the years. In 1937 the concern among policy makers had been that public housing would create a glut of low-cost housing and that congressional action was needed to ensure that clearance would keep up with public housing production. As a result, Congress demanded that a substandard house be eliminated for every unit of public housing built. By 1969, urban renewal was so widely used and demolition of low-cost housing so common, that Congress felt the need to ensure that public housing development would keep up with the removals.

One-for-one replacement remained a requirement until 1983 when the Reagan administration succeeded in removing it from the program in the midst of a larger policy shift away from subsidizing "hard units" and toward the use of household-based vouchers. Congress reinstated the requirement four years later in response to a growing lack of low-cost housing in the nation. HUD was given authority to waive the one-for-one requirement if there was evidence that the local housing market within which a petitioning PHA operated had a surplus of low-cost housing. Otherwise, PHAs were given six years to construct the replacement units for those they had been given approval to demolish. Even when the replacement requirement was not in effect, however, the other provisions of Section 18 applied, requiring the PHA to demonstrate that the units to be removed were obsolete. A portion of a project could be demolished if the PHA demonstrated that the removal of those units was necessary to preserve the rest of the project—the equivalent of amputating a gangrened limb to save the body.

Prior to the 1980s, very few public housing demolitions took place and there was not much pressure from PHAs to demolish or sell public housing units. Nationwide, new units were still coming online each year, and congressional intent during this period was to preserve public housing whenever possible. Of course, the notable and very significant exception to all of this was the implosion of the Pruitt-Igoe project in St. Louis in 1972. The skyrocketing vacancy rates at Pruitt-Igoe, the rapid physical decline of the buildings, and the dysfunctional social and living conditions that prevailed at the development presaged what would happen to many large developments during the 1980s. When these conditions emerged, PHAs began to press more frequently for demolition and HUD became more accommodating. Thus, the 1980s saw an almost imperceptible shift in the trajectory of the public housing program. Though there was no stated course reversal, and despite a continued trickle of new units coming online, PHAs across the country began to embrace the idea of demolition for projects that presented the greatest management or financial challenges. HUD largely acquiesced to this shift, frequently approving the demolition applications it received.

A report published in 1990 by the National Housing Law Project (NHLP) sheds light on this otherwise unknown and unannounced policy shift.[5] Surveying local housing authorities and reviewing HUD documents related to the disposition of public housing units, NHLP revealed that local housing authorities sold or demolished 14,990 units of public housing between 1978 and 1989. Another thirty thousand units were scheduled for demolition or sale by local authorities (the removal of eight thousand of which had already been approved by HUD) at the time of the publication of their report. In addition, NHLP identified another twenty thousand units in projects with very high vacancy rates that put them in jeopardy for future disposition.

Though this trend started out modestly (fewer than one thousand units were lost in 1980), the rate of loss was several thousand per year by the end of the 1980s. Although NHLP did not foresee the massive policy changes that would emerge in the 1990s, it nevertheless estimated that the rate of demolition and sale would pick up during the decade. In all, they identified around sixty-five thousand units of public housing that had either been lost or were in danger of being removed from the stock by housing authorities nationwide. This was roughly equivalent to the total production of new public housing units nationwide during the 1980s—an average of 7,149 units was being added annually nationwide during the last half of the 1980s.[6] Furthermore, NHLP documented an accelerating rate of demolition and sale by the end of the decade.

NHLP's numbers were likely an undercount. Though they were able to secure the cooperation of most of the housing authorities they surveyed, their study was not a complete review of PHAs across the country. Though their sample was heavily weighted toward the largest PHAs, and their findings showed that the largest PHAs were the most active in removing units, their study did not cover the actions of all local housing authorities. But several of the trends they reported foreshadowed the great explosion of demolitions that occurred in the '90s.

Most of the demolitions and sales they reported occurred in large family-housing projects. Senior public housing was, for the most part, not endangered in this first round of removal. In three-quarters of the removals they identified, local housing authorities removed only a portion of a project, a practice NHLP called "thinning." For example, in Kansas City the housing authority demolished the high-rise portion of the Wayne Miner project, but left the low-rise housing intact. In many cases, a thinning strategy indicated that the PHA was attempting to protect the rest of the housing stock by removing the worst. The relative emphasis on thinning versus complete abandonment shifted over the course of the decade, with the removal of entire projects becoming more common over time.

PHAs with more than 1,250 units (categorized as "large" PHAs by HUD) removed 84 percent of the units lost in the 1980s. Another 12 percent were removed by medium-sized PHAs (those with 500 and 1,250 units). PHAs on HUD's "troubled" list were also more likely than other PHAs to demolish or sell public housing units. A troubled PHA is one that has been judged by HUD to have significant deficiencies in its management capacities, achieving a very low score on the department's Public Housing Management Assessment Program (PHMAP). In most cases, the projects that lost units were severely distressed projects suffering from significant problems.[7] The removal of units from these projects, or the removal of the entire project, was thus an attempt to eliminate problem properties from the public housing stock.

Although gentrification became a major driver of public housing removal during the 1990s, this was not the case in the 1980s. In and around most public housing communities during the 1980s, housing markets were depressed and the communities themselves were immersed in problems associated with poverty and gang violence. Gentrification and a rebounding housing market did not seem viable scenarios in most cases. In fact, in only five of the thirty-four developments that were lost entirely during the decade did the public housing projects sit on highly valued real estate.[8] These five were all redeveloped as higher-income residential properties. The NHLP report indicated that race seemed to be a factor in determining which units would be removed from the public housing stock, because all of the projects slated for removal at the time of their report were majority nonwhite.

"De Facto Demolition"

The three-hundred-unit Fort Dupont public housing project in Washington, D.C., was situated in the city's far southeastern corner, a section with a predominantly black population and characterized by high levels of poverty and problems of crime and disinvestment. In 1977 the District of Columbia Housing Authority (DCHA) in Washington, D.C., made an application to HUD for modernization funds to fix up twenty-eight units at the development that were deemed uninhabitable. HUD approved almost a half million dollars for the project. The funds, however, were not spent immediately and by 1981 rising costs convinced the DCHA to pursue demolition instead. As a result the agency made an application to HUD to demolish the twenty-eight units. HUD did not immediately rule on the application and two years later DCHA increased the number of units it wanted to demolish to 112. In the interim, according to the tenants of Fort Dupont, the DCHA, anticipating demolition, had begun to systematically disinvest in Fort Dupont. The agency allowed the project to fall deeper into disrepair and made no attempt to rent out vacant units. By 1984, seventy-four of the 112 units designated by DCHA for demolition were vacant and DCHA was moving to empty the remaining thirty-eight units. Tenants who resisted moving out were threatened with eviction.[9] DCHA's interest in maintaining Fort Dupont continued to wane, and by 1985 more than half of the units in the entire project were vacant At that point, residents filed suit in federal court (*Edwards v. District of Columbia*) alleging that HUD's inaction, combined with the DCHA's neglect of maintenance at the project, constituted a de facto demolition of the project that reduced the stock of public housing units without going through the formal process of approval mandated by Congress in Section 18 of the original Public Housing Act of 1937.[10]

The argument in *Edwards* would become the foundation for similar cases across the country alleging de facto demolition. In essence, the claim is that the local PHA, having decided internally to demolish the units (but prior to receiving or in some cases even requesting approval from HUD to do so), discontinues normal maintenance at the site, deliberately engaging "in a systematic practice of vacating units and refusing to maintain [the development] so as to create *a fait accompli* and thereafter to obtain HUD's approval to demolish an abandoned and uninhabitable project."[11] Thus, de facto demolition is simultaneously the unauthorized removal of units from the active stock through abandonment and the creation of the very conditions of disrepair and obsolescence required for HUD approval of demolition.

De facto demolition was a strategy pursued by some PHAs in an environment where approval by HUD was necessary, and the demonstration of the specific need for and desirability of demolition was required. In the 1980s, prior to the nation's massive policy shift toward dispersal and deconcentration, the burden of proof for the need to demolish rested with the PHAs. De facto demolition emerged as a way of generating the proof necessary for HUD approval and of generating support for demolition among residents. During this time it was the typical process by which public housing units were lost in cities across the country. According to NHLP:

> Usually, the PHA's decision to apply for demolition and the filing of the formal application—not to mention HUD's review and approval process—is merely the last of a very protracted series of decisions and actions, all of which move inexorably toward that ultimate destruction.[12]

In a case of de facto demolition, a PHA in effect induces the physical obsolescence that is required for demolition approval through willful neglect of the public housing project, allowing physical problems at the site to go uncorrected, creating the conditions for vandalism by keeping large numbers of units vacant, and allowing major building systems to decline significantly to the point that repairs become prohibitively expensive. Thus, another term used for these cases was "constructive demolition." The assumption is that without this deliberate neglect on the part of the PHA, the project would have continued to be viable, inhabitable, and therefore continue to be a source of affordable housing for very low income families.

The second argument in the de facto demolition claim focuses on the immediate loss of units. The plaintiffs in *Edwards* claimed that by allowing the units to decline to the point where they were uninhabitable, and by keeping them vacant, the DCHA had in effect demolished them without HUD approval, without consultation of the tenants, and without providing any relocation assistance to the displaced families. In this way the tenant-protection requirements of the federal statute had been circumvented. Here the claim suggests that the effect of PHA neglect is the same as actual demolition; units of public housing are taken out of the stock and very low income families lose affordable housing opportunities. In contrast to actual demolition, however, residents are not consulted or provided with relocation assistance. Such action, when tacitly sanctioned by HUD and allowed by the courts, rendered the Section 18 requirements meaningless.

In a perfect application of catch-22, the U.S. District Court for the District of Columbia ruled in *Edwards* that since the DCHA's demolition application had not been approved, the law did not apply, and that "nothing in the statute prevents the District from seeking such demolition in the allegedly insensitive way it has chosen."[13] Without ruling on the factual merits of the case, the court dismissed it. The *Edwards* decision meant that as long as HUD did not rule on a PHA's demolition application, or as long as the PHA does not make a formal application to HUD for demolition, PHAs could take units out of the stock by allowing them to go unrented, and could take whole projects out of circulation by allowing conditions to deteriorate.

Congress, still interested in preserving public housing in the late 1980s, immediately responded to the decision in *Edwards* with an amendment— Section 18(d)—that prohibits a PHA from taking "any action" to demolish a public housing project unless approval has been obtained from HUD. Members of the House Committee that approved the amendment were clear about its intent, noting specifically that it was meant "to correct an erroneous interpretation of the existing statute...in *Edwards v. District of Columbia*."[14]

This new congressional amendment was soon invoked by the U.S. District Court in Connecticut in *Concerned Tenants Association of Father Panik Village v. Pierce*. In this case the tenants' de facto demolition claim was allowed.[15] Father Panik Village was a seven-hundred-unit public housing development in Bridgeport, Connecticut. The plaintiffs alleged that the Bridgeport Housing Authority had

> failed to repair broken windows, doors, electrical fixtures, appliances, radiators, pipes, showers, stairway railings, floors, walls, and ceilings; that defendants have failed to provide adequate security, including door locks, hallway lighting, and smoke alarms, which have resulted in frequent robberies of the tenants and use of vacant apartments by drug addicts and drug sellers; and that the hallways and stairs are filled with garbage and refuse and the apartments are infested with rodents and insects.[16]

In the case of the Newark Housing Authority (NHA) in New Jersey, de facto demolition seemed to be its central strategy during the 1980s. In 1978 NHA owned and operated over thirteen thousand units of public housing, only 587 of which were vacant (a 4.5% vacancy rate). Nine years later, NHA had 5,547 vacant units, a 42.7 percent vacancy rate. The number of vacant public housing units in Newark exceeded the entire stock of public housing in most cities. Tenants claimed that the agency deliberately created vacancies through lack of maintenance. According to NHLP, the vacancies occurred as the result of "a combination of intentional neglect and gross mismanagement on the part of NHA, and an absence of oversight on the part of HUD."[17] Newark had been granted modernization funds that it did not spend; instead, the NHA allowed vacant units to sit unrented for years. In the Scudder Homes project, two buildings were entirely vacant and the bottom floor of another building had been gutted two years before NHA even applied to HUD for demolition approval. Ultimately, the Newark Low Income Housing Coalition sued the NHA to stop demolition of two projects, alleging violation of the 1937 Housing Act provisions for approval of demolition.

In Kansas City, Missouri, the story was similar. The Housing Authority of Kansas City (HAKC) also engaged in the systematic practice of de facto demolition. In the Wayne Miner project, HAKC allowed two high-rise towers to empty completely, and it vacated the highest floors of the other three buildings in that project before applying to HUD for demolition approval. In the Theron B. Watkins project (a project ultimately demolished through HOPE VI), vacancies were allowed to skyrocket in the 1980s.

Other cases emerged across the country. Residents of public housing in Pittsburgh challenged demolition on the grounds that they were not consulted by the housing authority.[18] Residents of Allen Parkway Village in Houston alleged that the housing authority, despite receiving $10 million in modernization funds from HUD, spent less than $50,000 of that and instead let the project slide while first requesting approval for demolition and then for sale of the property. Allen Parkway would later be demolished in a HOPE VI project funded by HUD in the first year of the program.

Since the congressional amendment in 1987, the courts have, with one exception,[19] interpreted Section 18 of the Housing Act of 1937 as allowing a right of private action by tenants who claim de facto demolition. In *Tinsley v. Kemp*, tenants were successful in bringing a suit against HUD and the Housing Authority of Kansas City for the systematic neglect of the Theron B. Watkins Homes.[20] In this case, faced with a viable lawsuit against them, HAKC moved to settle the case, promising to renovate and maintain the project. After signing the consent decree, however, HAKC, a "troubled" PHA in HUD's parlance, reneged on its promises and was successfully sued for contempt of court by the tenants who were still attempting to force the agency to maintain the property.

Meanwhile, HAKC was allowing conditions at other developments to deteriorate. In 1992 the HAKC was confronted with a second de facto demolition suit, *Boles v. Kemp*, for its neglect of Riverview Gardens where vacancy rates had risen to 55 percent and abandoned apartments were left to deteriorate, not even properly boarded up by HAKC.[21] *Boles* was settled in 1993 with HAKC agreeing to fully modernize the development. When tenants had to go to court a third time in the *Tinsley* case (with a second contempt-of-court motion) to force HAKC to make the improvements committed to in the original consent decree, they asked the court to appoint a receiver. The court agreed and HAKC was put in receivership in 1993 and stayed there for more than fifteen years.[22]

From *Edwards* through *Tinsley* the courts had considered only whether Section 18 allowed tenants to bring a suit on the basis of a de facto demolition claim. None of these cases went to a final decision on the merits of the claim because settlements were reached in each. The first full adjudication of a de facto demolition case came in 1992 in *Gomez v. El Paso Housing Authority*.[23] In this case, the plaintiffs were on the waiting list for public housing and alleged that they had been harmed by the El Paso Housing Authority's failure to maintain hundreds of units that had become uninhabitable, therefore reducing the number of public housing units in the city. The court required the tenants to demonstrate that the El Paso Housing Authority intended to engage in de facto demolition. This was a major setback for tenants and for the strategy of bringing de facto demolition suits. Requiring a demonstration of intent, rather than merely the effect of demolition, was a high bar for plaintiffs to meet. HUD attempted to institutionalize the *Gomez* ruling on intent by proposing a final rule to implement Congress's 1987 revision of Section 18 that would require demonstration of intent. Affordable housing advocates responded strongly and forced HUD to withdraw that proposal.[24]

Other courts did not follow the lead of *Gomez*, however. In both *Velez v. Chester Housing Authority* and *Henry Horner Mothers Guild v. Chicago Housing Authority and the U.S. Department of Housing and Urban Development* the courts reversed *Gomez* and did not require proof of intent.[25] The *Velez* case went to full adjudication, while the parties reached a settlement in *Horner*. By 1994, then, the courts had generally determined that public housing residents could, in fact, sue local housing authorities and HUD for neglectful property management that led to severe deterioration of units and high vacancy rates. Furthermore, case law was converging on a second conclusion, also in the tenants' favor, that proof of intent on the part of the PHA in question was not required to show de facto demolition.

HUD's efforts to preserve the public housing stock and enforce adherence to congressional intent related to demolition were questionable through most of the 1980s. The agency routinely approved demolition applications, often merely accepting the assertion by PHAs that the projects (or units) in question were in fact obsolete—sometimes even without independent verification of the condition of units.[26] HUD waived the one-for-one replacement requirement on occasion, sometimes without bothering to establish whether conditions within the local housing market merited it.[27] Even when the requirement was not waived, it was unevenly and ineffectively enforced. In its assessment of demolitions in the 1980s, the National Housing Law Project found that in addition to being waived, the one-for-one requirement was "sometimes directly violated, sometimes evaded, or occasionally remained unfulfilled."[28]

In cases of de facto demolition, HUD's lax oversight allowed PHAs to cut off maintenance and generate skyrocketing vacancy rates. HUD, for its part, claimed that it could not prevent these actions among PHAs. But the process of de facto demolition rendered HUD preservation oversight meaningless, since by the time most PHAs filed for formal approval, the projects had been made uninhabitable by the concerted neglect of the local authority and the indifference of HUD. In the case of New Orleans, HUD was actually out ahead of the PHA in terms of recommending removal of public housing units from the stock. In 1983, citing HANO's overall lack of a maintenance plan, and the deteriorated conditions at two large projects in the city, HUD recommended the removal of 2,118 units.[29] Almost two decades before Katrina, however, HANO opted to hold on to all of its units. HUD's willingness to facilitate demolition during the 1980s was illustrated by the fact that the department approved several demolition applications in the days and hours before Congress reinstated the one-for-one replacement requirement in 1987.[30] The agency clearly did not want these demolitions inhibited by a requirement to replace the lost units on a one-for-one basis.

By the 1990s, the desire on the part of local PHAs to remove public housing from the stock was strong and within HUD it was growing, even though public policy changes were lagging. Although de facto demolition suits often forced PHAs into more responsible behavior regarding the maintenance of units in the short term, the policy environment in which demolition was considered only as an unavoidable last resort was about to change. In 1992 the National Commission on Severely Distressed Public Housing issued its report, and a year later Congress created the Urban Revitalization Demonstration (URD) program—the program that would become HOPE VI. The first set of de facto demolition cases (through *Velez*) occurred in an environment in which the value of demolition was strongly contested not only by residents but by housing and community advocates. These cases were also decided prior to the emergence of the mixed-income model of public housing communities. Thus, in most cases, the objective of the plaintiffs was to force PHAs to modernize the buildings and improve maintenance.

The *Horner* case, for example, emerged in Chicago, the first city to experiment with a mixed-income public housing model, and the case was settled at a time when Congress was actively considering elimination of the one-for-one replacement requirement that attached to public housing demolition. In fact, some argued that the one-for-one rule was actually *causing* de facto demolition because the statutory requirement for replacing all demolished units was too onerous for PHAs to meet. At the time the *Horner* settlement was being negotiated the HOPE VI demolition and redevelopment model was emerging. Thus, the consent decree in *Horner* focused not on forcing the CHA to modernize and upgrade the existing structures (mostly sixteen-story high-rises) but to proceed with demolition and redevelopment in a manner that protected tenants' rights, allowed them to stay on-site during a phased redevelopment, and to move into newly completed units as they were finished.

The complaint of the Horner tenants was similar to other de facto demolition cases. The vacancy rate at the development had skyrocketed in a short period of time from 2 percent in 1991 to 49 percent in 1993. Furthermore, CHA had not spent any of the $4 million in modernization funding it had received from HUD for the Horner project. CHA allowed extremely poor conditions to prevail at the site, failed to invest in the property compared to other CHA properties, and thus effectively abandoned the project to (not so) gradual ruin. The parties agreed to demolition of most of the site, to be completed in phases, and the decree mandated one-for-one replacement of the units demolished in Phase I. The parties further agreed that should Congress repeal the one-for-one requirement (as it was considering at the time), they would negotiate the degree of replacement housing that would apply to the rest of the phases of redevelopment.

The emergence of the HOPE VI demolition approach and the repeal of one-for-one replacement in 1995 altered the landscape for PHAs that were looking to demolish portions of their public housing stock. HOPE VI gave them the resources to accomplish the task, a model by which to do so, and in some cases the funding for large-scale redevelopment of the old public housing sites. The repeal of one-for-one eliminated the financial obstacle associated with actual demolition of public housing units. These policy developments of the 1990s have not eliminated de facto demolition. Residents continue to have to force local housing authorities to abide by the requirements of Section 18 of the Housing Act. In 2008, residents of Arroyo Vista, the only public housing complex in the city of Dublin, California, filed suit alleging that the housing authority had begun steps to demolish the project without notifying tenants or getting permission from HUD. Indeed, according to the tenants' claim, a developer had already been chosen and the PHA was asking tenants to move, "urging them to take Section 8 vouchers immediately, or to risk not being granted one later."[31] In 2007, tenants of Jane Addams Village in Rockford, Illinois, filed suit against the Rockford Housing Authority challenging the demolition of that eighty-four unit townhome project. The tenants alleged that the project was not obsolete as the RHA had asserted in its demolition application. HUD conducted its own engineering study and agreed with the tenants. RHA made a second demolition application on separate grounds and the parties negotiated a settlement that allowed demolition but required the replacement of seventy-seven units.[32]

Residents in post-Katrina New Orleans also filed suit to force the Housing Authority of New Orleans to reopen structurally sound public housing units that had been boarded up and allowed to sit vacant for years after the hurricane hit.[33]

Desegregation Suits and Dispersal

Whereas the evolving legal doctrine related to de facto demolition served to check the hand of PHAs in dismantling public housing, a number of desegregation lawsuits were having an opposite effect. In the late 1980s and early 1990s a series of lawsuits were settled in cities across the country that called for the demolition of public housing, the relocation of residents, and the expansion of so-called mobility programs to achieve a wider geographic dispersal of subsidized households. The genesis of these suits was a case in Chicago in which public housing residents alleged that the Chicago Housing Authority and HUD had illegally discriminated in the siting of public housing and in tenant selection policies.

The Civil Rights Act of 1964 ordered an end to racial discrimination in federally assisted housing. Using this leverage, a group of public housing residents in Chicago sued the Chicago Housing Authority and HUD for discriminating along racial lines in tenant selection and placement, and when making decisions about where to put public housing. The *Gautreaux v. Chicago Housing Authority* case made its way to the U.S. Supreme Court where, in April 1976, the Court ruled in favor of the plaintiffs and ordered HUD and the Chicago Housing Authority to initiate a metropolitan-wide plan of relief that would decentralize public housing assistance. The resulting Gautreaux demonstration program involved an agreement by HUD to make Section 8 housing certificates available to African American tenants of the Chicago Housing Authority to be used throughout the metropolitan area. The program included counseling and outreach to ease the transition of these residents to suburban areas.

The initial significance of *Gautreaux* was its reversal of public housing policy that had overtly served the cause of segregation for several decades. The program had been run under rules that explicitly sustained patterns of racial segregation. The so-called neighborhood composition rule, first applied by the Interior Department in the 1930s, required that the racial composition of public housing buildings had to match that of the neighborhoods in which the projects were located. This ensured that public housing would not integrate neighborhoods, and it led to a high level of segregation within public housing, as projects came to reflect the extreme racial segregation found in most U.S. neighborhoods.[34] In *Gautreaux*, the courts said that public housing would henceforth operate under different rules. Litigation across the country attempted to extend the thrust of *Gautreaux*.

By the mid-1980s efforts to desegregate public housing were being made nationwide. In 1983, federal courts required that twenty-five white and black families swap apartments in Clarksville, Texas. In 1984, HUD ordered Texas public housing authorities to stop their racially dual public housing systems. Efforts to desegregate public housing accelerated during the Clinton administration. The greater attention to desegregation was a policy objective of HUD under Secretary Henry Cisneros, and the result of a coordinated campaign by Legal Aid and NAACP lawyers that led to lawsuits in over twenty cities alleging segregation in public housing. HUD decided not to contest most of these suits, and instead negotiated settlements that provided for decentralization and desegregation of public housing units.[35]

In a case brought by public housing tenants in Allegheny County, Pennsylvania, HUD settled with the plaintiffs in 1994, agreeing to provide one hundred units of replacement public housing in areas of low racial concentration, to provide 450 new Section 8 certificates to be used in areas of low racial concentration, and various other efforts to upgrade the existing stock of public housing and provide tenants with the opportunity to escape segregated housing conditions. A similar consent decree in Minneapolis provided for the demolition of seven hundred units of public housing (built in 1939) and the provision of seven hundred replacement units to be scattered throughout the city and suburban areas, eight hundred new Section 8 certificates and vouchers for use metropolitan-wide, and counseling services for public housing tenants relocating to suburban areas. *Thompson v. HUD* in Baltimore, *Walker v. HUD* in Dallas, *Hawkins v. Cisneros* in Omaha, and others incorporated similar elements in their settlements. According to Roberta Achtenberg, HUD assistant secretary for fair housing from 1992 to 1995, these elements provided the framework for legal settlements of suits across the country.[36]

HOPE VI

Movement was occurring legislatively as well. After operating for more than a decade on its own and with little outside scrutiny, the Gautreaux program in Chicago was beginning to produce results that some reformers felt could be replicated in other places. Using the experience of the Gautreaux program as a framework, HUD officials began creating a national model in 1990 that became known as the Moving to Opportunity (MTO) program.[37] MTO provided residents of public and HUD-assisted housing with Section 8 vouchers and certificates that were to be used in low-poverty areas. Unlike the Gautreaux program, participants are identified by their income, not their race, and the areas to which they are relocated are defined by a low concentration of poverty, rather than racial composition. Although MTO was aimed at achieving dispersal for public housing residents who wished to leave, it did not address the problems that existed within public housing communities. Thus, parallel to the efforts to accomplish the desegregation of public housing, Congress established the National Commission on Severely Distressed Public Housing (NCSDPH) in 1989. The Commission was tasked with assessing conditions at the nation's most troubled public housing and making recommendations for addressing them.

The Commission took eighteen months to visit public housing developments and interview residents, local housing officials, and other experts. The commission's report led to congressional passage of the Urban Revitalization Demonstration (URD) program, which later became known as HOPE VI.[38] The Commission's report was issued in August 1992 and URD was enacted in October of the same year.

The Commission's Report on Distressed Public Housing

Given the evolution of HOPE VI and the expansion of efforts outside of HOPE VI to demolish public housing, there were several things notable about the report. First, the Commission's study of public housing suggested that "only 6 percent of the public housing stock is estimated to be severely distressed." Although the conditions in that 6 percent of the stock were "almost unimaginably" bad, and "that in human terms, only 6 percent is 6 percent too many," the Commission clearly saw their work relating to a small minority of public housing in the nation.[39] Though a small percentage, the degree of distress in those projects was, according to the commission, so advanced and deplorable that the commission called public housing "a national problem—a national disgrace."[40] As the report stated, "it is important to note that if 6 percent of the units are severely distressed, approximately 94 percent of the units are not in such a state; thus, the public housing program continues to provide an important rental housing resource for many low-income families and others."[41] The Commission thus offered a set of recommendations aimed at addressing the needs of roughly eighty-six thousand units out of a stock, at that time, of 1.4 million units of public housing. The HOPE VI program alone has demolished more than twice as many units, and when other demolition and disposal of public housing units is considered, three to four times that amount have been eliminated. Some will maintain, with some justification, that the Commission's numerical estimate was not precise, and that the problem might have been worse. But even doubling the number (and thereby suggesting that the commission's estimate was off by

100 percent) produces a number of units (172,000) that has been far exceeded by the 250,000 demolitions that have occurred.

Second, the Commission's recommendations focused on fixing the problems of severely distressed public housing. They began by noting that "traditional approaches to revitalizing seriously distressed public housing have too often emphasized the physical condition of the developments" and that "clearly, severely distressed public housing is not simply a problem of 'bricks and mortar.'"[42] Thus, the Commission called for attention to the needs of residents and recommended a series of resident support service changes and a more comprehensive and holistic approach to delivering human services in public housing.[43] The commission was particularly supportive of resident initiatives and resident-owned businesses. The report also included a smaller number of recommendations for improving the management of distressed public housing and for supporting PHAs by revising archaic accounting and funding systems to allow greater financial creativity in generating the resources necessary to manage the buildings effectively. Yet, in most respects, the HOPE VI program and the more general push for the demolition of public housing is exactly what the Commission criticizes—a solution that privileges physical change over meeting the human services needs of public housing residents.

Third, the Commission's recommendations related to capital improvement and upgrading the physical conditions of distressed public housing are especially noteworthy. Their first recommendation was to expand the Major Reconstruction of Obsolete Public Housing (MROP) program to include a program aimed specifically at severely distressed projects. "The program," argued the Commission, "should be *limited to the rehabilitation and replacement* of that portion of the public housing stock that meets the criteria of severe distress as defined by the Commission."[44] The Commission clearly envisioned a program of rehabilitation and renovation, one that did not diminish the size of the public housing stock nationwide. Indeed, the report did not recommend amending the one-for-one replacement requirement that was then in effect for public housing. In fact, the Commission suggested that "HUD should revise its policy on impaction rules and limitations to allow replacement units on the same site or in the surrounding neighborhood."[45] The HUD impaction rule was an attempt to ensure that new units of federally assisted housing be dispersed more widely throughout local housing markets and not be concentrated in neighborhoods that already had such units or that were predominantly poor. This recommendation by the Commission implicitly acknowledged that the replacement of public housing units had been hindered by the requirement that the units be placed in "non-impacted" neighborhoods. The replacement of any units lost or demolished in the rehabilitation effort was of such importance to the Commission that they specifically recommended that HUD sacrifice its dispersal objective in order to get the units replaced. The commitment to maintain the stock of public housing was strong. In fact, the Commission was even concerned that an expanded MROP not substitute for the further expansion of public housing. The report specifically stated that this program "must not detract from the development of new public housing but instead be promoted in addition to it."[46] HOPE VI and other efforts to improve public housing, however, have generally not been based on rehabilitation but on demolition—the one-for-one replacement requirement gave way almost immediately. In the end, the formula recommended by the Commission has been reversed; the dispersion and deconcentration objectives of public housing transformation are now in most cases achieved by reducing the stock of public housing.

The Evolution of HOPE VI

The main program objectives of HOPE VI were the improvement of living conditions for residents of public housing, physically transforming distressed public housing developments, and deconcentrating poverty.[47] The program operated as a competitive grants program that required applicants to demonstrate that the public housing projects proposed for redevelopment met at least one of the following definitions of "severe distress": (1) families in distress (including those with low incomes and a low number with earned income); (2) high levels of crime; (3) management problems (including high vacancy and turnover rates); and (4) physical deterioration of the project.[48] HUD reviewed grant applications using four criteria: (1) need for the redevelopment project; (2) the capacity of the local housing authority to carry out the proposed project; (3) the quality of the revitalization plan; and (4) the potential of the project to leverage other capital.

Several dimensions of the program evolved over time, including the relative importance of rehabilitation and demolition in redevelopment strategies, the relative emphasis on leveraging private-sector investment, and the allowable scope of the projects.[49] The program as originally established was limited to the forty largest public housing authorities and an additional twelve that were on HUD's list of "troubled" housing authorities. Subsequent changes opened up the program to all PHAs, though individual projects still had to meet the threshold of distress.

The most important part of the evolution of the HOPE VI program was how it moved from an orientation toward rehabilitation to a program that relies on demolition. HUD acknowledges that when the program was created it was "an embellished modernization program" for public housing, little different than the

existing MROP program.[50] Although PHAs had been demolishing public housing on a small scale throughout the 1980s, the official HUD and congressional
policy until the mid-1990s was to preserve public housing and demolish only
under extreme circumstances. Demolition efforts were constrained in the early
years of the program by the requirement that public housing be replaced on a
one-for-one basis. This made demolition financially challenging, and diluted the
deconcentration objectives of the program. In a relatively short period of time,
however, the program became more oriented toward demolition of existing public housing projects.

Coming out of the recession of the early 1990s, central cities were seeing a
resurgence of investment in real estate and in some cases significant growth in
population. Downtown housing markets especially were reviving in many cities.
Housing prices in most cities were rising outside of downtown as well—the
housing bubble expanded for another decade before bursting in 2007. Meanwhile, the midterm elections in 1994 posed a significant political threat to HUD
as the Republican takeover of Congress led to talk of possible elimination of
the agency. Henry Cisneros, the secretary of HUD at the time, moved to radically reinvent many of the agency's programs. HUD's "Reinvention Blueprint,"
issued in December 1994 as a response to the Republican threats, was a plan
for the complete reshaping of the agency and its programs. A central element
of the Reinvention Blueprint was reform of the public housing program and
a dramatic shift in the form of housing assistance away from project-based to
household-based subsidies. If adopted, the Reinvention Blueprint would have
converted all public housing tenants to certificate holders, halted federal subsidies to local PHAs and deregulated them. Public housing residents would have
been given the choice to stay in their apartments or move to units in the private
market, using their certificates as a subsidy. This would have been coupled with
an aggressive campaign to demolish uninhabitable and nonviable public housing projects. These changes would have brought an immediate end to the public
housing program and replaced it with a system of "portable" housing certificates
that residents could use in the private housing market.

For some, the overriding concern in fixing the most troubled public housing
in the nation was to not repeat old mistakes. Developer Richard Baron, who was
a member of the National Commission on Severely Distressed Public Housing,
argued that a new paradigm for public housing was necessary and possible. As
early as 1993, Baron attempted to convince HUD that for the full effect of transformation to occur, PHAs would have to go beyond the original objectives of
the National Commission and the URD legislation. Specifically, Baron argued
that physical upgrading and resident programs were insufficient to catalyze the
change that was needed. He suggested that two additional objectives should be

added to efforts to transform public housing—changing the demographic profile of projects and integrating sites into their surrounding neighborhoods.[51] To accomplish this, demolition and not rehabilitation was necessary, and a mixed-income model of redevelopment was needed. Baron's firm had completed some mixed-income communities by 1993 and was working with the Atlanta Housing Authority on plans to redevelop Techwood Homes.

HUD Secretary Cisneros was coming to his own conclusions about public housing. Touring public housing in Atlanta, Baltimore, Chicago, and other cities throughout 1993, Cisneros concluded

> that public housing in the form it took in many big cities was an unacceptable way to house the nation's most needy residents. It seemed, if anything, that the analysis of the National Commission on Severely Distressed Public Housing *had understated the severity* of the problem.[52]

By 1994, Cisneros was openly talking about the demolition of high-rises and dispersal of residents, and a year later he was advocating "revolutionary change in public housing" in testimony to Congress in order to "infuse market discipline into Washington's relationship with PHAs."[53] Faced with a hostile Republican majority in Congress that was ready to do significant and lasting harm to the department and its programs, Cisneros and his staff ultimately adopted the idea that URD as originally envisioned was not thoroughgoing enough to bring about a true transformation of public housing. Calls for greater leeway to demolish public housing fell on receptive ears in Congress, which seemed eager to drastically reduce the federal government's presence in the assisted-housing area. In 1995, Congress suspended the one-for-one replacement requirement and then permanently repealed it in 1998. This allowed demolition to become the centerpiece of the HOPE VI program, and allowed local housing authorities the latitude of tearing down units and replacing them with vouchers.[54] The HOPE VI program, born out of a national commission's recommendation for a strengthened rehabilitation program aimed at severely distressed public housing, soon became a program of demolition leading to large-scale displacement of public housing residents and the transformation of the communities into mixed-income neighborhoods. HUD adopted New Urbanist design principles that were aimed at creating more inviting, walkable, and safe neighborhoods that would be more integrated into the surrounding communities.

The acceptance of demolition quickly spread beyond the context of HOPE VI. In 1996, Congress directed local public housing authorities to impose a "viability test" on all public housing developments with three hundred or more units and

FIGURE 4. Demolition of Capitol View Plaza II in Washington, D.C., adjacent to the Capital Gateway HOPE VI redevelopment.

a 10 percent or higher vacancy rate. The crux of the test was an assessment of the relative cost of repairing and rehabilitating the projects or demolishing the building and providing tenants with vouchers for twenty years.

In a similar fashion, the HOPE VI program has evolved into one that is meant to generate significant spillover effects in the neighborhoods in which it operates. In 1995, HUD began to emphasize the leveraging of private-sector capital in HOPE VI projects. One year later, in 1996, the program began to allow mixed financing, allowing public housing authorities to use other public and private funds to build public housing, or to channel public housing funds to third parties to develop public housing units. HUD additionally encouraged local housing authorities during this time to be entrepreneurial and innovative, to "incorporate boldness and creativity" in their HOPE VI applications, fundamentally rethinking the public housing model that had prevailed for close to sixty years.[55] The emphasis on leveraging private capital that was incorporated into HOPE VI in the late 1990s has become, in practice, an incentive for projects located in neighborhoods ripe for private investment. By fiscal year 2002, local housing authorities were required to demonstrate how their proposed HOPE VI redevelopment would "result in outside investment in the surrounding community."[56]

The Dismantling of Public Housing Post-1990

The public policy changes of the 1990s greatly accelerated the rate at which public housing units were sold off or demolished by PHAs. The best estimate of the loss of public housing in the 1980s puts the number for the entire decade at less than fifteen thousand units. By the latter half of the 1990s that figure was being nearly matched on an annual basis, over 47,000 units were removed from 1996 through 1999. The removal of public housing units from the stock became the accepted and preferred means of dealing with the property management and financial challenges for many PHAs.

Selling Public Housing

The sale of public housing to residents has been a minor part of local housing authority programs for decades. For the most part, PHAs have not been anxious to participate in such programs because the units typically chosen for purchase and the families wishing to participate in the program are both the cream of the crop for local authorities. Significant sales of public housing would mean the loss of the PHAs' best housing stock and the loss of their best, most stable families. Thus, only a small number of sales have occurred. In 1998, the Quality Housing and Work Responsibility Act (QHWRA) revised the means by which PHAs could sell their units and did not limit the purchasers to existing public housing residents. These efforts to sell to residents, however, have never accounted for a large reduction in the public housing stock.

Starting in 2008, however, local public housing authorities, feeling a fiscal pinch because of budget cutbacks at HUD, have looked at the option of selling off part of their public housing stock in order to address budgetary problems. Local housing authorities receive funds each year to cover the gap between rent revenues and the full operating costs of public housing. The amount is determined by a federal formula, but the funds are not guaranteed. If Congress does not appropriate sufficient funds for the program, local housing authorities get only a percentage of the formula amount. For the two decades prior to 2003, PHAs received an average of more than 98 percent of the formula amount.[57] Beginning in 2003 funding dropped significantly, first to 95 percent of the formula amount, then to 89 percent in 2005, 86 percent in 2006, and 78 percent in 2007. Although funding levels are set by Congress, HUD's budget requests for the program during the last years of the Bush II administration did not even match what would be necessary to fully meet the formula obligations.[58] Local housing authorities also point to changes in the formula itself and HUD's requirement that PHAs shift to an "asset management" model as additional reasons for significant budget shortfalls in recent years.[59]

The Wilmington, Delaware, housing authority, for example, saw a $1.8 million drop in operating subsidies in two years. In St. Paul, Minnesota, the housing authority sold sixteen houses to raise $2 million to help pay for other units it operates. Other cities such as Salt Lake City and New York City have considered the same, only on a larger scale. In St. Petersburg, Florida, in 2008 the housing authority sold its largest development, a 486-unit project, to a private developer for conversion to condominiums. In September 2008 the Oakland Housing Authority moved ahead with a plan to sell more than a thousand units of public housing, converting the units to Section 8 in order to bring greater subsidies to the agency. The San Diego Housing Commission has divested itself of its entire public housing stock by transferring all of its public housing to nonprofit ownership.[60] In Fort Worth, Texas, the housing authority sold the 268-unit Ripley Arnold Homes to Radio Shack for $20 million. In places such as Woonsocket, Rhode Island, and Rochester, New York, scattered site units have been sold off to generate savings because of the relatively high operating costs of scattered units.[61]

Demolition

The most significant policy event in the dismantling of public housing was, of course, the creation of the HOPE VI program and its evolution into a demolition and redevelopment program. HOPE VI embodied the larger shift in public policy away from the objective of preserving public housing to one that directly financed large-scale removals in cities across the country. The evolution of HOPE VI in this direction was the result of the emergence of the mixed-income model and the belief among HUD officials that the design of older public housing was one of the core reasons for its decline. Since 1994, HOPE VI has financed the demolition of more than 110,000 units of public housing in cities across the nation. Only sixty thousand of the units have been or will be replaced in mixed-income projects subsidized by the program. The shift to large-scale demolition and replacement was aided by the suspension and then repeal of the one-for-one replacement rule. Though the rule was not so diligently enforced by HUD, it nevertheless stood as an obstacle to routine demolition. In 1996 Congress further encouraged demolition by requiring local housing authorities to prove that larger housing projects with high vacancy rates were worth saving. Failing the so-called viability test led to the demolition or disposition of the public housing units. In some cases, the local PHA moved more quickly than even HUD wanted. Woonsocket, Rhode Island, which had sold fifty-one units of scattered site public housing earlier in the decade, was told by HUD that it could not demolish another 180 units because they were still in decent shape.[62]

By 2010, the demolition of public housing had become routine. It is the dominant approach in several major cities but it is also being pursued in smaller communities. In Clarksville, Tennessee, the city's Smart Growth 2030 Master Plan calls for the demolition of the 210-unit Lincoln Homes public housing complex. In Rome, Georgia, the 150-unit Hight Homes was torn down in 2010; in its place will be a shopping center featuring a Publix grocery store. Danville, Illinois, put the demolition of the 326-unit Fair Oaks public housing in its 2010 Consolidated Plan.

Variations in the Rate of Removal

As of 2008, it was estimated that over 220,000 units of public housing had been demolished; thousands more had been sold off or converted to other uses. In this section I analyze data from HUD on public housing units lost between 1990 and 2007.[63] The rate of public housing demolition grew rapidly in 1995 when Congress suspended the one-for-one rule and HOPE VI converted to a demolition program. In 1995 four thousand units of public housing were removed nationwide, but from 1996 through 2005, removals topped ten thousand per year eight times, with the peak years of 2000 and 2001 seeing more than eighteen thousand units lost each year.

Within this national trend, however, there is a great deal of variation from one city to the next. The largest 150 cities in the U.S. together operated 642,873 units of public housing in 1996, or 48.5 percent of the national total that year. Among these 150 cities are thirteen large suburbs, generally located in the Southwest, that have no public housing. Only 102 of the 137 central cities (74 percent) have removed (demolished or disposed of) public housing between 1990 and 2007.[64] The average city in this group removed 880 units of public housing. Of the cities that removed any public housing, the average city has taken 1,190 units out of service through sale or demolition. The range of removal efforts, however, is wide, from two units sold off in Salt Lake City to Chicago's elimination of more than sixteen thousand public housing units, most by demolition. Across the board the scale of removal through demolition was many times larger than the loss of units through sale. Of the eighty-eight cities that demolished public housing over this period of time, the average number of units torn down was 2,131. For the sixty-nine cities that sold off public housing units, the average city took 169 units out of service in that manner. Just over one-quarter of the cities did not remove any public housing units, while another 10 percent removed between one and fifty units.

The scale of removal is greater in some cities simply because these cities had more public housing units to begin with. The three top cities in terms of units lost, Chicago, Philadelphia, and Atlanta, had very large inventories of public housing. At the same time, however, some cities with large public housing inventories took relatively few units out of service over this period. New York City, the largest PHA in the country, removed just over five hundred units, or less than 1 percent of its total public housing stock. Table 2.1 ranks cities that removed public housing by the absolute number of units and by the percentage of the cities' stock. Chicago far outstrips other cities in absolute numbers, having removed twice as many units as the second-place city (Philadelphia), and more units than the next two cities (Philadelphia and Atlanta) combined. However, Chicago does not appear among the top ten when percentage of the public housing stock is considered.

The right-hand column ranks cities by the percentage of public housing stock removed. Hartford, Connecticut, tops this list, having removed 56 percent of their public housing units between 1990 and 2007. Memphis, St. Petersburg, and Detroit have also removed more than half of their stock over this time period. The table reveals, however, that the absolute number of units removed and the percentage of a city's public housing removed produce two substantially different lists; only three cities—Atlanta, Detroit, and Memphis—make the top ten on both lists; that is, they have removed a large number of units both in absolute terms and as a percentage of their total public housing stocks.

TABLE 2.1 Cities with most public housing units removed, 1990–2007

HIGHEST NUMBER OF UNITS REMOVED		HIGHEST PERCENTAGE OF UNITS REMOVED	
Chicago	16,461	Hartford	56
Philadelphia	7,809	Memphis	55
Atlanta	7,160	St. Petersburg	55
New Orleans	5,628	Detroit	53
Baltimore	5,117	Atlanta	49
Newark	4,745	Tucson	48
Detroit	4,503	Hampton, VA	45
Memphis	3,912	Tampa	45
Pittsburgh	3,749	Little Rock	43
Washington, D.C.	2,856	Columbus	41

There is a variation in the degree to which cities removed public housing units that defies easy explanation. Though many older Rust Belt cities were very aggressive in dismantling their public housing system, other cities in that region were much more constrained. Providence, Rhode Island, and New York City removed less than 1 percent of their public housing stock, Cleveland just 12 percent, and Milwaukee only 16 percent. Two Florida Sunbelt cities, Tampa and St. Petersburg, are among the leaders in disposing of public housing, while two others, Miami and Orlando, removed only 5 percent and 18 percent of their public housing stock, respectively. In Arizona, Tucson removed 48 percent of its public housing while Phoenix disposed of only 2 percent.

In order to better understand why some cities have been more aggressive than others in dismantling their public housing, a multivariate regression technique was used (details of this analysis are contained in the appendix). We wish to examine the impact of a range of factors that might plausibly explain the variation in public housing removal. Specifically, we tested whether the following characteristics of cities were associated with the number of public housing units removed: the extent of concentrated poverty in the city, the violent crime rate, the condition of the housing market, the strength of progressive political movements and the union movement, the degree of racial segregation, the size of the black middle class, the degree to which public housing in the city is racially identified, and the strength of gentrification pressures within the city. Two different Poisson regression equations were estimated, one for the time period 1990–99, and the second for 2001–07.[65]

Crime, Gentrification, and Race

The analysis (data table shown in appendix) indicates that rates of violent crime were significantly related to public housing demolition in both decades. Where violent crime rates were higher, the rate of public housing demolition and disposition was greater. In cities with more acute crime problems, city officials and residents alike may have associated those problems with public housing and as a result moved more aggressively to demolish. Beyond the constant of crime, however, the story of public housing transformation in the two decades was importantly different. During the 1990s, gentrification pressures were also significant predictors of more aggressive dismantling of public housing systems. After 2000, however, gentrification recedes as an explanation and is replaced by race and by politics. Since 2000, more public housing units have been lost in cities in which blacks are disproportionately represented among public housing residents. Furthermore, political variables that measure union membership and the existence of progressive policy initiatives are both statistically significant and negative; where unions and progressive political strength are greater, fewer public housing units have been lost. Finally, the record of public housing removal since 2000 seems to be a continuation of the approaches used by cities during the 1990s, in that there is a positive statistical association between the percentage of the public housing stock removed in the 1990s and the removal of stock since 2000. City characteristics *not* associated with efforts to demolish and remove public housing in either decade include the quality of public housing management, the degree of concentrated poverty within cities, and the extent of racial segregation.

Thus, the story of public housing demolition has changed over time. During the 1990s, a time when central cities made a dramatic rebound in population and development, pressures for gentrification and redevelopment drove the removal of public housing from city to city. As many observers have noted, expanding central city real estate profit opportunities in the 1990s encouraged both private- and public-sector actors in the direction of radical transformation of public housing communities.[66] Gentrification of inner city neighborhoods led to conditions in which public housing projects were islands of poverty and distress in the midst of areas of wealth and renewal. In Chicago, for example, much of the notorious Cabrini-Green complex, long regarded as occupying potentially profitable space on the city's Near North Side, was demolished in the late 1990s as part of a large-scale redevelopment initiative that ushered in luxury housing and upscale commercial transformation. Similarly, on the edge of Houston's downtown, the Allen Parkway Village, home to nearly half of the city's public housing families, gave way to the wrecking ball and luxury condominiums.[67] In New Orleans, even before Hurricane Katrina provided local officials the opportunity to eliminate thousands of public housing units, the St. Thomas development, a community of impoverished, black public housing residents surrounded by more affluent white residents where housing costs were relatively high, was identified as a crucial missing link in a chain of revitalizing neighborhoods near the city's downtown.[68]

The fact that public housing demolition tracked gentrification pressures is not surprising given that the HOPE VI program emphasized redevelopment of areas that were most poised for higher income redevelopment.[69] Public housing demolition seems to have been an important element in local government efforts to reactivate or capitalize on a real estate resurgence in or around low-income neighborhoods.[70]

Thus, the rapid expansion of demolition that occurred in the 1990s was in large part a response to economic reinvestment opportunities in central city neighborhoods. These opportunities were great enough, and the problems of crime associated with public housing alarming enough, that a decades-long reluctance on the part of federal officials to sanction demolition was swept away. Once the policy environment had changed, however, the story of public housing demolition at the city scale became more racialized and political. Though crime remains a significant predictor of unit loss, public housing demolition and sale after 2000 becomes less a matter of gentrification and is more dependent on race and politics.

Since 2000, the greater the disparity in racial profile between public housing and the city's population at large, the greater the public housing demolition effort. To the extent that some cities have joined the bandwagon of public housing removal since 2000, or have taken greater prominence in the effort, they generally have been cities in which the racial profile of public housing residents is more distinctly African American in comparison to the city as a whole. This pattern is illustrated by the cities of Tampa, Nashville, and Portland, Oregon, where the representation of African Americans within public housing is three times or more greater than within the city population as a whole. Portland did not remove any public housing units during the 1990s and took out 456 after 2000. Tampa removed 273 through 2000 and 1,948 units afterward. Nashville's numbers were 280 and 1,528, respectively.

In addition to shifting somewhat to a racial strategy after the 1990s, the removal of public housing since 2000 has mirrored political conditions within cities more closely. The dismantling of public housing in recent years has been more aggressively pursued in cities where union strength is weaker and in cities with a less extensive history of successful progressive policy efforts. This suggests that after the first wave of demolitions in the '90s, the issue of public housing demolition has become more politically determined, and that constituencies supportive of public housing have been able to limit its dismantling, or that the pursuit of public housing demolition in the first place is more limited to cities in which those constituencies are weaker. The evidence presented here also suggests that the negative manifestations of concentrated poverty are more influential in leading to public housing removal than the mere existence of pockets of poverty. For example, crime was significantly related to changes in the public housing stock while the extent of concentrated poverty in cities was not. This is true for both decades analyzed.

The ways in which the dynamics of gentrification or crime play out in a city, or the ways in which racial politics affect public housing, depends a great deal on the historical context or the unique social and political characteristics of any given city. In the next chapter, we examine in greater detail three cities that have been at the forefront of efforts to dismantle public housing: Chicago, Atlanta, and New Orleans. Brief case studies of each are presented to illustrate how the dynamics of race and redevelopment are transforming public housing.

DEMOLITION IN CHICAGO, NEW ORLEANS, AND ATLANTA

Stephanie Mingo, who had been a 43-year resident of the now-closed St. Bernard project, blinked back angry tears as she spoke during her allotted three minutes. "You are hurting people. You are killing people," she said [to the New Orleans City Council]. "I don't know how y'all can sleep at night."

—Julia Cass and Peter Whoriskey, "New Orleans to Raze Public Housing"

If public housing is dead, it is Chicago that killed it. From the 1960s onward, projects all over the city declined into dangerous and alienating wastelands, with the CHA, paralyzed by "staggering mismanagement," unwilling or unable to do much about it.[1] In 1982 a HUD-commissioned report concluded:

> In every area we examined, from finance to maintenance, from administration to outside contracting, from staffing to project management, from purchasing to accounting, the CHA was found to be operating in a state of profound confusion and disarray. No one seems to be minding the store; what's more, no one seems to genuinely care.[2]

The Robert Taylor Homes on the South Side and the Cabrini-Green development on the North Side gave Chicago a matching pair of internationally renowned debacles: intense concentrations of poverty and racial segregation that spiraled downward into nightmares of roach- and rat-infested housing, crumbling infrastructure, economic deprivation, and gang violence. All that had failed about public housing in America was manifest in the city's high-rises, all the dysfunctionality brought to its highest level of expression there.

HUD put the CHA in receivership in the 1990s, concluding that it was fundamentally incapable of managing itself and its stock of more than forty thousand units. The failure of CHA was, in fact, the nation's biggest public housing collapse. Its housing was so bad that when Congress imposed the viability tests for public housing, more than nineteen thousand units in Chicago failed; this was more units than any other city, except New York, even *had*.

New Orleans provides a second example of dysfunctional public housing leadership. The Housing Authority of New Orleans (HANO) also went into receivership in the 1990s when the federal government determined that HANO had no plan for ongoing maintenance and upkeep of its housing stock. In 1996, the U.S. General Accounting Office noted that "for nearly two decades, HANO has been one of the country's poorest performing housing authorities" and for 1995 was the lowest ranking in HUD's performance management evaluation system. As in Chicago, public housing residents were forced to live in deplorable conditions. HANO came late to demolition, not moving decisively until Hurricane Katrina forced thousands of public housing residents from their homes. Given the opportunity, however, the city simply condemned the properties and never let those families back in. By 2010 HANO had decided to demolish and redevelop all of its large public housing projects. Though residents resisted demolition in Chicago, the opposition in New Orleans produced scenes of violence not matched elsewhere. Former residents and their supporters were beaten back by police on the night the city council voted to tear down most of the city's public housing.

In Atlanta, as in Chicago and New Orleans, public housing had been allowed to deteriorate until living conditions in most of the projects were deplorable. The Atlanta Housing Authority (AHA) was on HUD's "Troubled Agency" list in the early 1990s and had proven itself incapable of effectively managing the thousands of units in its stock. New leadership at AHA, appointed in the mid-1990s, committed to a complete redefinition of public housing in that city, fully adopting the model of mixed-income development that was then emerging. Atlanta is the largest city in the country to commit to tearing down all of its old public housing.

These three cities then represent the vanguard of public housing transformation in the new century. They are not necessarily unique; other cities, such as Washington, D.C., and Memphis, have also committed to almost complete transformation of public housing and to dramatic reductions in the number of units available to very low income families. Chicago, Atlanta, and New Orleans, however, provide opportunities to examine how the factors leading to the dismantling of public housing across the nation identified in the previous chapter, including crime, race, and gentrification/redevelopment initiatives; have played out within specific historical and political contexts.

Chicago

The Chicago Housing Authority has been for a large part of its existence the poster child of public housing dysfunction. Forced by local politicians to funnel projects into slum areas of the city to maintain and reinforce racial segregation, and besotted by mismanagement and cronyism for most of the 1960s and 1970s, the CHA allowed its properties to sink into a hellish nightmare of crime and disrepair.[3] Mayor Harold Washington during the 1980s said that the "CHA didn't have a problem, they *were* the problem."[4]

But just as Chicago set the bar nationally for dysfunction and failure, so, too, has it been a leader in producing the displacement, dispersal, and demolition policy paradigm that has dominated since the early 1990s. In the aftermath of the *Gautreaux* court cases, the city was home to the first large-scale mobility program that allowed public housing residents to move out of the projects using Section 8 subsidies and into "non-impacted" neighborhoods of the city and the surrounding suburbs. The outcomes of this program led policy makers to create the Moving to Opportunity (MTO) program that virtually duplicated the Gautreaux program in a select number of other large American cities.

The city was also an early innovator in the "mixed-income" development experiment, producing the first-in-the-nation experiment, Lake Parc Place, in 1991. The CHA's executive director, Vincent Lane, was the coleader of the National Commission on Severely Distressed Public Housing that ultimately led to the creation of the HOPE VI program. Chicago received one of the first HOPE VI grants, $50 million in 1994, to redevelop Cabrini-Green. When HUD took over operation of CHA in 1995 it had its biggest opportunity to test the new set of ideas about public housing. As HUD Secretary Henry Cisneros declared, "the national system of public housing is on trial in Chicago."[5]

The (Mis)management of Chicago Public Housing

As the 1990s began, the forty thousand units that CHA operated housed over 145,000 people. If Chicago public housing had been a separate city, it would have been the second largest in the state of Illinois. Most of the units dated from the 1950s and 1960s, and the CHA had built thousands of units in high-rises.[6]

The city's public housing strategy had always heavily emphasized slum clearance and the city council had assumed responsibility and authority over the siting of public housing almost from the beginning.[7] The shift in resident demographics to a black and mostly welfare clientele that characterized most cities was more rapid in Chicago than elsewhere. Though few public housing residents were on public relief during the 1940s, the CHA fairly quickly oriented itself toward serving the neediest within the city. When the CHA lowered its rents in 1940 it made one-quarter of the existing tenant's income ineligible. These tenants, all of whom were white, were evicted.[8] After the war, as incomes steadily rose, the CHA continued to strictly implement income guidelines and evicted households who were improving their economic situations. The opposition to public housing within white and middle-class neighborhoods was such that virtually all of the CHA's housing was situated in predominantly black neighborhoods. Racial tensions within the city led to severe segregation and a shortage of quality housing options for blacks. By the mid-1950s, with most of the developments located in minority neighborhoods, demand for public housing among whites declined significantly. The shift in resident demographics was complete by the end of the 1960s, cementing public housing's image as a home of last resort for the most marginal residents among the city's black and welfare population.

The city kept adding large high-rise projects throughout its South Side and West Side black belt during the 1950s and 1960s. In one stretch from 1957 through 1968, 96 percent of the family public housing built in Chicago was in high-rise buildings.[9] The city's Near South Side, including a single corridor along State Street from Cermak Road (20th Street) to 53rd Street, became a long and virtually uninterrupted series of mid- and high-rise public housing projects that contained over twelve thousand public housing units. Here the Robert Taylor

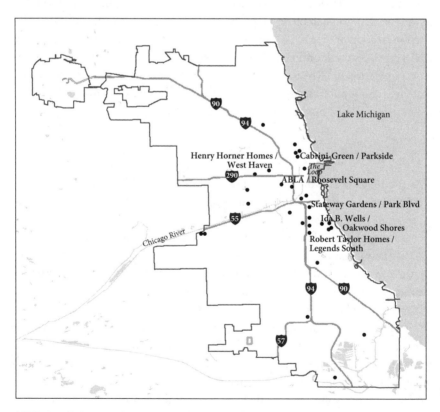

MAP 1. Chicago public housing sites

Homes dominated the landscape, over four thousand units stretching for two miles from 39th Street to 53rd Street. In the same vicinity, CHA placed Stateway Gardens (sixteen hundred units), Dearborn Homes and Ickes Homes (both over eight hundred units), the Ida B. Wells project (sixteen hundred units), and several other developments accounting for thousands of other units.

The quality of public housing in Chicago was affected by the marginalization of the CHA within city government. The CHA and the projects it created and oversaw were never fully integrated into the city administration. As one Chicago ex-official put it, "the CHA was like a separate universe" within the city government.[10] There was no coordination of services with other city departments, there was little to no career movement of executives across department lines into or out of CHA. Congress designed PHAs as quasi-independent agencies to insulate them from local political pressures; in Chicago the CHA was dominated by the city's politics but insulated from the rest of the city's administrative and policy structure. The outcome was the worst of both worlds as the city's public housing was concentrated in declining, segregated neighborhoods surrounding the urban core, the only places allowed by the political power structure, while its operations were ignored by other city departments, leaving the communities virtually bereft of the services and benefits of city government. CHA management jobs were doled out as patronage to political supporters of the mayor who were not up to the challenges of maintaining thousand of units of low-income housing located in many of the most disadvantaged neighborhoods in the city. Problems of maintenance and crime spiraled out of control, and the CHA, mired in disarray, was unable to respond to deteriorating conditions.

Over time management and the local police largely ceded the grounds of public housing estates to gangs who controlled the projects and fought among themselves for control of the local drug trade. Families lived in constant fear, devising plans for what to do when the next gun battle broke out between rival gangs.[11] Vincent Lane, a private-sector real estate developer, who took over as executive director of CHA in 1988, aggressively attacked the problems of Chicago highrise projects. His anticrime efforts were especially innovative and only partially constitutional.[12] He introduced identification badges for residents, guarded entryways, and initiated apartment sweeps aimed at rooting out crime. The residents of Chicago public housing were in effect asked to surrender many of their civil rights in order to enjoy a less dangerous environment. Conditions in Chicago public housing were such that many of the residents did this willingly. The sweeps, unfortunately, had only a marginal effect.[13] The private security guards hired by CHA were ineffective in reducing the control of gang members at most buildings.

When Congress imposed the viability test in 1996 to determine whether rehabilitation was more cost-effective than outright demolition, over nineteen thousand CHA units failed. The viability test presented the CHA with the prospect of tearing down virtually all of its family public housing (including all of the city's family high-rises). The new congressional rules meant, in effect, wholesale transformation of the Chicago public housing stock. This, however, was a realization that CHA had been coming to on its own.

Vincent Lane was an early devotee of mixed-income redevelopment. In fact, under his leadership, CHA had pioneered the concept of mixed-income redevelopment of public housing projects. In response to lobbying by the CHA, Congress had included a small demonstration program of mixed-income public housing redevelopment in the 1990 National Affordable Housing Act.[14] Chicago was the only PHA to run the experimental program, using the federal funds to rehabilitate the Victor Olander Homes (a development of two sixteen-story high-rises) into Lake Parc Place. The project incorporated some design upgrades over previous HUD standards for high-rises, but the income mix was limited to public housing tenants and "moderate-income" wage-earning families at 50 to 80 percent of the area median income. Although these were modest first steps—"modernization" of units rather than demolition and redevelopment, limited deviation from the spartan design guidelines then in place for public housing, and an income mix that did not include market-rate or homeownership units—Lane and the CHA had, by 1991, completed one of the nation's first experiments in mixed-income public housing redevelopment.

In the same year that Lake Parc Place opened, CHA was sued by residents of the Henry Horner Homes, a public housing project on the city's West Side.[15] The plaintiffs in this case alleged that the CHA had engaged in de facto demolition by leaving the units vacant and allowing them to deteriorate. The parties to the suit began to negotiate a settlement (ultimately signed in 1995) that would turn the Horner Homes into West Haven, a mixed-income community that replaced the Horner high-rises with a lower density townhouse development. Work began in time for some of the redevelopment to be completed in advance of the 1996 Democratic National Convention, which was held at United Center, across the street from the old high-rises. When the HOPE VI program was first created, Chicago was an early and frequent subscriber. Cabrini-Green received $50 million in 1994, ABLA received $24.5 million in 1996, while Horner received $18.4 million in 1996, and the Robert Taylor Homes $25 million in the same year. In the first eight years of the HOPE VI program, Chicago received $200 million in grants, more than any other city in the country.

Despite the considerable energy of the Lane years, and the initiatives in crime prevention and redevelopment, the city's public housing projects were still plagued by crime, financial mismanagement, and decline. The historian Bradford Hunt recounts a memorable scene in 1995 in which a frustrated Lane, meeting with

HUD officials, "threw his large set of keys across the table at HUD assistant secretary Joseph Shuldiner, and told him the federal government could have Chicago's projects if it wanted them."[16] HUD, after years of watching the CHA flounder, took him up on the offer.

The HUD Years

In 1995 HUD assumed control of Chicago's public housing system, acknowledging decades of mismanagement, fiscal irresponsibility, and misguided and ineffectual CHA policies. The CHA had been on HUD's list of troubled agencies since 1979 but there was some worry within HUD that the scale of dysfunction at the agency, the third largest PHA in the country, was beyond the capacity of HUD to reverse.[17] HUD assigned its top public housing official, Assistant Secretary for Public and Indian Housing Joseph Shuldiner, to the Chicago case. Shuldiner had previously been the director of the New York City Housing Authority and the Housing Authority of the City of Los Angeles before joining HUD. Within two years, he had CHA off of HUD's "troubled agency" list and had improved the agency's management and accounting systems. He continued to aggressively pursue redevelopment funds, while managing the redevelopment processes at Cabrini, Henry Horner, ABLA, and the Robert Taylor Homes. By the time HUD handed back the CHA to the city of Chicago in 1999, there were five HOPE VI projects under way in the city, accounting for more than $150 million in federal funding. Yet, if anything, the viability tests meant that Chicago would have to expand and accelerate its public housing redevelopment efforts in the near future. Congress had mandated that buildings failing the viability test would have to be torn down and redeveloped within five years. Given the sheer number of units of Chicago public housing that had failed (the city's failed units were 16 percent of the national total of failed units[18]), this requirement was unrealistic in the Chicago case. The city's first task, upon reacquiring responsibility for the operation of its own housing authority, was to finalize a plan for the remaking of public housing within the city.

The Plan for Transformation

The city of Chicago submitted its Plan for Transformation (PFT) of public housing to HUD on January 6, 2000. One month later HUD approved the plan and made a commitment to provide the Chicago Housing Authority $1.5 billion over ten years for demolition and rehabilitation of thirty-eight thousand units of public housing.[19] Under the plan the number of public housing units in the city would be reduced from thirty-eight thousand to twenty-five thousand, with essentially all of the reduction coming from the stock of family housing. Only the ten family projects that had passed the 1996 Viability Test would avoid the wrecking ball; these projects would be rehabilitated and continue to operate as "traditional" public housing. The rest of the city's stock of family units would shrink considerably and operate under the new mixed-income model. Management of the properties would be shifted to private companies, and new and stricter tenant screening policies would be adopted.[20] A total of fifty-one high-rise buildings were scheduled for demolition according to the plan.[21]

The plan was announced with great fanfare by the city and by HUD. Secretary of HUD Andrew Cuomo called it one of the highlights of his administration.[22] The MacArthur Foundation pledged millions of dollars in support of the plan. Table 3.1 details the pre- and post-transformation landscape of family public housing in Chicago.

The PFT in Chicago was not merely an effort to remake public housing. It became the city's major urban redevelopment initiative of the new decade and the largest public works program in the city's history. The plan, in a complete reversal of previous practice in the city with respect to public housing, was to be a coordinated effort of several city agencies, including the CHA. As one former city official said, "the Mayor said 'this [the Plan for Transformation] is the major urban redevelopment initiative in the city'—he made it every agency's highest priority."[23] The redevelopment sites would see new and upgraded city streets and infrastructure, parks and recreation facilities, and in some cases new or improved elementary schools, all of which had been systematically denied to public housing complexes in the past. The city allocated 50 percent of its Low-Income Housing Tax Credit funding to public housing redevelopment sites, and 50 percent of its annual Community Development Block Grant (CDBG) allotment for community improvements. The design of the sites, as in HOPE VI projects across the country, would reintegrate public housing into the fabric of the community by reestablishing street grids, scaling down developments (turning high-rises into row-house and townhome developments), and mixing incomes so that public housing residents would never be the majority of residents in any given development. The PFT would subsume and expand on all of the previous redevelopment efforts that had been completed or begun in the city prior to 2000.

Community Impacts

The PFT has been by any estimate a massive undertaking. Chicago had invested heavily in the high-rise model of public housing and had concentrated the developments in such a way that they dominated several South Side and West Side communities. The demolition of these projects, the relocation of thousands

TABLE 3.1 Summary of Chicago family public housing pre- and post-transformation

FAMILY PUBLIC HOUSING DEVELOPMENTS	NUMBER OF PUBLIC HOUSING UNITS	
	PRE-	POST-
Mixed-income developments		
ABLA Homes (Roosevelt Square)	3,235	1,467
Cabrini-Green (Parkside et al.)	2,625	1,200
Henry Horner Homes (West Haven)	1,743	824
Hilliard	346	117
Ickes Homes	312	0
Lakefront Properties (Lake Park Crescent/		
Jazz on the Blvd.)	604	441
Lathrop Homes	925	400
Lawndale Complex (Ogden North)	187	100
LeClaire Courts and Extension	610	0
Madden/Wells/Darrow (Oakwood Shores)	2,891	900
Robert Taylor Homes (Legends South)	3,284	851
Rockwell Gardens (West End)	1,136	264
Stateway Gardens (Park Boulevard/Pershing)	1,644	439
Subtotal	**20,042**	**7,003**
"Traditional" public housing rehabilitation projects		
Altgeld Gardens	2,000	1,998
Bridgeport Homes	141	111
Cabrini Rowhouses	586	586
Dearborn Homes	800	660
Lake Parc Place	300	282
Lawndale Gardens	125	125
Lowden Homes	128	127
Trumbull Park Homes	434	434
Washington Park Low-Rises	378	330
Wentworth Gardens	422	343
Subtotal	**5,314**	**4,996**
Grand total	**25,356**	**11,999**

Source: Business and Professional People for the Public Interest. 2009. *The Third Side: A Mid-Course Report on Chicago's Transformation of Public Housing* (Chicago: BPPPI); Chicago Housing Authority.

of residents, and the complete remaking of the physical environment at the demolition sites would consume years and billions of dollars of federal and local investment. As one aldermanic aide said, "this whole city is being transformed economically and racially by this Plan for Transformation."[24] Any public works project of this magnitude would send ripple effects throughout the entire city; the PFT did so in at least three ways. First, it was part of a significant revalorization of inner city real estate in Chicago. In some cases, neighborhoods were poised to take off in land value and simply awaited the removal of public housing as in the Near North neighborhood surrounding the Cabrini-Green project. In other cases, public housing demolition has generated unmistakable gentrification trends in South Side and West Side neighborhoods by the sheer size of the redevelopments taking place. The demolition of units along the State Street corridor has helped to trigger gentrification in the Bronzeville neighborhood and in surrounding communities once dominated by Stateway Gardens and the Robert Taylor Homes.

Second, the demolition of thousands of units of public housing has necessitated the relocation of thousands of very low income households. Except for the Henry Horner Homes redevelopment, where the CHA was forced by a lawsuit to phase the redevelopment so that residents could remain on-site while construction was taking place, redevelopment of public housing communities has pushed thousands of low-income families into the private housing market. The scale of the PFT produced a concern early on that the housing market would be unable to absorb all of the households displaced by public housing demolition. A market study by researchers at the University of Illinois at Chicago reinforced those concerns. The plan began at a time when the rental vacancy rate in the Chicago area was less than 5 percent.[25] Through 2009, almost four thousand CHA households relocated with vouchers; most moved into the city's high-poverty, predominantly black neighborhoods on the South and West sides, reinforcing the overall pattern for the Housing Choice Voucher program in Chicago.[26] Between 1995 and 2002, 82 percent of the displaced families using vouchers moved to neighborhoods that were more than 90 percent African American, and half moved to neighborhoods with poverty rates in excess of 30 percent.[27] In fact, the independent monitor for the plan, former U.S. Attorney Thomas Sullivan, reported in 2003 that there were significant problems with the city's relocation assistance. Families were hurried out of their public housing homes, there were too few relocation counselors to handle the workload, and too many families relocated to poor-quality housing. Shortly after that report, residents sued the CHA for failing to live up to its obligation to assist residents in the relocation process and for violating Fair Housing laws in the process.[28] The result has been an improved relocation effort in which families have had access to "enhanced mobility counseling" in an effort to move out of segregated, high-poverty neighborhoods. It is unclear, however, whether the enhanced counseling will result in dramatically different spatial patterns among families displaced from public housing in Chicago. Families who moved away from the Henry Horner Homes had access to special relocation counseling, social services, and van tours in an effort to guide them to "opportunity neighborhoods," yet only 6 percent of the enrolled families made such moves. The majority moved to predominantly black neighborhoods, high poverty neighborhoods, or to both.[29]

The reception of neighborhood residents to the influx of public housing families was mixed at best. Complaints about public housing newcomers have been the greatest in more middle class neighborhoods,[30] where property owners are concerned about protecting their real estate investments. The conflicts between homeowners and public housing residents reveal a significant split in several communities on the city's South Side. Both sides felt threatened by the other, with public housing residents worried about being displaced by gentrification and the middle-class property owners threatened by the prospect of living near concentrations of poverty.[31] Especially in areas where new investment was occurring, as in the city's Bronzeville neighborhood on the near South Side, black middle class homeowners and gentrifiers were concerned about what they consider to be the problems associated with public housing—crime, social disorder, and declining quality of life within the community. The studies of Michelle Boyd, Mary Patillo McCoy, and Derek Hyra document the divisions within the South Side black community based on class and housing tenure.[32]

The third ripple effect of transformation was the displacement of crime from the sites of demolished public housing into other neighborhoods. Reduction of crime *at the redevelopment site* is a common outcome in public housing transformation; studies of HOPE VI redevelopments have documented this effect in a range of cities and circumstances.[33] Crime reduction at the redevelopment site, however, does not mean necessarily a reduction in crime citywide. Indeed, the major effect of redevelopment is not to reduce overall crime in the city, but to push it into different areas. The displacement of crime could reflect two phenomena. First, the displacement of public housing residents who were engaged in gang and criminal activities at the original site simply move their criminal activities to their new residences. In this case, one would see a spike in crime in so-called destination neighborhoods that receive displaced residents. In fact, there does not seem to be much evidence to support this particular dynamic.[34] Second, demolition and displacement removes a very low income population preyed upon by criminals and eliminates community design elements that make for easy environments in which to conduct criminal activities. When one inviting environment is taken away through demolition, crime moves to other promising areas. In Chicago, the crime displacement effects were notable.[35] The neighborhood where the Robert Taylor Homes once stood saw a large drop in homicides from 2000 to 2008, while two miles south the murder rate tripled.[36] A local expert attributes the spike in crime to gangs who had controlled the Taylor Homes "trying to establish new territory" after the demolition of the project.[37] For their part, CHA officials argue that fluctuations in neighborhood crime rates cannot be reliably attributed to the Plan for Transformation and the intracity migration it has induced.

In some cases, the displaced households themselves were put at risk when they were moved out of their public housing community. The relocation of public housing residents into other neighborhoods and sometimes into other public housing projects at times moved gang members into the heart of another gang's territory. Even when a resident was not a member of a gang, the gang dominance of their original project was enough to taint them in the eyes of their new neighbors. Investigative reporters in the city "found several murders that were linked to" disputes stemming from gang rivalries induced by the relocation of public housing residents.[38]

Resident Opposition

One of the more striking images of public housing transformation in Chicago was the sight of residents carrying signs protesting the demolition of the Cabrini-Green project. The prevailing discourse of disaster that circulated around Cabrini and most of Chicago public housing suggested conditions so bad that residents would be grateful to see the place demolished and grateful for the opportunity to leave. In fact, however, organized opposition to the demolition of public housing in Chicago emerged fairly early in the process. In 1996, Wardell Yotaghan and other residents of public housing organized the Coalition to Protect Public Housing (CPPH) to serve as a voice for CHA families. Chicago public housing residents have a history of organizing; residents have been involved in management activities since the 1960s. The CHA's system of resident management is the oldest public housing resident management organization in the nation. Organizing among CHA residents dates back to the formation of the Chicago Housing Tenants' Organization in 1970 to protest what it felt was the misuse of modernization funds and mismanagement.[39] As Feldman and Stall argue in their study of life in the Wentworth Gardens project on the city's South Side, Chicago public housing residents did not passively acquiesce to worsening conditions in CHA buildings.[40] They organized grassroots efforts to prod the CHA into better management, and when that did not work they took on the effort themselves. By the 1990s there was little trust between the residents and the CHA. When residents were told that their units were to be demolished and they would be relocated with Housing Choice Vouchers until they could return to the completed redevelopment site, they were skeptical. They were doubtful about whether there would be enough replacement housing built for them. They were unconvinced that the Housing Choice Vouchers would work in the local housing market, and they questioned the quality of the neighborhoods and the housing to which they would be moved. Finally, they disagreed with CHA about the need for large-scale demolition to turn around their public housing communities.

Opposition to demolition by public housing residents in Chicago, as elsewhere, was not an effort to maintain status quo conditions. No one knew the deficiencies of existing public housing in Chicago as well as the residents. Have been ill-used by the CHA for decades, residents easily envisioned the multitude of further harm that could befall them in a displacement and relocation effort managed by that same entity. CPPH was formed to advocate for positive change in the living environments of public housing that would provide existing residents the chance to benefit. By 1996, when CPPH emerged, the CHA was in the midst of redevelopment activities at the Henry Horner Homes and just beginning planning at Cabrini-Green. HOPE VI grants had just been announced for ABLA and the Robert Taylor Homes as well. It was clear that large-scale change was in the works for Chicago public housing, because four years before the Plan for Transformation was announced thousands of CHA units had failed the HUD Viability Test. At first, CPPH focused on a series of informational meetings at which residents from various developments could trade stories about what was happening to them and their communities. Specific concerns began to emerge, including an increased rate of evictions in 1997 and 1998. Some saw this as a way of emptying the buildings to ready them for relocation and demolition, a continuation and spread of the de facto demolition techniques the CHA had used at the Henry Horner Homes years before. The CHA, run at the time by the HUD caretaker Joseph Shuldiner, said the evictions were simply a reflection of better management.[41]

CPPH organized demonstrations at HUD and CHA offices to demand a demolition and redevelopment process that was more resident-friendly. Specifically, they demanded assurances and rights similar to those that were won through legal battle by the residents of the Horner Homes. The consent decree governing the Horner redevelopment called for phased redevelopment so that residents could remain on-site until such time as they could move directly into their new units. The Horner settlement guaranteed a one-for-one replacement of the public housing units demolished, and the newly redeveloped site, though managed privately, was not to be governed by restrictive tenant screening policies. Thus, the original residents of the project had better prospects of actually being able to reside in the redeveloped community and to directly benefit from the upgraded physical environment and better public services in the new community. CPPH was negotiating with Shuldiner on these points at the time that control of the CHA was returned to the city. Negotiations were cut off at that point and soon thereafter the city announced "The Plan."[42]

Once the PFT was announced, CPPH focused their efforts on opposing the absolute reduction in the number of public housing units being envisioned. CPPH's position was significantly undercut, however, when the traditional mouthpiece for resident concerns, the residents' Central Advisory Committee (CAC), endorsed the CHA plan.[43] The organization experienced a setback when its first leader, Wardell Yotaghan, died of a heart attack in 1999. CPPH continued its efforts to preserve Chicago public housing and to bring attention to the concerns of displaced tenants. In 2009 the organization worked with other national groups to bring the United Nations special rapporteur on the right to adequate housing to Chicago to examine the displacement of public housing residents. CHA continues to work with the resident representatives from the Local Advisory Committees (LACs) and the CAC, who on occasion have, themselves, been vocal in criticizing the implementation of the PFT. In December 2009, at the ten-year celebration of the PFT, CAC members unveiled a video that focused on the tenant experience. While acknowledging improved conditions at the newly redeveloped sites, the video described the disruption to residents' lives and the loss of community they had suffered in the process. At the event CAC member and CHA board member Myrna King called for a moratorium on further demolition until more replacement units were built.[44]

The completed redevelopment sites in Chicago are, for the most part, striking in the degree to which they have altered the physical landscape of public housing. Handsome two- and three-story brick walk-ups, with various architectural amenities, stand where neglected and imposing modernist high-rises once dominated. The great wall of public housing that paralleled the Dan Ryan Expressway on the South Side is now gone. Although large swaths are still vacant, attractive new housing has been built on part of the land previously occupied by the Robert Taylor Homes and the neighborhood shows signs of economic rebirth. Homeowners and the middle class are returning to the South Side; on the Near North Side, prior to the housing crash in 2007, condominiums were selling for $750,000 in the neighborhood where Cabrini-Green once stood. New shops, a park, a new public library, and a new fire station also have gone in near the Cabrini site.

The irony of the Chicago case is that the considerable achievements in coordinating city services were realized in public housing communities only after their demolition. For most of its history, public housing in Chicago was not a priority for public officials. It was, in fact, something of the opposite, at best a necessary evil. Public housing in Chicago, shunted to declining and segregated communities when first approved, marginalized by cost-cutting and excessive frugality when built, and slowly asphyxiated by mismanagement and neglect during its lifetime, would, upon demolition, finally become the city's top priority. The city that had proven so monumentally inept at providing public housing for its poorest citizens has proven quite adept at removing that housing and creating mixed-income redevelopment sites in its place.

New Orleans

The city of New Orleans was one of the more active in building public housing in the early years of the program; six projects were in place by 1940. The Housing Authority of New Orleans (HANO), like many public housing authorities at the time, carefully segregated its projects. Of the original developments, St. Thomas and Iberville were for white residents, while Magnolia (later called C. J. Peete Homes), Calliope (later called D. W. Cooper Homes), Lafitte, and St. Bernard were for blacks. These early projects were notable for their design features and solid construction. Iberville and Lafitte, the two projects adjacent to the city's downtown district, were especially distinctive architecturally. The projects consisted of three-story red-brick blocks with, according to a *New York Times* architectural critic, "detailed brickwork, tile roofs and wrought-iron balustrades representing a level of craft more likely found on an Ivy League campus" than in public housing.[45] The projects fit the scale of the surrounding neighborhoods, and incorporated a street grid with pedestrian paths shaded by large oaks. The construction was solid and high quality, producing housing with a physical foundation and strength much greater than its political foundation.

FIGURE 5. Lafitte public housing development in New Orleans. In the wake of Hurricane Katrina, 896 units were vacated and never reinhabited. It was demolished in 2008 and replaced by Faubourg Lafitte, a mixed-income community. Courtesy Louisiana Landmarks Society.

Initially, as in most cities, public housing was reserved for the lower-income working class. HANO filled their buildings according to a strict formula, reserving spots for households with incomes in each of five tiers, ensuring both a mix of incomes and a sufficient base of working families to keep the projects financially solvent. As families increased their incomes, especially after World War II, HANO forced them to move out to make way for other families. The strict application of income restrictions meant the cycling out of the highest income tenants, though HANO's strategies were never as forceful as those used in Chicago and elsewhere where evictions pushed thousands of working families out of public housing in the '40s and '50s.

The Decline of New Orleans Public Housing

Despite the general success of its early public housing developments, HANO had difficulty finding locations to build new projects. Neighborhood resistance led the authority to ever more isolated locations and to a strategy of simply expanding the size of the original projects; within twenty years of their initial construction Cooper, Peete, and St. Bernard had doubled in size while St. Thomas had grown by over 50 percent. Each of these developments became home to around fifteen hundred households by the time their expansions were completed.[46] In addition to the original projects, four additional large complexes were completed by 1964. By the end of the 1960s, the public housing stock in New Orleans was a mix of projects that were well sited, close to downtown job and activity centers, and others that were isolated developments far from the city center, in low-amenity neighborhoods, walled off from the rest of the community by railroad tracks, industry, and highways.

Severe housing segregation and employment discrimination in New Orleans from the 1930s through the 1960s gave lower-income whites greater upward mobility and greater housing choice than blacks who lived in public housing. As a result, turnover in the white buildings was consistently higher than in the black buildings. When HANO moved to desegregate its housing stock after passage of the 1964 Civil Rights Act, forcing the integration of white and black residents within the same buildings, public housing slowly lost its racial diversity. Lower-income whites, with other housing options in the local market, "simply stopped viewing the projects as housing they were willing to accept."[47] The socioeconomic profile of residents also changed during this time period as HANO, like other local housing authorities across the country, focused their resources on a more welfare-dependent population. Waiting lists were dominated by the jobless as working class blacks also began to leave the projects. By the end of the 1960s, public housing in New Orleans was almost exclusively inhabited by very low income African Americans.[48]

Patterns of white flight, suburbanization, and continued residential segregation left New Orleans more generally with a much poorer and predominantly black population. During the 1960s New Orleans lost 16 percent of its white population to suburbanization. A Brookings Institution study of social hardship in central cities in the mid-1970s ranked New Orleans as the third-most-distressed city in the country.[49] It had a large and growing black underclass, poor public schools, low rates of employment, and high rates of violent street crime. The poverty and crime continued to grow throughout the '70s and '80s, generating further decline in the public housing stock and in the city's poorer black neighborhoods.

Over time HANO showed little ability to manage the growing problems of physical decline in its housing stock or the social problems that were overwhelming its developments. A 1983 HUD audit concluded that HANO had no overall plan for the maintenance of its buildings. Conditions had deteriorated so badly in the Desire and Fischer developments that HUD recommended removal of 2,118 units from those communities.[50] A 1988 management review by HUD found 241 deficiencies in HANO operations. Six years later, in June 1994, another audit of units found violations of quality standards in every single unit randomly chosen for examination.[51] HANO still had no preventative maintenance program, and vacated units sat empty for months, costing the agency millions of dollars in lost revenue each year. In 1996, HUD took over the Housing Authority of New Orleans to correct systemic problems of mismanagement.

The precipitous decline in the conditions of public housing in the city coincided with increasing pressures for redevelopment and the expansion of upscale residential development in closer proximity to some projects. Political scientist Alexander Reichl maintains that the two trends were not unrelated: "Gross neglect serves the expressed political interest of displacing public housing populations. The battle to dismantle public housing in New Orleans is arguably half over at several housing developments."[52] Reichl wrote those words in 1999, six years before Hurricane Katrina.

Redevelopment Pressures

The only asset held by several New Orleans public housing projects that had actually appreciated over time was location. Iberville and Lafitte were next to the French Quarter, within walking distance of Bourbon Street and the heart of the city's tourist-dependent economy. St. Thomas, located near the Mississippi River east of downtown, was an isolated community of impoverished blacks surrounded by higher income whites, in the middle of a "chain of economically valuable neighborhoods" and directly in the path of the city's revitalization efforts.[53] Developers and city leaders were covetous of the land occupied by these projects.

In 1986, an advisory report to the mayor recommended a drastic reduction in the density of all public housing projects in the city. The mayor's report suggested that vacancy rates at the time (made worse by HANO's inability to maintain its housing stock) would allow the removal of one-third to one-half of all public housing units at its biggest developments without reducing the number of families then being served.[54] The report also contained a recommendation that the mayor assume authority over all HANO decisions, essentially eliminating the agency as an independent decision-making body. The mayor's plan was to remove public housing to make way for moderate-income housing or commercial development. In some cases, no plan for reuse of the public housing site was offered.[55] Though the mayor's recommendations were never implemented, public housing in New Orleans was in a precarious political position.

St. Thomas, in particular, was vulnerable. Vacancy rates had risen to 29 percent in the project by 1990 and plans for its redevelopment were openly considered by developers and the city. As came to be the case with many public

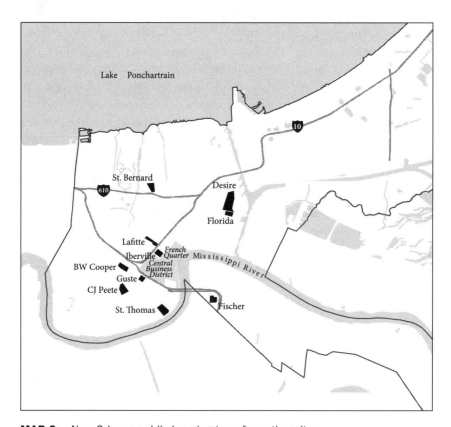

MAP 2.   New Orleans public housing transformation sites

housing projects across the country, the private sector saw the project as an impediment to investment in a neighborhood that was otherwise poised to take off.[56] The move toward demolition in New Orleans at this time still lacked sufficient support to move forward. The decisive factor proved to be the orientation of the federal government. The 1994 HUD audit of HANO depicted an organizational disarray so complete that it recommended privatization of "the entire operation of the authority."[57] HANO was one of the first PHAs to win a HOPE VI grant (for the Desire project), and when the federal government lifted the one-for-one replacement rule HANO asked for and received from HUD the authority to shift funds that had been earmarked for modernization to demolition. In 1996, HANO received its second HOPE VI grant, this one to carry out the long-anticipated demolition and redevelopment of St. Thomas.

Hurricane Katrina

When Katrina hit in August 2005, it devastated the city's poorest neighborhoods. Already in the midst of an affordable housing crisis prior to Katrina (56 percent of very low income families paid more than half of their income for housing), the city saw flooding in three-quarters of its poorest neighborhoods, where 80 percent of the residents were nonwhite.[58] Six large public housing developments were shuttered immediately after the hurricane. Though efforts to begin rebuilding middle-class homeownership-oriented neighborhoods in the city began immediately, rebuilding in the black, low-income Ninth Ward lagged. The loss of rental units produced significant rent increases across the city, which made Section 8 vouchers more difficult to use. HUD adjusted fair market rents upward by 39 percent from 2005 to 2006, but advocates argued the real increases were twice that high.[59]

Katrina caused some damage to the city's public housing stock, but most developments escaped significant structural harm. Nevertheless, public housing residents returning to the city in the weeks after the hurricane were kept from reoccupying their units, even in developments that sustained no structural damage from the storm winds or flood waters. In most cases they were not even allowed back in to retrieve belongings. The projects were fenced off and protected against intruders and against their previous inhabitants with razor wire. Residents were provided with "disaster relief vouchers" to subsidize other accommodations or were moved into other public housing developments. An unknown number became homeless or did not return to the city.

Katrina provided the opportunity for a final push to close down public housing in the city and move toward redevelopment. At the very least, the hurricane presented an opportunity for the city to rid itself of the blighting influences that most of those projects had become. As Republican congressman Richard Baker of Baton Rouge said, "we finally cleaned up public housing; we couldn't do it, but God did."[60]

With residents scattered and slowly trickling back to the city and with the units already vacated and arguably damaged by the natural catastrophe, proponents of redevelopment and demolition had the advantage. They also had the support of a HUD eager to implement its vision of mixed-income communities. From the very beginning, as public housing residents fought to be allowed back into their homes, Secretary of HUD Alphonso Jackson broached the subject of a complete dismantling of public housing in the city. To him and to others, the opportunity to radically reshape the city's public housing landscape presented by the evacuation forced by Katrina was an ideal chance to address the high levels of poverty and crime in the city. The racial dimension of this "opportunity" did not escape him. Indeed, Jackson suggested that post-Katrina New Orleans would not "be as black as it was for a long time, if ever again."[61] In November Jackson publicly promised to build $1.8 billion of public housing along the Gulf Coast, noting, however, that "it will not be traditional public housing."[62] Mayor Ray Nagin also took the opportunity provided by Katrina to advocate for a more comprehensive and complete program of public housing demolition and redevelopment than had existed prior to the hurricane.

The Fight to Preserve

Residents and their advocates began a series of protests in the months after Katrina that were to last the better part of four years. They demanded access to their homes and argued that the public housing closings were exacerbating the city's affordable housing crisis. In early 2006 rallies were held to demand the reopening of St. Bernard, Iberville, Guste, Cooper, and C. J. Peete. In June 2006, however, HUD announced plans to demolish over five thousand units of public housing in what became known as the "Big Four" developments—C.J. Peete, D. W. Cooper, St. Bernard, and Lafitte. HANO announced it would reopen one thousand units in other public housing complexes across the city—though these had existed before Katrina and therefore did not offset the demolition of the five thousand units. The decision to demolish was in part based on HUD's contention that rehabilitation of the projects would cost a prohibitive $130 million, a figure questioned by the residents and affordable housing advocates.[63] HUD and HANO, furthermore, pointed to the HOPE VI redevelopment of St. Thomas (now called River Gardens) as an example of the possibilities of full-scale demolition and renewal of public housing. Advocates pointed to the same example (and its reduction of public housing units from fifteen hundred to less than two hundred on-site) to highlight the severe reduction in public housing units that they felt would likely result from further redevelopment.[64] The HUD announcement triggered a lawsuit to block the demolition, and protests outside of the closed public housing projects intensified. In August 2006 residents and advocates attempted to reoccupy Lafitte; nine were arrested.[65] The next month former residents of C. J. Peete reoccupied units in that development without HANO permission. In January 2007, advocates temporarily reoccupied units at St. Bernard, only to be forcibly evicted by a SWAT team from the New Orleans Police Department. The next month, advocates repeated the effort at C. J. Peete. Advocates protested outside the home of city council members, attempted to disrupt HANO board meetings, and protested at City Hall.

The residents received support from advocates across the country, and from some members of Congress. In February of 2007, Representatives Maxine Waters (D-CA) and Barney Frank (D-MA) introduced the "Gulf Coast Hurricane Housing Recovery Act of 2007," giving residents the right to return to their public housing units and stopping demolition until a plan for one-for-one replacement of the units was developed. The House passed the measure in March. Ultimately, the bill was killed in the Senate by Louisiana's Republican senator, David Vitter, who argued that fewer public housing units were necessary in a city in which only two-thirds of the original population had returned.[66] Speaker of the House Nancy Pelosi (D-CA) and Senate Majority Leader Harry Reid (D-NV) called on President Bush to halt the demolitions in New Orleans in 2007, and to develop a plan to produce full replacement of the units that were to be removed. As a presidential candidate in 2007, Barack Obama did the same. Obama's open letter to Bush read in part, "No public housing should be demolished until HUD can point to an equivalent number of replacement units in the near vicinity."[67]

When demolition at B. W. Cooper began in December 2007 protesters stood in front of the backhoe, attempting to stop the tear down. The demolition resumed the next day while protesters marched to City Hall and the federal courthouse. Simultaneously, advocates filed suit to impose a restraining order to halt the demolitions. Two days later, Pelosi and Reid sent their letter to Bush. Meanwhile, HANO negotiated with the plaintiffs in the lawsuit and agreed to stop the demolition of three of the Big Four unless and until the city council explicitly permitted it. Demolition at Cooper was allowed to proceed because demolition of that project had been approved pre-Katrina.[68] These events set up a climactic city council vote that would decide the final disposition of the public housing developments that advocates and residents had been trying to preserve for more than two years. Prior to the vote, HUD made it clear to New Orleans council members that should they vote to halt the demolition of one of the projects, Lafitte, HUD would withdraw nine hundred housing vouchers targeted for the displaced residents of Lafitte. "Any action that would prevent the demolition of Lafitte will deny housing assistance to the displaced tenants, which...would likely make it very difficult for them to afford to pay their own rent," said Jackson.[69]

On December 20, 2007, as hundreds of people crowded into the council chambers, and hundreds more confronted police outside, the council heard more than four hours of public testimony on both sides of the issue. Official tenant representatives said the demolition of these projects was long overdue, and that public housing residents had been subject to substandard living conditions for years. Other former tenants expressed support for the demolition. "No one deserves to live in these conditions; it's inhuman. I am for demolition," said the president of the C. J. Peete residents' council.[70] A resident of the Cooper development said she wanted a better home and better schools: "If you don't rebuild then the rest of the city and the neighborhood behind you will not rebuild.... It's about us walking into a house and saying, 'this is a house, it ain't a project.'" Protesters, on the other hand, complained of a lack of voice in the decision-making process, of the loss of homes, and their lack of trust in HANO and HUD to provide enough housing assistance for all who had been displaced. As police battled protesters with pepper spray and taser guns outside of City Hall, the council voted unanimously in four separate votes to approve the demolitions. Mayor Ray Nagin called the decisions made by the council "ones of compassion, courage, and commitment to this city."[71] City council president Arnie Fielkow said, "It's my hope that the word 'project' will never again be used in place of what should be 'transitional homes.' Every citizen deserves a safe and affordable place to raise a family."[72] Demolition proceeded immediately at Cooper and shortly thereafter at C. J. Peete. The St. Bernard project began to come down in February 2008. The last of the Big Four, the Lafitte project, began demolition in April of the same year. Of the four, the Lafitte project was the bitterest loss for public housing advocates. The project sustained only minor damage in the hurricane and flood, and was relatively well maintained and almost fully occupied at the time of Katrina. This made it one of the more functional of the public housing developments run by HANO. Architecturally, the project "had a distinct elegance," according to the head of the local office of the National Trust for Historic Preservation (NTHP), including tile roofs, solid brickwork, and ironwork.[73] Walter Gallas, director of the New Orleans Field Office of NTHP, said:

> Any arguments I tried to make for the retention and continued long-term use of any of the buildings on the basis of historic preservation, architectural merit, structural soundness or sustainability were fruitless in a public arena filled with rhetoric about the evil nature of

the buildings, their dilapidated appearance, the alleged high cost to remediate and repair, and the success of national developers at showing examples of their work in other communities.[74]

Dismantling New Orleans Public Housing

Residents and their advocates continued to protest, holding signs and shouting with bullhorns outside the fences of the projects being bulldozed. But much of the tension had gone out of the protests by then, with the federal government and the city's power structure having decisively weighed in on the side of demolition. In the end, the preferences of the residents, whether in favor or opposed to demolition, were not important in how public housing demolition played out in post-Katrina New Orleans. There was a policy consensus among officials and analysts that public housing in the city would not be reoccupied. HUD, HANO, and city officials within New Orleans were in general agreement about the future of public housing in the city in the months and years following Katrina. HANO had already been in the process of demolishing and redeveloping projects prior to the hurricane. The redevelopment of the St. Thomas project (into River Gardens), and Desire (transformed into Abundance) were complete by the time the storm hit. Demolition had been approved for Cooper. Katrina did not initiate a new direction for city public housing policy; it merely provided the opportunity to expedite the complete dismantling of the city's public housing stock, an objective that had been decided by the city's political leaders years before.

In 2011, HANO received $30 million in federal funds (from the Choice Neighborhoods Initiative, the successor to HOPE VI) to redevelop its final remaining public housing complex, Iberville. The Iberville Homes are situated along a streetcar line, adjacent to the French Quarter and near a biomedical campus and hospital complex planned by Louisiana State University. The redevelopment of Iberville, according to business leaders, was "pivotal to revitalizing Canal Street" and the centerpiece of "a much more complete and responsible redevelopment" of the entire area.[75] Elimination of Iberville will be the last step in a complete shift away from traditional public housing in the city. Though the city actually gained subsidized housing because of the large increase in HUD vouchers after Katrina, the city, as of this writing, still suffers from extreme shortages of affordable housing as a result of stock lost in the storm. The conversion of housing subsidies from public housing to vouchers, furthermore, has generally not meant a greater dispersion of subsidized residents. There is evidence that, as in other cities, displaced families using vouchers have largely moved to other high-poverty, highly segregated neighborhoods. According to one study, "the areas with the largest concentrations of Section 8 units and the best access to public transportation, grocery stores and functioning parks are near former public housing sites."[76]

The transformation of public housing in New Orleans post-Katrina was complicated politically because of the larger racial conflicts playing out in the city. The debate over public housing demolition in New Orleans took place in a highly volatile setting in which accusations of racial engineering were made back and forth. Advocates for the poor argued that government officials were trying to remake the color line in New Orleans and inhibit the ability of blacks, especially low-income blacks, to repopulate the city. Racial conflict had played out in ugly ways in the immediate aftermath of the storm. Just three days after Katrina had rendered much of the city uninhabitable, a group of evacuees, most black, attempted to leave the city by way of the U.S. Route 80 bridge that crosses the Mississippi into the predominantly white suburb of Gretna. The group was met on the bridge by Gretna police with guns drawn and ordered to turn around. The next day a different group of refugees faced the same response, this time watched by a police helicopter hovering just above.[77] In the weeks that followed, race and poverty shadowed every decision about how to rebuild the city. Efforts to build affordable housing met frequently with political and regulatory obstacles. In mostly white St. Bernard Parish, officials passed an ordinance in late 2005 banning renovation of multifamily housing and a year later enacted another law that would restrict the rental of single-family homes to blood relatives only.[78] After having been ruled in violation of the Fair Housing Act and ordered to repeal the blood-relative ordinance, St. Bernard Parish issued a moratorium on the construction of apartment buildings.

Public housing was 100 percent black in New Orleans at the time of Katrina. The boarding up of these projects, and the efforts made to keep the old residents from returning to their homes, were seen by the residents and their advocates as part of an effort to redefine the racial and socioeconomic landscape of New Orleans. This was not a wild-eyed conspiracy theory; indeed, it was the expressed objective of some officials who did little to hide or conceal it. It was reflected in HUD Secretary Alphonso Jackson's comments about the likely racial makeup of post-Katrina New Orleans, and in the Louisiana congressman's comment that about the divine intervention in cleaning up public housing in the city. It was also apparent in Jackson's successor at HUD, Steven Preston, when he claimed that he did not "want to replicate what we had if that would mean bringing back certain problems we know about," and that "New Orleans must be safe and more secure."[79] There is little ambiguity among those advocating for public housing transformation in New Orleans; speaking about the St. Bernard project, the spokesman for the developer said in 2009, "This will not be the redeveloped St. Bernard. This will be a high-end residential neighborhood where St. Bernard once stood."[80]

It was Katrina that led a coterie of liberal policy analysts to suggest that the natural disaster had provided a perfect opportunity to disperse the city's poor black population in order not to replicate patterns of concentrated poverty within the city. Over two hundred scholars signed a petition in the weeks following Katrina urging a program of poverty dispersal in New Orleans to avoid allowing the concentrations of poverty that had existed in New Orleans from simply reconstituting themselves.[81] It was columnist David Brooks who wrote about the "silver lining" in the Katrina storm clouds, calling the storm, the flooding, and the mass displacement "an amazing chance to do something serious about poverty," and an opportunity for rebuilding whose first rule "should be: Nothing Like Before."[82]

The city had had almost fourteen thousand units of public housing in 1996. At the moment Katrina hit, nine years later, that number had been cut in half through demolition and redevelopment. The St. Thomas project, Desire, Florida, and Fisher had all been redeveloped prior to the storm. Demolition at C. J. Peete had begun before Katrina, reducing the size of that project by half—at the time the hurricane hit, only 146 families lived in that project.[83] The redevelopment of the Big Four after Katrina dropped the number of public housing units in those developments by 80 percent, from five thousand to fewer than seven hundred.[84] Four years after Katrina, there were still no public housing units, new or old, occupied in any of the Big Four projects. By 2011, when three of the four redevelopments were reoccupied, only 7 percent of the original residents were rehoused in the new communities.[85]

In a relatively short period of time New Orleans has eliminated thousands of units of low-cost public housing, all of which had been inhabited by low-income African Americans. In New Orleans the dismantling of public housing was part of a larger dynamic about race and poverty in which transformation played a central role in a conscious effort to deconcentrate poverty and disperse low-income blacks. The New Orleans case illustrates how public housing removal is key to efforts to redefine the city. The remaking of New Orleans was put into stark relief by the rebuilding effort after Katrina. Questions about how black or how poor the city should be were given explicit attention in ways that did not occur in other cities. Yet the effort to reduce concentrations of poverty and disperse low-income black residents was similar to Chicago's Plan for Transformation. The dismantling of public housing in both cities is part of a fundamental redefinition of the city and a forced mobilization of the poor and of people of color to suit a different vision of what the city should be.

Atlanta

The city of Atlanta is home to the first completed public housing project in the nation, Techwood Homes, constructed in 1935. The project cleared eleven blocks of slums, called Techwood Flats, near downtown Atlanta. Techwood Flats had been home to mostly white, low-income families, and a center of crime, disease, and infant mortality in the city. It was situated adjacent to Georgia Tech University and the headquarters of the Coca-Cola Corporation. Its existence led one city leader of the time to wonder "why such an untended abscess should fester between the lovely campus of our proudest school and the office buildings in the heart of the city."[86] Techwood Homes was well built and well designed. Each doorway had a canopy, and the buildings were solid and trimmed in stone. The project was designed to open up the environment to light and space, using a physical plan that designers thought would create more favorable social conditions. Applicants were carefully screened for employment history and general "deportment."[87] Rents were set above what the previous residents of the Flats could have afforded. In all, over six hundred families were housed in a combination of two-story rowhouses and three-story apartment buildings. Over the years, the project was noted for its historical importance and placed on the National Register of Historic Places. In 1993, a study of the project concluded that "it had fulfilled its 60-year life expectancy and could go for another 60."[88] Two years later Techwood Homes was demolished.

The city of Atlanta was one of the pioneers in public housing. In addition to finishing the first public housing project in the nation, the city added thousands of units in subsequent years. The Clark-Howell project, for example, added another 624 units immediately adjacent to Techwood Homes in 1940. Two more projects were added in the same area in subsequent decades. Throughout the 1950s and '60s Atlanta engaged heavily in urban renewal activities. More than sixty-seven thousand people were displaced in the city as a result of freeway and urban renewal construction, more than three-quarters of them were black. Public housing was built in the previous slum areas and on vacant land in various parts of the city to meet the demand for housing among blacks displaced through urban renewal. By the time it had stopped building new units, Atlanta had more public housing per capita than any other large American city: about one resident of Atlanta in ten lived in public housing.

By the 1970s Atlanta had become a majority black city, the white population having fled to the suburbs of the north. Between 1970 and 1990 the city continued to lose population, declining by one hundred thousand residents over that time period. Despite the active urban renewal agenda Atlanta was a city in economic decline throughout this period. With more affluent whites leaving for the suburbs, the income profile of the city plunged relative to the rest of the region. The poverty rate in the city was almost four times the suburban rate, and the median income of the city relative to the surrounding suburbs fell from 80 percent in 1969 to 59 percent in 1989.[89]

As in some other large cities, public housing in Atlanta was not well managed. The same patterns of concentrated poverty and civic neglect that plagued PHAs in some larger U.S. cities affected Atlanta's public housing. In 1980, Techwood and Clark-Howell had almost ten thousand code violations between them, attracting a $17.2 million grant for modernization from HUD. But conditions there and at other AHA projects only worsened during the 1980s. The crack cocaine epidemic hit hard in the 1980s and gangs vied for control of the projects. Gunfire at the East Lake Meadows project, which was a relatively new project that had been built in 1970, was so common that the project was nicknamed Little Vietnam. The AHA, meanwhile, had no answers for residents who wanted conditions in their communities improved. Maintenance orders were left undone, plans to improve security were never fully implemented, and the agency sank under the weight of

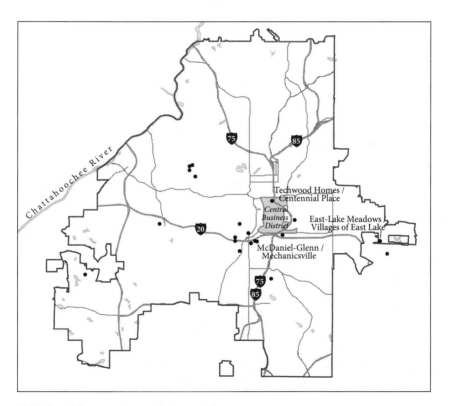

MAP 3.   Atlanta public housing transformation sites

corruption and inefficiency. By 1994, AHA had distinguished itself as one of the country's worst PHAs.[90]

The Olympic Legacy Program

In 1990 the city of Atlanta was chosen to host the 1996 Olympic Games. Mayor Maynard Jackson and other city leaders saw the Games as an opportunity to leverage public and private financing for revitalization efforts within the city. The Olympic Village, housing the athletes for the Games, was located across the street from the Techwood Homes public housing project. Although some called for the demolition of Techwood Homes, Jackson favored rehabilitation, calling Techwood "fundamentally sound, close in, and historically important."[91] The city and AHA made an application for funds from the brand-new federal HOPE VI program. HUD approved the city's application in 1993 calling for the rehabilitation of Techwood and Clark-Howell and the preservation of most of the site. Another public housing project, East Lake Meadows, 650 units in a more remote part of the city, received a $33.5 million grant for renovation from HUD in 1992. Within months, however, the political stars would realign themselves and the future of Techwood Homes, Clark-Howell, East Lake Meadows, and all of Atlanta public housing would change dramatically.

A new mayor, Bill Campbell, was elected in 1993 and he appointed Renee Glover to head AHA. Glover was a corporate finance attorney who had worked for Campbell's campaign staff. Her vision for public housing, supported by the new mayor, called for more fundamental and thoroughgoing transformation. The plans for Techwood and Clark-Howell shifted away from rehabilitation and preservation to total demolition and replacement. The East Lake Meadows renovation was put on hold and in fact never occurred. Although HUD had in 1992 rejected a transformation proposal for Techwood in part because it included too little replacement housing, the agency signaled its willingness to relax replacement requirements, especially with Congress considering a suspension of the one-for-one replacement requirement (an idea they followed through on in the following year). With HUD officials beginning to consider a much more sweeping form of transformation in the HOPE VI program, the plans for Techwood, Clark-Howell, and East Lake Meadows changed. All three, it was quickly decided, would be demolished, the residents relocated, and the sites redeveloped into mixed-income communities.

Following a classic pattern of de facto demolition, vacancies at Techwood skyrocketed in a short period. In 1990, months before the announcement that Atlanta had been chosen to host the Olympics, Techwood Homes was 93 percent occupied. Fourteen months later occupancy had dropped to 82 percent.

By April 1993 it was more than half empty, and only 38 percent occupied by August 1993. The vacancies created a self-reinforcing dynamic as families moved out because of the heightened security concerns created by previous vacancies. By the time official relocation activities had begun, only 44 percent of the original residents in Techwood and Clark-Howell were around to benefit from relocation assistance offered by AHA. The site was quickly cleared and redevelopment begun in time for a portion of the new development, called Centennial Place, to be completed for the 1996 Olympic Games. Between the demolition of public housing and the related real estate speculation spurred by the neighborhood changes taking place, an international housing rights group estimated that as many as thirty thousand residents, mostly poor, were displaced from their homes in Atlanta because of preparations for the Olympics.[92]

In fact, the AHA saw the Olympic Games as an opportunity for widespread transformation of older public housing projects. The agency announced an "Olympic Legacy Program" that expanded the demolition agenda far beyond Techwood and Clark-Howell. The Olympics and the change in political leadership within the city had brought forth an ambitious plan to demolish over a dozen public housing communities and transform them into mixed-income residential developments. The city secured seven HOPE VI grants from the federal government between 1993 and 2005, but also pursued other financing sources and redeveloped several other projects without HOPE VI funding.

The Atlanta Model

The AHA itself was transformed under Glover's leadership. From an ineffective, almost moribund operation overwhelmed by the multiple and varied problems facing it's properties, problems that were in large part induced by the agency's incompetence and indifference, AHA has been largely privatized and streamlined. It shifted dramatically from a public social service agency to a real estate development firm, assembling financing from various public and private sources to build mixed-income communities that it hands off to private firms to manage. Much of its internal operations are also subcontracted out to private firms.

Glover became a national spokesperson for public housing transformation, an enthusiastic supporter of the model with an evangelical faith in the redeeming effects of forced displacement. She speaks at national conferences and visits other cities to share the lessons of the Atlanta experience. Her official biography even credits her with creating the redevelopment blueprint used by HUD in HOPE VI projects across the country. Her statements about large-scale demolition and displacement are strong and unequivocal: "I find it incredible that so many people don't comprehend the awful, corrosive impact of intensely concentrated poverty and the dehumanizing low standards and expectations" associated with it. "We know with 100 percent certainty that people's lives will transform if their environment is transformed and we invest in people. Environment matters."[93] Yet, it is clear that Atlanta's effort goes well beyond merely an attempt to improve the living conditions for public housing residents. When Glover and HUD announced the plans to take down all of the city's family public housing stock, she said, "Make no mistake. When...the...large family housing projects come down, Atlanta will have made a great step on behalf of *all* Atlanta citizens."[94]

Though Glover declares that the corrosive impact of concentrated poverty is the reason behind Atlanta's effort to transform public housing, gentrification pressures played their part as well. In the case of Techwood and Clark-Howell, those projects had been targeted for demolition years before the arrival of Glover and the emergence of the new AHA. The projects occupied valuable land next to the Georgia Tech campus and Coca-Cola headquarters. When Atlanta desegregated its public housing in 1968, the two projects began a rapid change from all white to nearly all black occupancy. As the change was taking place, Coca Cola officials first proposed the demolition of the projects, and "Central Atlanta Progress," a downtown business group, also weighed in to support the demolition. Mayor Jackson, who served from 1973 to 1993, was against the idea and kept demolition pressures at bay during his terms in office.[95] But, as previously noted, the election of Bill Campbell in 1993 brought an end to the protection Jackson was able to provide. The revitalization of downtown Atlanta was a top agenda item for Campbell, as was preparation for the Olympics. Glover wanted Techwood and Clark-Howell to be part of the new administration's downtown agenda.

With Techwood and Clark-Howell cleared, and the publicly funded Centennial Olympic Park in place (which had redeveloped blocks of blighted and underutilized warehouse and commercial land nearby), Coca-Cola invested millions in an interactive corporate museum/attraction called World of Coca Cola and the city located the new Georgia Aquarium nearby. The Atlanta Police Department constructed a new substation near the site, and a new school was built where the children wear uniforms and Georgia Tech faculty help interview prospective teachers. The transformation of Techwood and Clark-Howell into Centennial Place, a transformation that reduced the number of public housing units from twelve hundred to 360 and introduced 311 units of upscale housing in a new mixed–income community, made these corollary investments possible. As one developer involved in the redevelopment said, "Without Centennial Place the area might not have been attractive enough for Georgia Aquarium and 'World of Coca Cola.'...None of that would have been built if Techwood Homes was there. Nobody was going to invest real money with 60 acres of that."[96]

Similarly, gentrification pressures played a role in the demolition of East Lake Meadows (ELM), a project located in a more remote residential area of the city. Little Vietnam was one of the more neglected projects of the AHA and over time became an island of crime and pathology with a drug trade operating on the site that took in an estimated $38 million annually.[97] In 1992, former president Jimmy Carter went to East Lake Meadows to launch the Atlanta Project, a private-sector antipoverty initiative that leveraged millions of dollars in corporate contributions for comprehensive community-building initiatives throughout the city's low-income neighborhoods. The announcement site was appropriately chosen. ELM was the epitome of neighborhood decline, disinvestment, and neglect in the city. Built and then mostly forgotten by AHA, not served well by city or county services, the project offered a relatively hassle-free environment for gangs and drug dealers, and made life miserable for residents. Carter was able to announce that ELM had received a $33.5 million grant from HUD for renovation and there was hope that the community could be improved to provide a decent living environment for its residents.

In 1993, however, a private developer bought the East Lake Country Club and "by the following year the East Lake neighborhood had been rediscovered by higher-income whites" who began to purchase properties in the area for renovation and upgrade.[98] As property values began to rise, the profile of the neighborhood changed, the housing stock improved, and the rehabilitation plans for East Lake Meadows changed. The HUD-funded renovation never occurred. Instead, Glover and the AHA demolished the 650-unit project and replaced it with 406 single-family homes, duplexes, and garden apartments and christened it Villages of East Lake. The new project included 271 public housing units, with the rest a mix of shallow subsidies and market-rate units. The number of public housing units put back on-site was increased only after residents sued the authority to stop the redevelopment. Demolition began in the fall of 1996. Over the following six years the neighborhood saw a 20 percent annual increase in property values, the most precipitous rise in the entire Atlanta metropolitan area.[99] Estimates are that the demolition of public housing in Atlanta and the conversion of those communities into mixed-income areas, combined with the spillover development that has followed, has increased the tax base by $2.4 billion.[100]

Resident Outcomes and Response

Though received enthusiastically by the city's political elite, the demolition agenda of the AHA has not had the full support of the residents of Atlanta public housing. Part of the resistance put up by residents is project-specific.

For example, residents objected to the rushed relocation and demolition of the first HOPE VI project, Techwood Homes. Moving quickly to complete a substantial portion of the project before the 1996 Olympic Games, AHA emptied the buildings well in advance of actual relocation efforts. Most of the residents who were living at Techwood at the time of the announcement of the Olympic Games never received any relocation assistance or benefits. The residents of East Lake Meadows pointed to the Techwood example when they sued to slow down the process at their redevelopment and improve the relocation assistance provided by AHA. In this their actions were similar to those of Chicago public housing residents who sued to improve relocation efforts there. One resident leader at ELM complained at the time that "a lot of the residents feel like this is a sneaky way to get rid of us."[101] Of the negotiations at East Lake Meadows, the former head of the residents' association noted that "the housing authority walked all over us and pushed people out."[102]

As in most places where public housing demolition is taking place, the majority of residents are relocated using the Section 8 Housing Choice Voucher (HCV) program. Also similar to other metropolitan areas, the spatial distribution of HCV users is heavily tipped toward high-poverty neighborhoods and racially segregated neighborhoods.[103] "Vouchers are a ticket to nowhere," said one activist in Atlanta, noting that disadvantaged neighborhoods are the main options for displaced families.[104] Reflecting the complexities of relocation, however, a detailed analysis of the 2007 relocation from the McDaniel-Glenn HOPE VI redevelopment showed that despite the patterns of relocation noted above, most residents moved to lower-crime areas and reported satisfaction with their new housing. Ninety percent of the McDaniel-Glenn residents did not leave the city limits of Atlanta, and there is some evidence that families that did move farther away from the original site are moving back.[105]

The suboptimal relocation outcomes of displaced public housing residents became an issue in Atlanta as it did in Chicago. Also as in Chicago and most other cities, very few of the original public housing residents have made their way back to the newly redeveloped communities. In testimony before Congress in 2003, Glover described a planning session with AHA residents who just couldn't bring themselves to believe that the redevelopment of their public housing homes was *for them*: "I will never forget meeting with a committee of residents whose community we hoped to revitalize. When we showed them the architectural designs of what a new community would look like, one said to me, 'I know you're not planning that for me because that's too nice.' All of her neighbors agreed."[106] Glover was using the skepticism of the residents to make a point about the high quality of AHA's redevelopments and to suggest that the agency was delivering benefits that the resident regarded as unbelievable. This could be considered an effective rhetorical device but for the fact that the unnamed resident and her neighbors were largely accurate in their skepticism—the new developments in Atlanta are generally *not* for them; only 17 percent of Atlanta's former public housing residents have returned to the mixed-income communities since 1995.[107]

Nevertheless, AHA pushed ahead vigorously with its plans to expand the transformation of public housing in Atlanta. In 2008 the AHA announced that it would demolish all of the city's old public housing and that in some cases new mixed-income communities would be developed in its place. One element of the transformation effort is the use of private property management firms and the institution of more rigorous tenant screening criteria and behavior guidelines. In 2004 AHA imposed a work requirement on all residents. When the agency attempted to press forward with evictions of those who had not complied, the residents resisted. Tenant leaders felt that residents had not been given enough time at some of the developments, and that AHA had not informed tenants how the policy would be implemented: "We want the whole thing to stop because they never told us anything. They never came to the resident advisory boards."[108] Resident representatives also questioned the assumption that all AHA residents would be able to find employment, citing a large number of disabled tenants for whom employment was not a realistic expectation. In April 2007 residents disrupted the agency's annual plan public hearing. Residents were joined by a range of advocacy groups and some local elected officials. Councilmember Felicia Moore took up the cause of the residents, vowing to "personally intervene [with] ... the Housing Authority for people to be treated with dignity."[109] After another protest before an AHA public hearing, the agency announced it would moderate the eviction policy. In a letter to resident leaders, Glover acknowledged that some families "may face unique or special challenges" in meeting the work requirements, and that the agency would work with these households rather than move directly to eviction.

The advocacy of the residents picked up more momentum in June 2007 when the Fulton County Board of Commissioners adopted a resolution asking AHA to stop demolition until all senior and disabled residents were placed in safe and decent housing. The plight of seniors was especially important given the fact that AHA was moving to demolish even the senior buildings in its stock. The majority of seniors did not want to move out of their housing and were afraid of what awaited them in the relocation process. Later in June, public housing activists from Chicago came to Atlanta to join the protests. In August 2007, the citywide Resident Advisory Board filed a civil rights complaint with HUD, alleging that AHA's plan to eliminate all public housing violates the "Fair Housing Act of 1968 by discriminating against residents of public housing, virtually all of whom are black." One resident leader pointed out that "most of the public housing is predominantly black and we're the ones they're trying to move out."[110]

In early 2008, the citywide residents' board voted unanimously to oppose the demolition of any more public housing. City council members began to question whether AHA needed to be reined in a bit. In January of that year, the city council considered a nonbinding resolution asking AHA to stop demolitions until residents and the council could review the demolition applications. The mayor vetoed the nonbinding resolution to stop the demolitions, but was overridden by the council. Throughout the first part of May, resident groups opposed the demolition in letters, e-mails, and a resolution to HUD requesting delays until their concerns could be discussed and addressed. The resident leader at one senior high-rise located next to the revitalized Techwood Homes said:

> Please do not shut us out of this process; this is our home and the seniors want to have a voice. My residents are still saying they don't want to move. They don't want to go anywhere. We stayed here during the time it was so bad you couldn't walk the streets. Why can't we be here to enjoy the beautiful location of Techwood now?[111]

At the same time the city council considered an ordinance that would have given it oversight over the demolition plans of the AHA. The oversight ordinance would have provided the Council with a real role in AHA operations and was vehemently opposed by the agency. The oversight ordinance was ultimately withdrawn and AHA retained its full independence. In the end, the agency went ahead with all of its demolitions. At the staged event marking the demolition of the Bowen Homes in 2009, a former resident wondered about the clapping and celebratory mood: "What are they clapping about? Clapping for a demolition? You've had generations behind generations behind generations living in this public housing. This is not a time for celebration."[112]

"Racing" to Demolition

Chicago, New Orleans, and Atlanta are notable for the size and the extent of their transformations and for the extent to which they illustrate the empirical conclusions from chapter 2. The high crime rates in Chicago, Atlanta, and New Orleans reflect trends across the country associated with large-scale public housing demolition and disposition. Gentrification pressures were critical in all three cities, though Chicago stands out in this regard. In Atlanta and New Orleans the large-scale dismantling of public housing was more opportunistic, arising out of the planning for a mega-event (the Olympics) in Atlanta and from a natural disaster in New Orleans. Importantly, the political regime in each city lent decisive support to the PHA's efforts to transform public housing. In Chicago, the mayor's office under Richard M. Daley became closely identified with the Plan for Transformation and made the Plan the city's major redevelopment initiative from 1999 through 2010. In Atlanta, the close ties between the AHA under Glover and the mayor's office led to a coordinated effort to boost the fortunes of downtown and to expand the transformation of public housing citywide. Though there was less leadership from the governing regime in New Orleans, the city council provided the critical approval in 2007 that cleared the way for dismantling the city's public housing system. In each city there was a clear understanding that public housing transformation would facilitate significant private-sector reinvestment and trigger neighborhood upgrading.

Common across these three cities, too, was the resistance of residents to the large-scale transformation of public housing. None of the three housing authorities enjoyed much credibility with their residents; suspicion of PHA motives was high in each. In each city, of course, the resistance of residents was ultimately unsuccessful in halting the demolitions.

Finally, there is the fact that public housing in these three cities was almost exclusively occupied by African Americans, that the projects had become, in the words of Douglas Massey and Nancy Denton, reservations for poor blacks.[113] Chicago has a history of racial animosity that includes race riots in 1919 and the fairly regular firebombing of black residences during the 1940s and 1950s in order to maintain lines of residential segregation.[114] Martin Luther King famously said of Chicago after bringing his civil right campaign to that city, "people in Mississippi should come to Chicago to learn how to hate." Chicago's public housing became racially identified as early as the 1950s and the subsequent siting of new projects was restricted virtually without exception to black neighborhoods.[115] Chicago's public housing was the "other city," almost exclusively black, poor, and systematically neglected by city leaders, a physical articulation of its unresolved racial hostilities.

In Atlanta and New Orleans, blacks had been part of the governing coalition since the 1970s, yet public housing in the two cities suffered from mismanagement and disregard that rivaled the dysfunction in Chicago. In both cities, leaders decided to remake their cities in part by eliminating what had become the neglected repositories of the cities' poorest people of color. In Atlanta the reimaging began in the context of a mega-event that would attract worldwide attention, in New Orleans it was pursued in the wake of a natural disaster. In New Orleans especially, the question of race was laid bare during the dismantling of its public housing system. The evacuation of the city after Katrina and the subsequent steps taken to discourage resettlement by the low-income African Americans who had occupied the city's public housing led to the surfacing of a number of disquieting questions about who the city is for, and how race and disadvantage will be accommodated in post-Katrina New Orleans.

The experiences of Chicago, Atlanta and New Orleans suggest that public housing transformation is more than simply a policy shift from one model of subsidized housing to another. In these cities the full-scale attack on public housing was employed as a means of eliminating entire communities of poor black residents. These cities suggest a racial strategy in the transformation of public housing that is more fully examined in the following chapter.

"NEGRO REMOVAL" REVISITED

Gladys Showers raised eight children at Bluegrass-Aspendale [public housing complex in Lexington, KY]. She said she missed her friends who have all dispersed since the demolition. "We was happy," said Showers, 89. "I lived long and I lived good."

—Josh Kegley, "New Neighborhood Rises from City's First Public Housing Community"

On July 3, 1999, the city of Baltimore used five hundred pounds of dynamite to implode the George B. Murphy Homes. The Murphy Homes, 758 public housing units arrayed in fourteen-story high-rises, had been built in the 1940s. The city planned a parade of local residents and officials, and a "Murphy Homes Implosion Party" to mark the event.[1] Though 92 percent of Baltimore's public housing was occupied by African Americans at the time, Murphy Homes was even more segregated—99 percent of its residents were African American the year before it was blown up.

In Denver, Colorado, in 1999, the Curtis Park and Arapahoe Courts public housing projects were demolished. Prior to their demolition, 61 percent of the Curtis Park public housing project residents were black, as were 65 percent of the Arapahoe Courts residents. Though this is not particularly high by public housing standards, it was high for public housing in Denver where citywide only 25 percent of the city's public housing units were occupied by African Americans.

Also in 1999, the Knoxville Community Development Corporation, the city's public housing authority, demolished Lonsdale Homes, a 320-unit public housing project. Though the city's public housing stock was only 47 percent occupied by African Americans, Lonsdale Homes was 90 percent black. The Elizabeth Park Homes in Akron, Ohio, demolished in 2000, were 90 percent black while the city's overall public housing resident profile was 52 percent black. McConaughy Terrace in New Haven, Connecticut, was also disproportionately occupied by African Americans the year before it was torn down. So were the Bryant high-rises in Minneapolis, Parkside Homes and Dunbar Manor in Dayton, Addison Terrace and St. Clair Village in Pittsburgh, Pleasant View in Omaha, and Scott and Carver Homes in Miami. One can, in fact, point to dozens of projects across the country that share two characteristics with all of the projects listed above—they contained a disproportionately high percentage of black residents compared to other public housing in their cities, and they were demolished.

One of the defining characteristics of the old urban renewal program was its deleterious and disproportionate impact on African American residents of central city neighborhoods. Urban renewal displaced an estimated one million people from the time of its enactment in 1949 to 1965.[2] The impact on African American communities was so disproportionate that the program earned the nickname "Negro Removal." So, too, the development of the interstate highway system, as it carved its way through central cities, tended to disrupt largely black areas, displacing families and disrupting communities.[3] And now, the dismantling of public housing is producing a similarly disproportionate impact on black families. Households displaced by public housing demolition are predominantly African American, far in excess of their proportion in the American population, and far in excess of their representation among city residents in those cities where demolition is taking place. Though public housing in general is disproportionately occupied by people of color and by blacks specifically, the effort to demolish public housing has targeted African Americans *even accounting for their over-representation among public housing residents.* Projects that have been torn down in city after city have had significantly higher percentages of African American residents than those left standing in the same cities.

The Fact of Race

Public housing in the United States is disproportionately occupied by people of color, predominantly African Americans, and it is disproportionately located in minority neighborhoods. In 2000, 48 percent of the residents of public housing nationwide were African American, despite the fact that blacks made up 12.9 percent of the national population. In cities with the most public housing (larger jurisdictions with local public housing authorities that own and operate more than five thousand units) blacks made up 66 percent of public housing residents. In some cities, notably Birmingham, Detroit, Memphis, New Orleans, and Washington, D.C., HUD data show that 99 percent of the residents of public housing in 2000 were African American. In fact, a number of southern cities have public housing systems that are virtually entirely black, including Jackson, Shreveport, Richmond, Tallahassee, and Montgomery. These are cities in which public housing has become essentially the exclusive domain of blacks. The only nonsouthern city comparable in this respect is Detroit, Michigan.

In most large American cities the concentration of African Americans in public housing is highly disproportionate to their representation within the city as a whole. For example, in Indianapolis, where only 25 percent of the population was African American in 2000, fully 87 percent of the public housing was occupied by African Americans. Similarly, Tallahassee, Florida, is one-third African American, but its public housing is 98 percent black. This phenomenon occurs in cities of all sizes and types, and is one of the legacies of racial segregation and discrimination in the American housing market. Patterns of racial residential segregation dominated American cities in the immediate postwar years. Though segregation has declined slightly over the past decades, it remains a central characteristic of most urban areas even today. In many cities, the limited housing choices of African Americans and the lack of suitable housing in the postwar era led many blacks to public housing as a safe, affordable, and high-quality housing option.[4] As the United States emerged from the Depression during the 1940s and the economy (and local housing markets) expanded in the 1950s, white families of all income levels enjoyed greater housing choices, while blacks faced continued shortages of decent housing. Thus, demand for public housing waned among whites while increasing among blacks during this time period. The pattern became self-perpetuating as the racial turnover in public housing led more and more whites to avoid it. Public housing increasingly became known as housing for African Americans, leading many whites who might otherwise have been attracted by the lower rents to stay away because of racial attitudes.[5]

Across the largest 137 cities in the United States, in only five cities (two in Massachusetts—Springfield and Worcester, and three in Texas—Brownsville, El Paso, and Laredo) is the concentration of blacks in public housing less than in the city as a whole. In 62 percent of the cities, blacks as a percentage of public housing are at least two times their proportion of the citywide population. In fact, in the average large city in the United States, the share of public housing occupied by blacks is 2.6 times the share of the population of the city as a whole. In one-third of the cities, the ratio is greater than 3:1, and in 10 percent of the cities the ratio is greater than 4:1. In Lexington, Kentucky, and in San Francisco, the ratio is 5.7:1, the highest among the nation's largest U.S. cities. The rest of the cities with high ratios of blacks in public housing compared to citywide are cities with relatively small black populations such as Wichita, Kansas, Lubbock, Texas, and Aurora, Illinois, with black populations at or below 10 percent and public housing populations that are around 50 percent black.

Given the clear and consistent overrepresentation of blacks in the public housing of America's largest cities, any action, positive or negative, directed at public housing will have a disparate impact on African Americans. Had Congress, or HUD, or any of the presidential administrations from 1970 through 2010 attempted to systematically improve public housing, the beneficiaries would have disproportionately been African American. Conversely, however, because HUD and Congress have both passively allowed and actively pursued the demolition of public housing since the 1980s, the impact of the forced displacement has been disproportionately felt by black families.

Disparate Racial Impact

Though the NHLP report on demolition in the 1980s did not examine the racial breakdown of projects already demolished, it did look at the race of residents in projects that were being considered for demolition (twenty thousand to twenty-five thousand units at the time of their report). The NHLP observed that "race seems to be a factor in the units being considered for demolition. All of the projects slated for demolition are majority non-white." Specifically, the higher-than-average occupancy by African American households might have been a factor in determining which projects were torn down.

There are several potential standards against which to judge whether public housing demolition has had a disproportionate impact on blacks, each one corresponding to a more restricted spatial scale. To judge the displacement of blacks from public housing against the representation of blacks in the national population would show tremendous disparity owing to the overrepresentation of blacks in public housing. A second possible standard is the proportion of blacks in public housing across the nation (49 percent). This too would produce a conclusion of highly disparate impact. But this too is a less than adequate standard because we know that public housing demolition is concentrated in larger cities, places where blacks typically make up a higher percentage of public housing residents. In the average large city in the United States in 1996, 59.7 percent of public housing residents were African American. By this standard, there is still a very large disparate impact, since the average demolished project was 79.7 percent African American. Thus, demolished projects contained 33 percent more (79.7/59.7 =1.33) African Americans as a proportion of all residents than would have been expected had demolitions occurred in projects that were representative of public housing in all cities in the sample.

Restricting the referent standard to large cities would produce a more targeted comparison, but would still not indicate that individual PHAs are tearing down projects that have higher rates of black occupancy than the projects they leave standing. To demonstrate that, one must compare demolished projects to other projects in the same city in the same year; that is, one must use the overall racial distribution of a given city's public housing stock as the reference for the demolitions that took place in that city.

One example should suffice to explain the method. The Bernal Heights Dwellings in San Francisco were demolished in 1997. In the year prior to its demolition the 208 units in the Bernal Heights Dwellings were 93 percent occupied (193 households), and 69 percent of households at Bernal Heights were African American.[6] If 69 percent of the overall public housing stock in San Francisco that year was occupied by blacks, then the Bernal Heights demolition would be judged to not have had a disproportionate impact on African Americans. In fact, however, public housing citywide in San Francisco was only 49 percent Black in 1996. Thus, we conclude that the Bernal Heights Dwellings demolition did have a disproportionate impact on African Americans.

The degree of the disparate impact is calculated by a "disparity ratio" in which the numerator is the proportion of the demolished project occupied by blacks and the denominator is the citywide percentage of public housing occupied by blacks in the year prior to demolition.[7] A ratio over 1.0 indicates a disparate impact. In the Bernal Dwellings example, the disparity ratio is 1.41 (69/49). The Bernal Dwellings demolition affected 41 percent more African American households as a percentage of all households displaced than would have been expected had the project reflected all public housing units in San Francisco.

For each demolition occurring between 1997 and 2007 a disparity ratio can be computed and then aggregated for all public housing projects. The information on resident demographics comes from HUD's online database, "A Picture of Assisted Households."[8] There were, over this time frame, 394 public housing projects demolished in the 137 largest U.S. central cities. These projects accounted for 163,393 units of public housing (an average of 415 units per project). Of these units 110,227 (67 percent) were occupied during the year for which we have occupancy data. The HUD data contains resident demographic information for 313 cases, or 87,251 households. The average size of the projects in the sample is 397 units, though the median is 293. The mean is skewed upward by a relatively few large projects; one quarter of the projects had more than 515 units prior to demolition. The total number of people displaced in the 313 projects for which resident information is available is estimated at just under a quarter of a million (239,844).[9] Assuming that the units for which no resident data are available are similar in household size to the units for which information exists, then all of the public housing demolished in these 137 cities over this time period directly displaced more than three hundred thousand people (303,002).

The majority of cases in the database are HOPE VI projects (228, or 73 percent of the projects for which we have resident information). Although HOPE VI projects are on average larger than the rest of the public housing developments that have been demolished (a mean of 421 units compared to 327),[10] the data show that the HOPE VI projects and the other demolitions were statistically identical in terms of resident demographics. On seven indicators (percent of residents earning less than $5,000, percent with wage incomes, with welfare income, percent seniors, disabled, minority, and African American) there was no statistical difference between the HOPE VI and the other demolitions. As a result, it is reasonable to consider all of these projects as a single group regardless of whether they were HOPE VI-funded or not.

The overwhelming majority of households directly displaced by public housing demolitions across the country are African American. Of the 87,251 displaced households for whom we have demographic information, 71,373 households (or more than 192,000 residents given average household size in these projects) were African American, or 82 percent. The average demolition displaced 229 African American households (or 641 African American residents). In half of the demolished projects, furthermore, African Americans made up 95 percent or more of the households. Are these figures higher than one would expect to find in these cities during these years? Table 4.1 compares the demolished projects with the rest of the public housing stock in the same cities.

The data suggest a disparate racial impact of public housing demolition across more than three hundred demolitions in these large American cities. The average project that was demolished was 79.5 percent African American while other projects in the same cities were 73.2 percent African American on average. For Hispanic residents, however, there was no disparate impact; the average demolished project was 11.5 percent Hispanic, while the rest of the public housing stock in the cities averaged 11.2 percent Hispanic.

The data in table 4.1 also provide evidence of other statistically significant differences between the projects that have been demolished and other public housing. In the average demolished public housing project, 32.2 percent of the residents had incomes of less than $5,000, compared to only 25.2 of the residents in the comparison projects. Thus, demolition tended to target projects with significantly greater percentages of extremely low income residents. At the same time however, demolished projects had higher relative populations of wage earners and residents with welfare income. This is likely due to the fact that demolished projects also had significantly fewer seniors and disabled households than public housing that was not demolished. These findings show that demolished public housing projects looked significantly different than other projects on a range of resident-demographic measures.

TABLE 4.1 Demographic characteristics of demolished public housing, 1997–2007 (%)

	BLACK	HISPANIC	MINORITY	INCOME LESS THAN $5,000	WITH WAGES	WITH WELFARE	FEMALE-HEADED HOUSE HOLDS	SENIOR	DISABLED
Demolished projects	79.5	11.5	94.2	32.2	24.9	28.6	82.8	15.4	16.9
Other public housing projects	73.2	11.2	87.5	25.2	22.2	21.5	78.5	25.9	20.2
sig.	***	–	***	***	***	***	***	***	***
N	305	306	306	296	296	296	305	304	304

Notes: *** p < .001. Figures in the table are unweighted means.

The disparity ratio for individual projects ranges from 0 (in projects that displaced no African American households) to 5.08. The unweighted average disparity ratio for the 305 projects for which all data are available is 1.096, indicating that the average public housing project demolished had 9.6 percent more African American households as a percentage of all households than other public housing in the same cities. Twenty-two percent of the demolished projects had ratios of less than 1.0, meaning that there were fewer African American households in those projects compared to other public housing in the cities studied. Just over one-third of the projects (36.7 percent) had disparity ratios between 1.0 and 1.10, one-quarter (24.6 percent) had disparities from 1.10 to 1.25, and the rest (16.7 percent or one-in-six) had disparity ratios of 1.25 or more.

The *overall disparity ratio* is determined by dividing the total number of black households displaced in all 305 projects by the expected number displaced, where the expected number is simply the citywide percentage of public housing residents who are black applied to each project. In the Christopher Columbus Homes example, in Paterson, New Jersey, if there had been no disparate impact on blacks, one would expect that 70 percent of the 314 households in that project would have been black because 70 percent of the rest of the city's public housing was black in 1999. This would have meant 220 African American households would have been displaced. In fact, 97 percent of the project was African American, or 305 households. Thus, this project displaced eighty-five more African American households (or 39 percent more) than would have been expected given a nondisparate outcome. Summing this calculation across all 305 projects, we obtain a weighted disparity ratio of 1.077; in the aggregate, projects that have been demolished in these 137 cities have displaced 7.7 percent more African Americans than would have been the case had there been no disparate impact. The weighted ratio is less than the unweighted average because of large projects in cities such as Chicago, Detroit, and Baltimore where virtually all public housing residents are black and therefore the individual-project disparity ratios are close to 1.0.

This last point highlights a limitation of the disparity analysis as used here; disparity ratios are bounded on the upper end by the initial overrepresentation of blacks in public housing in most of the large cities in this sample. For example, in cities such as Washington, D.C., Memphis, and Detroit, where 98 percent or more of all public housing residents are African American, there is *essentially no possibility of a disparate racial outcome* as it is defined here. Since both the numerator and the denominator in the disparity ratio have maximum values of 100, as the denominator (the citywide percentage of public housing residents who are black) approaches 100, the possibility of a ratio above 1.0 diminishes. The very high percentage of black residents in all public housing in these and other major cities, such as Atlanta (92 percent), Philadelphia (92 percent) St. Louis (95 percent), and Cincinnati (95 percent), have the effect of limiting the overall disparity ratio. Thirteen percent of the demolitions in the sample (or forty projects) took place in cities in which blacks make up 99 percent of all public housing households. In one-third of the demolitions (more than one hundred projects), blacks make up more than 90 percent of all public housing households citywide.

When all cases are included in the analysis, the unweighted disparity ratio is near 1.1 (1.096). When cases are eliminated at the upper end, that is, cases are removed where the percentage of citywide public housing is 98 percent or above, the average disparity ratio increases. When cities where 90 percent or more of the citywide public housing is inhabited by African Americans are removed from the analysis, the ratio is 1.15. The overall disparity ratio tops out at 1.18 when the analysis is restricted to cases in which the citywide public housing population that is African American is 75 percent or less.

National figures mask a wide range of outcomes from one project to the next. The highest disparity ratios occurred in cities in which African Americans made up half or fewer of all public housing households. Demolitions in those cities, nevertheless, affected some projects with very large proportions of African American residents. The largest disparity ratio belonged to the Springview Apartments complex that used to stand in San Antonio, Texas. Though the city's public housing was only 12 percent African American, the Springview Apartments complex was 61 percent black, producing a disparity ratio of 5.08. Four of the top ten projects, as ranked by the size of the disparity ratio, were located in Denver, Colorado, and two were in Knoxville, Tennessee. In Denver, blacks made up roughly one quarter of the residents of public housing citywide, but accounted for between 61 and 71 percent of all residents in four projects demolished between 1995 and 2007. In Knoxville, blacks made up just less than half of citywide public housing residents, but were 90 percent of the occupants of two projects dismantled in that city.

Other cities have fewer African American households in their HOPE VI projects than would be expected given the overall racial makeup of public housing in the city. There are two extreme examples of this in El Paso, Texas, and Los Angeles (disparity ratios of 0.17 and 0.22, respectively) where public housing demolition has generally affected projects with higher Hispanic populations. And though San Antonio, Texas, has the project with the single greatest disparity ratio in the nation (Springview Apartments), overall the city has not targeted projects with a disproportionate number of African American residents for demolition (a disparity ratio of 0.76 over eight demolitions).

It is possible that the disproportionate impact on African Americans is not due to a targeting of blacks per se, but to the fact that public housing demolition and redevelopment has focused on the most dysfunctional public housing units and that these units happened to be occupied by African Americans. This, of course, does not eliminate disparate impact, it simply pushes it back one step. That is to say, one would need to ask why blacks occupy the worst public housing. Are they steered into the worst of the public housing stock? Or do local housing authorities systematically neglect the management and upkeep of public housing occupied by blacks? If one assumes that the earliest HOPE VI projects and the earliest non-HOPE VI demolitions were the most distressed and dysfunctional public housing in the nation, then it is possible to examine whether the disparate impact on African Americans is due to an emphasis on the most distressed public housing.[11] If the disparate impact of demolition on African Americans is due mainly to the fact that African Americans occupy the worst public housing in the country then we would expect the percentage of black residents in demolition projects to be highest in the early years and to decline over time. This has not been the case, however. The percentage of residents in HOPE VI projects, and in all public housing developments demolished between 1995 and 2007, who are African American remained steady over that time period. This suggests that the racial breakdown of residents is probably not a function of the level of distress in projects that are demolished.

In order to definitively demonstrate a disparate impact one must be able to control for the other factors that could lead to demolition. A fixed-effects logistic regression analysis of public housing demolition and disposition between 1996 and 2007 was undertaken to see whether the racial composition of residents was a significant predictor of demolition net of other factors. The other factors that were controlled for in the model include the size of the development (in number of units), the vacancy rate, the percentage of residents over the age of sixty-two, and the median rent.[12]

The findings (data shown in the appendix) indicate that in large U.S. cities that account for the majority of public housing demolition, the public housing projects that were demolished tended to be larger on the whole than those that have been maintained, they had higher vacancy rates, lower rents, fewer seniors, and more African Americans as a percentage of all residents. Some of these findings are not surprising. PHAs have often manipulated vacancy rates when engaging in de facto demolition in order to induce the conditions that lead to greater acceptance of actual demolition. A higher vacancy rate was one of the factors identified by the National Commission on Severely Distressed Public Housing (NCSDPH) as a direct indicator of distress and thus was directly used to identify developments suitable for demolition.[13] Projects with lower rents were also more likely to be demolished than other projects. This is consistent with the interpretation offered in chapter 2 that cities are clearing the way for more lucrative land uses through the demolition of public housing.

The data indicate that the percentage of residents over the age of sixty-two is an important predictor of whether a project was subsequently chosen for demolition. Projects with more senior residents were less likely to be demolished. This suggests a marked propensity on the part of PHAs to demolish "family" projects and to preserve projects set aside for seniors. Sometimes the tendency is so pronounced that even HUD requests an explanation for why a PHA has "focused on eliminating 'so much of its family housing but none of its elderly/disabled housing.'"[14] Although the Atlanta case study showed that in some places even senior housing is being removed, the data indicate that for every additional percentage point increase in senior residency in a building, there is a reduction of over 3 percent in the likelihood of demolition.

Finally, the data show that, controlling for all other resident characteristics measured in this database, projects with greater proportions of African American residents were more likely to be demolished over the time period of this study. The magnitude of the effect for the African American variable suggests that for every additional percentage increase in black residency, the likelihood of demolition increases by 1.1 percent. A public housing project that is 80 percent African American thus is 44 percent more likely to have been demolished than an otherwise identical project that was 40 percent occupied by African Americans.

The analysis presents strong evidence that there has been a disparate impact of demolition on blacks and that this disparity goes beyond the mere overrepresentation of African Americans in public housing. The findings show a statistically significant tendency across more than twenty-five hundred public housing projects in 137 cities for projects with greater percentages of African American residents to be demolished compared to those with relatively fewer African American occupants. This pattern is a national one, and exists despite all of the differences that exist across the large cities in the sample.

Negro Removal Updated

To secure congressional passage of the public housing program in 1949, advocates joined forces with groups interested in creating a federal initiative aimed at revitalizing the downtown cores of the nation's cities.[15] As a result, the public housing program became tied to what became known as the urban renewal program. Urban renewal proceeded to fund massive redevelopment projects that from 1950 well into the 1960s involved total clearance of slums and blighted areas of central cities. The program was supposed to produce low-cost, public housing on a portion of the sites cleared in order to provide new housing for the slum dwellers. The program never fulfilled that promise and in the end demolished much more low-cost housing than it ever built. In many cities, most of the residents of that housing were African American families. Thus, the program took on the nickname of Negro Removal. Fifty years later, the HOPE VI program swept in for another round of clearance in many of the same neighborhoods that had experienced urban renewal a half century earlier. The numbers quite clearly indicate that the current round of demolition and the HOPE VI program in particular has been an updated version of Negro Removal.

The current efforts to dismantle public housing are only the most recent contribution to a troublesome legacy of disparate racial impacts in public housing. In its early years public housing was operated so as to reflect and reinforce patterns of racial segregation. The program reinforced racial segregation within cities and repeated those patterns within its own developments. Later, as the population of public housing became increasingly black in most cities, the program suffered from mismanagement and neglect. As the years went on and the problems of public housing in some major cities continued to mount, it was low-income blacks who bore the burden. This most recent phase of public housing history, the displacement and demolition phase, has also, as a matter of course, most heavily affected African Americans, both because they are generally overrepresented in public housing and also because they seem to have been targeted by the effort.

The forced removal of a household from its home is one of the most intrusive exercises of state power. The disruption to families is significant and the sense of loss, loss of home, of community, of a sense of identity and belonging

can be profound in cases where people have developed strong place attachment. Forced displacement can also have negative effects on self-sufficiency
and well-being regardless of place attachment, simply from the disruption
of social support networks and survival strategies designed and employed by
people living on the economic margin. For these reasons, the United Nations
Human Rights Council (HRC) and the international Centre on Housing Rights
and Evictions (COHRE) have both weighed in on the displacement of public
housing residents. The HRC conducted a fact-finding mission to several locations in the United States and COHRE has called for a moratorium on public
housing demolitions.[16]

It is not at all clear, however, that the intentional targeting of African Americans in the transformation of public housing, should such intention exist, would
necessarily be malicious. The demolition of public housing is embraced by many
local officials as a necessary step in improving the communities of public housing and improving the lives of families in public housing. The proponents of
HOPE VI and public housing transformation might not be surprised or troubled
by the findings reported in this chapter. To them, demolition and displacement
is a benefit, an opportunity for families trapped in public housing to escape the
stifling and dangerous environments of public housing and to move to neighborhoods of opportunity. Thus, to some extent, the degree to which the targeting of
"black projects" for demolition is a problem is dependent upon the experience
of the displaced. How many are able to move back into the finished redeveloped
neighborhoods? What are the neighborhoods like that displaced persons inhabit?
Are the benefits that they experience significant enough to balance or outweigh
the disruptions of forced removal? Are there reasons to distinguish this mass displacement of African Americans from the one that occurred as a result of urban
renewal during the 1950s and 1960s? It is to these questions that we now turn.

THE FATE OF DISPLACED PERSONS AND FAMILIES

We're not fighting for the status quo to keep these raggedy buildings....We're fighting to be able to stay in the community....We've
stayed there during the hard times. Now we're going to up and move
now that they're going to redevelop it?

—Wardell Yotaghan, Coalition to Protect Public Housing, Chicago

The controversy over the displacement of low-income families in the urban
renewal projects of the 1950 and early 1960s ultimately led to changes in the
way that program operated. From a heavy reliance on demolition and clearance,
an approach that led to the displacement of tens of thousands of central city
residents nationwide, urban renewal shifted to a rehabilitation strategy that was
less disruptive and kept more people in their communities. Displacement in the
urban renewal era was seen as a problem to be mitigated, a disruption to be
endured for the sake of the community revitalization that might be achieved by
thoroughgoing redevelopment.

In the era of public housing dismantling, according to HOPE VI program architects and advocates, displacement is not so much a problem as it
is a solution. The public housing-as-disaster discourse suggests that public housing residents would be very anxious to leave their communities for
something, anything, better. The model of public housing transformation
embodied in HOPE VI leads, furthermore, to the expectation that residents
relocate to "neighborhoods of opportunity" that bring them closer to the available jobs and bridging social capital necessary for upward mobility, and that
just as importantly removes them from dangerous, crime-filled, resource-
poor neighborhoods.[1] Finally, the advocates of public housing transformation argue that because of these moves, families are better able to thrive,
to become economically self-sufficient or at least more financially secure,
and to benefit in a number of different ways from reduced stress, increased

physical health, better educational experiences for children, and to enjoy a much greater sense of safety on a daily (and nightly) basis. Some residents are anxious to leave, some do move to better neighborhoods with real opportunities, and some do see real and personal benefits from displacement and relocation.

Were these outcomes to occur systematically and to a consistent majority of displaced persons, the disparate racial patterns of displacement described in the previous chapter would not constitute a public policy problem. If displacement were invariably, or even predominantly, a benefit to public housing residents, then the disparate impact of displacement could be interpreted as the targeting of a program benefit, and our perception of the information presented in the previous chapter would be quite different. But, in fact, the experience of very low income families displaced from public housing does not allow such a conclusion.

The Experience of Displacement

Alice and Ross Llewellyn, both in their sixties, had lived in the Harbor View public housing project in Duluth, Minnesota, since 1976 (all names of Duluth public housing residents and family members used in this chapter are pseudonyms). They had raised two children there. Ross drove a taxi for most of his working life but never made enough money at it to move the family out of Harbor View. The kids grew up and moved away; Billy, the oldest moved south and died of shotgun wounds in a hunting accident. Carly, the youngest, lives nearby in Duluth with her two kids. The Llewellyns have seen Harbor View go through a lot of changes, including a time during the 1980s when the development became what Alice called "party central." Drug dealing, loud parties, and lots of strangers and outsiders walking through the development made them feel unsafe and bothered. With the help of the Duluth Housing Authority (DHA), the Llewellyns and other neighbors started a patrol in 1987. "The place up here changed like night and day," said Alice in an interview in 2004.

> When we first started the patrol, there was a party in every building—in fact, in every apartment almost. We used to have fun bothering people and calling and chasing kids that were running around at nighttime. And the police had fun because we helped them catch a bunch of kids. And now it's quiet; I mean *quiet*. We'd walk around at nighttime on the patrol and it's like walking around a senior citizens area.... It's been getting boringer and boringer. We walk around and nothing is going on. It's been that way for a few years now.[2]

When the Duluth Housing Authority sponsored tenant meetings to plan for a HOPE VI redevelopment project at Harbor View, the Llewellyns took a wait and see approach. Having lived at Harbor View for twenty-eight years they had the longest ties to the neighborhood of anyone involved. When DHA officials assured them that they would have first pick of the new units on-site they were hopeful. "I hope we'll be more comfortable," said Alice. "It'll be nice to live in a building that looks nice, that's brand new for once. Never lived in a new building. It would be nice once they get done; if it looks anything like what the architects drew, it'll be beautiful. It'll blend in with all the neighborhoods."

The Harbor View public housing project was built in 1951, overlooking the picturesque Duluth harbor and Lake Superior. The twenty-acre site is located in a working class area in the hills north of downtown and consisted of forty-five barracks-style buildings containing a total of two hundred housing units. In 2003, the DHA received a $20 million HOPE VI grant to demolish and redevelop Harbor View. In some ways, the Harbor View HOPE VI was unusual and does not represent the typical public housing redevelopment. First, the project was to be a phased redevelopment in which some residents would remain at Harbor View while demolition and redevelopment took place elsewhere on-site. Upon completion of the first phase, the internally relocated families were to move directly into the newly built units. Such phasing minimizes displacement and the disruption to public housing families, but it is not a widely used technique in HOPE VI projects. With the most seniority of any residents at Harbor View, the Llewellyns had the option of staying at Harbor View while redevelopment began in order to move into the very first units completed.

Another unusual aspect of the Harbor View project is that the DHA pledged to replace all two hundred units of public housing. In fact, the project was to result in a net increase of subsidized low-cost housing in the city due to HOPE VI-funded development on three additional sites throughout Duluth. One-for-one replacement, of course, is not only not required of PHAs in HOPE VI projects, but its elimination as an obligation of PHAs is often regarded as one of the factors that has allowed the HOPE VI program to expand into the demolition-based approach that has been predominant over the history of the program. In most cities, HOPE VI leads to a significant reduction in the public housing stock. But not in Duluth, Minnesota.

In other respects, however, the Harbor View redevelopment was very typical of HOPE VI projects across the country. The redevelopment involved demolition of all of the old public housing units. The new site plan and the new units built on-site incorporate New Urbanist design ideas that reduce the institutional look of the architecture, bring units closer to the street, and individualize the space on-site. And, of course, the new site will be a mix of incomes that integrates market-rate units with public housing and other subsidized housing. The experience of the original families at Harbor View is also broadly representative of what happens to public housing residents when displaced from their homes.

FIGURE 6. Construction of Harborview in Duluth, Minnesota, in 2006. The Duluth Housing Authority replaced the demolished public housing units on a one-for-one basis.

John and Rochelle Quinn had lived in Harbor View for five years before being moved to a Section 8 home in the east Hillside neighborhood in March 2004. At the time of their move they had four children ranging in age from an infant to a thirteen-year old. Two of the children are from their marriage and the older two are from John's life before Rochelle. Rochelle works for a nonprofit organization and John wants to start a business of his own. When asked what he thought about the HOPE VI project, he was skeptical. "Well, usually people like us don't get a break," he says, trying to account for his skepticism. But their relocation went smoothly, and they don't miss living at Harbor View.

The move from Harbor View did not work so well for Cynthia Barker. Cynthia lived in Harbor View with her son and nephew, both teenagers. The three of them were relocated just a couple of blocks from the Quinns in the east Hillside neighborhood. Cynthia, too, was doubtful about the changes HOPE VI would bring. "To tell you the truth, I thought it was bullshit. Things that sound too good to be true usually are too good to be true," she said in 2004, several months after being relocated. She likes her new apartment and neighborhood just fine, but she lost her job in the move when the community center at Harbor View where she worked, cut back on hours and staff. She has been unable to find another job in the two years since being displaced.

Deborah Stefanovich misses the Harbor View Community Center where her teenage daughters spent a lot of time. Deborah has become something of an advocate for the original residents of Harbor View, wondering out loud at public meetings whether they are being treated in the way they were promised. She too thought the plans for Harbor View were "too good to be true" when she first heard them. As families were moved out and as the structures began to come down, Deborah monitored the actions of the developer and DHA closely, pushing them on details that she felt were important to the residents of Harbor View. From her personal standpoint, the biggest negative effect of the project was the loss of community and the scattering of people who were friends and who had built relationships over the years.

The experiences of these and other families in being forcibly removed from their public housing homes defy easy generalizations, either positive or negative. The Duluth case, as all cases do, points up a variety of individual stories and outcomes that do not conform well to expectations of program advocates or to the blanket criticisms of opponents. Some families thrive as a result of moving out, some suffer. Some are able to finally escape a living environment they regard as dangerous and unhealthy. Others fight the move, not wanting to leave the community they have built for themselves and unsure of what awaits them in other neighborhoods. A few move back into the redeveloped areas and share in the benefits of the redevelopment. Others move into bad housing in nearby poor and segregated neighborhoods.

For thousands of families displaced by public housing demolition we simply do not know what happened. Studies tracking residents have been done on only a small percentage of HOPE VI projects. Families and households displaced by non-HOPE VI demolition or conversion are largely untracked, even though they may receive relocation assistance.[3] In cases of de facto demolition, where residents are induced to leave by systematic neglect of management responsibilities, the displaced go entirely untracked and unassisted. Even tracking studies funded by the government do not follow all of the residents. Those who move early and who drop out of the assistance system or are forced out by eviction—their outcomes are unknown to us. The evidence we have is for a small number of residents in cities across the country. Finally, where surveys are used, we only know about those who answer the phone or fill in and mail back the questionnaires.

The Desire to Move

On December 20, 2007, public housing residents in New Orleans tried to force their way into a city council meeting to keep the city from tearing down several public housing projects in that city. Police used taser guns and pepper spray to keep the protesters from disrupting the meeting. In Chicago in 2007, one hundred public housing tenants marched on the local HUD office to protest the displacement of public housing residents. Residents of the Alice Griffith Homes in San Francisco protested that city's plans to demolish the project. In Minneapolis in 1996, recent Southeast Asian immigrants and residents of the Sumner Field Homes also protested the demolition of that development and the loss of their community. In other cities, such as Miami, Pittsburgh, Seattle, and Atlanta, residents have resorted to lawsuits in attempts to stop demolition. As these episodes suggest, demolition and displacement is not universally regarded by residents as the solution to the problems of living in declining and neglected public housing complexes.

On the other hand, some public housing residents look at demolition differently. In Duluth, when relocated families were asked what they missed about their old Harbor View community, 19 percent said "nothing."[4] Newspaper accounts of demolitions across the country almost invariably include a quote or two from an ex-resident such as Lorraine Ledbetter of Baltimore, who burst into tears at the sight of the Lexington Terrace high-rise being demolished in 1996. Though she was tearful when thinking of the good friends who had lived there with her, she was glad to see the towers go: "Good riddance. I won't miss those buildings one bit."[5] They are more than ready to say good-bye to living environments that were hostile, dangerous, segregated, and devoid of economic opportunity. Some were convinced that demolition and displacement were necessary and that what replaced it would be a much better home for them and for their families.

In Duluth, less than a quarter of the residents said that prior to announcement of the HOPE VI project they had wanted to move out of Harbor View. Over half said that they did *not* want to move while the remaining quarter was uncertain.[6] The desire to stay is typically a reflection of two different realities for residents. First, for many the public housing in which they lived provided real and tangible benefits to them that have been either misunderstood or discounted by the officials calling for demolition. Second, many fear the consequences of moving into other neighborhoods where they may not be welcome, or to other housing that will cost more and be more difficult for them to keep. Barbara McKinney, another ex-resident of the Lexington Terrace high-rises in Baltimore, said in the months before their demolition that "the people here are looking out for each other. Moving out of here scares me."[7]

WHAT IS LEFT BEHIND

Very common among persons forcibly displaced from their housing is the feeling that they have been wrenched from their communities. Since the early 1960s, researchers and planners have been aware of the seriously disruptive nature of forced relocation for lower-income households. Marc Fried's work on the psychological costs of relocation, published in 1963, described the grief experienced by families forcibly relocated through urban renewal.[8] Forced relocation and the loss of a home and an entire neighborhood, according to Fried, shatters both a sense of spatial identity and a sense of group identity that are dependent on connection to a place and the stable social networks formed with neighbors:

> On the one hand, the residential area is the region in which a vast and interlocking set of social networks is localized. And, on the other, the physical area has considerable meaning as an extension of home, in which various parts are delineated and structured on the basis of a sense of belonging. These two components provide the context in which the residential area may so easily be invested with considerable, multiply-determined meanings....This view [among working class families] of an area as home and the significance of local people and local places are so profoundly at variance with typical middle-class orientations that it is difficult to appreciate the intensity of meaning, the basic sense of identity involved in living in the particular area.[9]

Although acknowledging that reactions to relocation can vary significantly and that grief reactions can be entirely absent among some, Fried notes that "grieving for a lost home is evidently a widespread and serious social phenomenon following in the wake of urban dislocation."[10] The grief can occur even when the home has problematic aspects. A reporter for the *Pittsburgh Post-Gazette*, describing in 2009 the impending demolition of the last of the St. Clair Village public housing units, portrayed for readers a largely inhospitable and dangerous environment (in part induced by the previous demolition of several hundred units at the site). "And yet," the article went on, "most residents of St. Clair are 'devastated' that the Pittsburgh Housing Authority is moving them out, said Cynthia Grace, president of the tenant council. One's home is home, she said, no matter what it looks like to someone else."[11]

Herbert Gans documented the urban slum of Boston's West End before it was demolished in the late 1950s through urban renewal. Where middle class reformers saw dilapidated housing and physical blight, residents saw a functioning community that provided affordable housing and social supports that they valued highly. Gans argued that the advocates of demolition and redevelopment "failed to make a distinction between *low rent* and *slum* housing."[12] The residents of the West End, on the other hand, valued the neighborhood for its affordability and did not regard it as a slum. The proponents of urban renewal, in that case, either failed to recognize the positive elements of life in the West End as experienced by residents or ignored them.

In a much more recent analysis, Mindy Fullilove updates the work of Fried and Gans by advancing the concept of "root shock," which she defines as the "traumatic stress reaction to the destruction of all or part of one's emotional ecosystem."[13] Beginning with the elementary observation that places are more than "simply bricks and mortar that provide us shelter,"[14] Fullilove argues that we all establish routines for navigating the external environment in order to satisfy basic needs (finding food, maintaining shelter, and coexisting with others). For all people, these routines represent the result of trial-and-error experiences that produce the most efficient and effective patterns of getting along and getting by. For people of limited means, these routines are critical because of the slim to nonexistent margins on which they live. Access to the correct bus routes, to jobs, to services, and to supportive informal networks is most critical for people with limited means because of the relative costs and difficulties of reestablishing these strategies once they have been disrupted.

Connections to place, and the sense of spatial identity and group identity that they foster, are extant even in the worst public housing conditions.[15] Researchers in Seattle and Portland, Oregon, have found that place attachment is strong among public housing residents and it affects their willingness to move some distance away from the projects from which they were displaced.[16] Place attachment, these researchers found, is often connected with the material and psychological benefits that families receive and the support systems that they establish when negotiating work demands, family obligations, and child care.[17]

Though the design of public housing is frequently blamed for the deterioration of living conditions Alexandra Curley's interviews with displaced families from Boston's Maverick Gardens indicates that the arrangement of buildings and common spaces in that community encouraged the development of trust, interactions, and neighborhood ties. Common entryways and living spaces, and the superblock configuration with walkways and open space between buildings, fostered "dense, overlapping networks [that] enhanced residents' support systems and contributed to their collective efficacy."[18] Danya Keene and Arline Geronimus find that close social ties are more common and stronger in public housing than in other forms of assisted housing.[19] Not all of the social relationships left behind are, of course, positive ones. Curley's Boston study also showed that women displaced from public housing sometimes welcome the fact that they can leave behind "draining" social ties—friends or family who constitute more of a burden than a resource.[20]

In Duluth, when asked what they would miss most about Harbor View, 36 percent of displaced residents referred to friends and neighbors, while another 14 percent said they would miss the community activities that took place at the community center on-site. As in all communities, some people were enmeshed in neighborhood life and others were not. Half of the residents reported having no close friends in Harbor View, and two-thirds had no close family members in the development. One-third had neither close friends nor family members nearby. But for the other two-thirds, displacement meant moving away from close friends or family, and moving away from what some of them regarded as a close-knit community. Equally important, displacement meant being taken out of an environment in which one felt at home or comfortable; an environment in which one comfortably carried out daily tasks. As one resident wrote, she missed "friends, the yard out front, the safe neighborhood, the community center, hanging laundry outside, the place to barbecue, having a porch to sit on, [and the] sense of community."[21]

In the case of Harbor View in Duluth, 23 percent said they would miss the convenient location of the community. Harbor View is situated on the hillside above downtown Duluth. The HOPE VI application called the community isolated because it was separated from other residential communities on the east and south by a four-lane highway. To the north was a steep hill connecting to a high school, and to the west was undeveloped land. Residents saw it differently; they described it as being conveniently close to Central High School, to downtown Duluth, and accessible by bus. The residents found Harbor View convenient because they had built their routines around its location. Displacement to them meant greater difficulties and inconvenience in completing those tasks, or in the establishment of entirely new patterns of travel, shopping, and schooling. For example, for Cynthia Barker's nephew, who had walked less than a quarter of a mile to high school every day, the move meant having to rise an hour earlier each day and take two buses to get to school. Deborah Stefanovich tenaciously held on to her Harbor View unit until her youngest daughter graduated from Central High so that she wouldn't have to change schools or take multiple buses to get to class.

In addition to the community and the location, the third most commonly "missed" aspect of Harbor View was the housing unit itself. This is somewhat surprising since HOPE VI projects are supposed to target projects that are physically obsolete and dysfunctional. Indeed, the Harbor View HOPE VI application characterized the units as not meeting current minimum size and amenity standards.[22] Yet, when asked what they would miss most about Harbor View, 20 percent of Duluth relocatees mentioned some aspect of their dwelling unit. Most often in this regard, respondents mentioned the size of the unit, though a small number of residents said they miss the low rents most of all. Larger low-income families, even those with Section 8 subsidies, typically have a difficult time finding large enough housing units in the private marketplace. The units at Harbor View were roomy enough in the living area, but also featured basements for storage that many residents highly valued. As one respondent wrote, "Harbor View may have had a bad rap, but you can't find another apartment where you have an upstairs, main floor, and a basement. I really miss those apartments. They were very accommodating to a family." Many residents were unable to duplicate those living arrangements in their postrelocation housing.

Harbor View was also blessed with a singular amenity that several former residents mentioned prominently among the things they missed. Located on the hillside above downtown Duluth, the community offers a view of the entire Duluth harbor to the south and southwest, and the great expanse of Lake Superior to the southeast. Displacement from Harbor View meant losing that view and the pleasure it provided. Much of the public housing demolished in U.S. cities over the past two decades has had some similar type of locational advantage, sometimes having to do with proximity to geographic amenities, sometimes simply based on proximity to downtown and to revitalizing neighborhoods. In fact, it is the very existence of these amenities that can in some cases generate the pressure for redevelopment in the first place.

MISTRUST OF HOUSING AUTHORITY MOTIVES

Harbor View's advantages contributed to a significant sense of cynicism about the true motivations for the redevelopment. A number of residents felt that the HOPE VI project was simply a way to remove low-income people from a prime parcel of real estate. Some made reference to gentrification and what, from their point of view, was a barely disguised attempt to take this land from them and hand it over to wealthier residents. As one respondent said:

> This whole HOPE VI project was and still is about money and the rich. Where myself and my neighbors lived was one of the most beautiful areas in Duluth—the top of the Hillside complete with beautiful grass, trees, and a stupendous view of Lake Superior, Aerial Lift Bridge, and the other two bridges. Some greedy people decided that it was a choice area and decided to get rid of low-income families.

Duluth is a city, however, without strong gentrification pressures. The Harbor View redevelopment has not triggered any large-scale real estate reaction in the surrounding blocks. Yet, even in the absence of development pressure, some residents were quick to question the Housing Authority's motives. The suspicions voiced in Duluth are repeated in cities across the country. In Flint, Michigan, where the land market is very weak, all eight of the city's public housing projects failed HUD inspections, leading the director of the Flint Housing Commission to suggest that some will have to be torn down. The feeling among some public housing residents in Flint is that the Housing Authority has allowed the developments to decline in order to get more federal dollars for the fix up. "It boils down to money," said resident Ronnesha Holmes. "If you keep the appearance low then you can get more money" from the federal government for the demolition or rehabilitation.[23] This type of distrust is fairly common among public housing residents facing displacement. Even in New York City where the public housing is well run and the PHA has demolished less than 1 percent of the stock, residents are quick to suspect the NYCHA of clearing land for more lucrative development options.[24]

In many cities, of course, the concerns about gentrification have been realized, as have the worries of the original residents that they would not be allowed back into the new development. Frequently there is a sense among residents that they are being pushed out of an area that is about to be redeveloped into something nice. As one resident of the Earle Village public housing complex in Charlotte, North Carolina, said to housing authority officials, "this is prime land. You're just running a game on us to get us to agree and you'll move the rich people into the community."[25] In Chicago, in the words of one resident, the concern is about both gentrification and racial turnover: "We feel like, man, they trying to like take over our neighborhood.... Y'all moving these white folks over here. We've been here for like twenty-five years and now you going to tell us we have to leave because you're moving these white folks here?"[26] In Duluth, where the PHA was pursuing a redevelopment strategy designed to be sensitive to tenants' concerns by phasing the work to keep people on-site and to minimize displacement, replacing the public housing units on a one-for-one basis, even there residents dug in their heels, resisted the disruption to their lives, and questioned the motivations of the PHA.

Mistrust of the PHA can also be generated by the perception among residents that the agency allowed the public housing community to decline over time in order to pave the way for demolition and redevelopment. This is reflected in the number of de facto demolition lawsuits that have been and are still being filed across the country. The belief that PHAs willfully allow conditions to decline to the point where demolition is necessary is a common one among public housing residents. Watching Lexington Terrace come down in Baltimore in 1996, former resident Janice Dowdy said, "It didn't have to come down. They just let it deteriorate. I believe it could have been saved."[27] Activists opposed the demolition of the Connie Chambers Homes in Tucson on the same principle.

THE DISRUPTION OF DISPLACEMENT

The desire to remain in public housing is not necessarily a signal that a resident is satisfied with the living conditions there. Cynthia Barker complained loudly and often about the conditions at Harbor View. She felt that the DHA was an unresponsive landlord. By comparison, her new unit is "very nice" and she likes her neighborhood. Her reluctance to move, however, derived from a fear that her financial situation and that of other displaced residents would suffer. Indeed, she is worried about paying her bills in the new unit she moved to from Harbor View. But her biggest concern is the troubles that she says *other* families are experiencing: "One woman had four or five kids [and] she had to move because they are tearing down her unit. That woman today is homeless because she couldn't afford to live where they put her. The utilities cost too much. You have to pay more with Section 8 because you have to pay utilities. She was in scattered site housing. You have to pay utilities there, too. HOPE VI is a disaster for some people."

In Chicago, much of the opposition to demolition was based on similar concerns for the economic security of displaced families, and the neighborhoods to which families would be relocated and rehoused.[28] Many public housing residents in that city had little faith in the promises made to them by the CHA about either the adequate availability of replacement housing, or whether moving with a voucher would put them in a better situation.[29] Some of the concern is that the first move may create financial hardships that may result in additional moves, setting off a prolonged period of residential instability. This potential is nowhere better illustrated than by what happened to Lucy Hollman, the lead plaintiff

FIGURE 7. One of the last families leaving the Glenwood Townhomes on the North Side of Minneapolis. Most families from the project relocated elsewhere on the city's North Side or in high-poverty neighborhoods on the South Side.

in a Minneapolis lawsuit that led to the demolition and redevelopment of 880 public housing units in that city. In the years after she left public housing she bounced from unit to unit, losing a section 8 subsidy, losing a home after becoming ill and falling behind on payments, and falling victim to a flipping scam in which she purchased a home for close to twice its appraised value and for more than ten times the amount paid by the speculator who had purchased it two years earlier.[30]

Though public housing residents are often told that being displaced is for their own good, they do not always concur with that assessment. They often see value in remaining in public housing where public officials cannot or do not. Even when they agree that conditions in the public housing project are subpar, they may not regard demolition and displacement as the best solution. They are acutely aware of the difficulties of finding adequate housing in the private market and worry that displacement will initiate significant disruption in their housing situation and in their lives. They worry about making ends meet while facing new and significant utility costs. In short, they worry about all of the challenges faced by very low income families in the search for decent, safe, and affordable housing.

The Move

In cases where the public housing authority simply demolishes a building or project, families are given relocation assistance and moved elsewhere. Typically a portion of the families move on to the Housing Choice Voucher program and lease a unit in the private market. Another segment of the displaced group moves to other public housing. The final group of tenants moves out of publicly assisted housing altogether, an outcome that can occur for several reasons. Some families do not wait for the formal relocation phase to begin and move away without any assistance. This is particularly the case when the local housing authority has moved over a period of months or years to empty the building through a process of de facto demolition. These families, of course, are not tracked by the PHA because their leaving is interpreted as a voluntary move out. They are typically not tracked by researchers in any way because their mobility often occurs prior to the commencement of research and their destination after leaving public housing is unknown. In some cases, with access to PHA data, the size of this early-mover group can be estimated. Thus, in the redevelopment of Techwood Homes and Clark-Howell in Atlanta, Larry Keating and Carol Flores concluded that only 44 percent of the original respondents received relocation assistance from the PHA.[31] In Chicago's Henry Horner Homes, the CHA had allowed more than eight hundred units, half of the entire project, to empty through neglect and by failing to rerent apartments, before seeking approval to demolish. The eight hundred families received no relocation assistance, nor were their movements tracked by CHA or by researchers. Some families become ineligible for relocation assistance by violating the terms of their occupancy during the relocation period. A small number will receive relocation assistance but nevertheless move into market-rate housing, either in homeownership or to another rental accommodation. When demolition is followed by redevelopment, as in many HOPE VI projects, residents have an additional option—to move into the newly constructed mixed-income development that replaces their old public housing community.

MOVING BACK ON-SITE

The option to return to the rebuilt site is attractive because many families have an attachment to their public housing community and the neighborhood, and because they are encouraged in the belief that they will be able to return to the redeveloped community. The redevelopment process for most HOPE VI projects includes significant resident participation in the planning stage. Design teams are brought in who question residents about the qualities of their homes that they like, and about what features they would like to see in the new, redeveloped community. The residents are shown architectural and design renderings of what "their community" will look like after redevelopment. They are encouraged to imagine what it will be like to live in the new development. As Deborah Stefanovich said, "they asked us to 'dream your biggest dream—your most perfect neighborhood.'" A Baltimore public housing resident reports that the public housing commissioner "told us to dream, dream about what this neighborhood could be, he didn't tell us…that the dream meant we wouldn't be included."[32] Residents are told about homeownership opportunities that may or may not be realistic for them or are told that they "are going to be able to move into affluent, upscale communities."[33] They are encouraged to be co-producers of the vision that will guide redevelopment. And while some, perhaps most, begin the process skeptical and remain so throughout, months of planning and design review, focus groups, and public meetings begin to implant the idea that the redevelopment is for and about them. Though PHA officials may inform residents that new screening requirements will apply after redevelopment, meaning that some of them will not be able to return and live in "their" newly constructed community, they are not told that if the nationwide experience holds true in their case, only two or three out of ten will return. They are not told that in some places it is fewer than that. They are not told that based on national averages it will be several years longer before the new units are built than what is set out in the plan. Nor are they told that the plan itself will almost certainly change over the period of redevelopment because of changes in the funding and financing environment, or to respond to unpredictable increases in the cost of materials or changes in the housing market. The number of assisted units is likely to fluctuate, the size of the units themselves may change, and important design features of the units and of the redevelopment are also likely to change. Most families make the mistake of thinking that the PHA and the developer, who together received millions of dollars from the federal government and who likely also announced millions of additional dollars in leveraged financing from the private sector or other public sector sources, can impose their will over the course of the entire development process. Most families make the mistake of thinking the redevelopment "plan" is more than just a plan.

In the end, however, for most families, displacement from their public housing home is the only program intervention they experience.[34] Estimates from national studies indicate that the percentage of original residents who return to the redeveloped site ranges from 14 percent to 25 percent.[35] In the Park Duvalle redevelopment in Louisville, fewer than 5 percent of the original residents returned to the site.[36] In the Earle Village redevelopment in Charlotte, North Carolina, only 2 percent of original residents went through the process set up by the local PHA to qualify for resettlement in the new community. PHA officials expressed disappointment that so few residents "chose" to do so.[37] But the rate of return is low for a number of reasons, few having to do with the choice of residents. The rate of return is low because the redeveloped sites typically have fewer public housing units than the projects they replace, the public housing units they do have are generally smaller than those they replaced, new management standards make it difficult for previous residents to pass tenant screening criteria, and the long time span between displacement and the completion of redevelopment means that many previous residents have resettled into new communities and wish to avoid the disruption of moving again.

Alice and Ross Llewellyn took advantage of the option to stay on-site during the redevelopment of Harbor View. Having more seniority than any other household, the Llewellyns were moved to a vacant unit on the site's East Side in 2003 where they stayed through much of the demolition and redevelopment. There they witnessed the gradual emptying of the project as other families were relocated away from Harbor View. They lived there through the demolition of two-thirds of the development, and then through the construction of the new units going up on the westernmost portion of the site. Construction delays and cost increases, however, led the DHA and its developer to redesign most of the units and the site, which reduced the size of individual units and increased the number of duplexes and triplexes planned. Alice began to worry about whether the new units would work for them. Ross was connected to an oxygen machine at all times, his lung having been accidentally cut during a surgical procedure many years earlier. Their living room was full of the equipment that Ross needed to live.

When the couple previewed a completed unit just weeks before demolition of the final Harbor View units was to begin, they realized they would not fit into the unit. The demolition schedule gave the Llewellyns one month to find a new place in a housing market they had not negotiated in three decades. In their sixties, and with Ross's significant mobility constraints and health problems, they started looking for housing. At this point they decided to merge their household with another, taking on as a roommate a young man, Kevin, who had lived alone in Harbor View and had been a friend of their son's. With Kevin around to help shovel and clear snow, and to take the garbage out and bring groceries in, the Llewellyns felt more secure in moving. Fortunately, Duluth's loose housing market worked in their favor and two months later they relocated to the city's West Side with a section 8 voucher.

In other cases, the new management regime may make it difficult or impossible for families to move back into the redeveloped site. Sometimes residents face difficult choices between keeping their family intact or moving into the redeveloped site. Sheri Wade of Chicago split from her husband because he had a criminal record; given the screening criteria, that would have been enough to keep her out of the new, redeveloped community.[38] In a similar case, the *Chicago Tribune* reported about Pam Stewart who had not decided whether she wanted to move back into the development that replaced Stateway Gardens in Chicago:

> Stewart doesn't know whether she wants to move into Park Boulevard, but she has made a difficult choice that many families face in this process. Because two of her sons have criminal records, she doesn't allow them in her home, for fear that they might be considered residents, fail the criminal background check and ruin her shot at one of the new units. "Don't get me wrong, I love my boys," Stewart said. But "it was either them or me."[39]

RELOCATION TO OTHER SITES

Most relocatees move into other public housing or receive housing vouchers to subsidize their rent payments in private-sector housing. Thus, the neighborhood to which a family moves is often determined by where other public housing exists, where rental units exist that qualify for the voucher program, or where landlords are willing to accept such vouchers. Most relocatees are therefore limited to other lower- and lower-middle-income neighborhoods. These constraints can be reinforced by the relocation assistance residents are offered, and/or by resident preferences for familiar areas and neighborhoods with the supportive infrastructure, including transportation, upon which they rely.[40] Indeed, the evidence on HOPE VI and other instances of forced displacement from public housing suggests that displaced residents typically move nearby.[41] Studies in Chicago, Portland, Buffalo, Philadelphia, Minneapolis, Durham, Newark, the District of Columbia, and Richmond, Virginia, show that displaced residents typically do not even make it out of the central city.[42] In Chicago, less than 2 percent of the first three thousand families displaced by public housing redevelopment left the city.[43] In Minneapolis, 87 percent of families displaced by a HOPE VI-like demolition remained in the central city, over half within a three-mile radius of their original homes.[44] Nearly all of the households who were moved out of public housing in Buffalo as a result of the *Comer v. Cisneros* deconcentration plan remained in the city, moving an average of 1.5 miles from their previous residence.[45] In the Harbor View HOPE VI project in Duluth, 23 percent of the families moved out of Duluth. This is a bit higher than national averages, but among displaced families in Duluth 7 percent relocated to the central cities of Minneapolis or St. Paul. Thus, overall, only 16 percent of the displaced families left central city environments, closer to the national norm. Nationally, HOPE VI displacees moved a median distance of 2.9 miles.[46] Though the distance is longer in some places,[47] families tend to remain within communities with which they are familiar, and in which they maintain social or historical ties. Research from Seattle suggests that the social networks of residents and the complex set of trade-offs residents face when moving work to restrict the spatial dispersion of displacees. Rachel Kleit and Martha Galvez argue that "a combination of wanting to foster personal community stability, depending on information from relatives … and perceptions of which neighborhoods will accept them" is responsible for the mostly short-distance moves made by displacees.[48]

Sometimes the mobility options available to public housing residents are constrained by the active opposition of those living in neighborhoods to which they might move. In Huntsville, Alabama, residents of south Huntsville protested city plans to demolish public housing concentrations in that city and move some residents into south Huntsville.[49] In Cincinnati, residents of neighborhoods surrounding the English Woods public housing development organized in opposition to the Housing Authority's plan to demolish it and provide Section 8 vouchers to the residents. "We're not saying we don't want low-income people, we're just saying that we have enough. We're already overburdened," said one neighborhood leader.[50] Displaced public housing residents in Chicago have faced opposition in several South Side neighborhoods.[51] In Baltimore, suburban officials opposed the movement of Baltimore public housing residents to the suburbs after a proposed court settlement was announced that would help move 1,342 families from public housing in the city to "better neighborhoods" in the city and surrounding suburbs. The county executive leading the opposition was careful to explain that "this is not a racial issue."[52]

Despite the prevalence of moves to nearby neighborhoods, receiving neighborhoods for HOPE VI and other public housing displacees tend to have much lower poverty rates than original neighborhoods.[53] In fact, in the Urban Institute's study of five HOPE VI locations across the country, the subset of residents who received vouchers moved from neighborhoods that averaged a poverty rate of 61 percent to neighborhoods with 27 percent poverty.[54] The neighborhoods to which displaced families move also tend to have lower rates of unemployment and public assistance participation.[55] But while the changes in neighborhood characteristics are real, there is some question as to whether they are significant enough to trigger the beneficial outcomes envisioned by policy makers. For example, though poverty rates are lower than in originating neighborhoods, poverty in the new neighborhoods remains higher than the city average in virtually all cases.[56] The HOPE VI Panel Study found that 40 percent of displaced residents who did not return to the redeveloped HOPE VI sites lived in high-poverty census tracts (those with poverty rates over 30%), and that for all HOPE VI relocatees in five cities, the average poverty level in their new neighborhoods was greater than 20 percent.[57] Furthermore, in many receiving neighborhoods poverty is increasing over time, meaning that reductions in neighborhood poverty experienced by displaced families might be transitory.[58]

John and Rochelle Quinn were relocated away from Harbor View in 2004. They moved into a spacious house on the eastern edge of the Hillside neighborhood of Duluth and received a Section 8 voucher to help pay the rent. They like the home and the neighborhood. The area they relocated to had a poverty rate of 35 percent, lower than the 45 percent poverty rate at Harbor View but more than two times the rate for the city of Duluth as a whole (15.9%). The median income of the neighborhood they moved to was $22,592 compared to $17,500 at Harbor View, an improvement but still only two-thirds the median of the entire city ($33,766). Unemployment among residents of their new neighborhood was 9 percent, better than Harbor View (11.7%) but worse than citywide (7.5%). The Quinns found themselves in a typical situation for families displaced from public housing. The statistics said that their new neighborhood was "better" than the old one, but it was still a relatively poor, disadvantaged neighborhood compared to the rest of the city of Duluth—and Duluth is a city that on the whole had pretty high poverty and unemployment numbers in 2000.

The subsequent mobility choices of displaced families must also be considered, though here the evidence is inconclusive. The experience in some cities has been that families tend to make further moves to neighborhoods that resemble their original neighborhoods. Families that are relocated to the suburbs, for example, will return to the central city and those that moved to substantially different (low-poverty, predominantly white) neighborhoods, will over time move back to higher poverty, more racially segregated neighborhoods.[59] On the other hand, there is also evidence in some cases that once families are removed from the most disadvantaged neighborhoods, they will continue to make mobility choices toward less segregated and more middle class areas.[60]

Although displaced families make some, albeit limited improvements in the poverty profile of their neighborhoods, the evidence suggests that their moves do not frequently involve crossing the color lines in local housing markets. Families typically do not escape neighborhoods that are racially segregated when they are displaced from public housing. In Chicago, for example, families displaced from public housing "are not distributed throughout the City of Chicago, but instead are concentrated in poor black neighborhoods on the south and west sides of the city."[61] In a national sample of displaced families who used Housing Choice Vouchers and thus had the best chance to move to more diverse neighborhoods, the average neighborhood to which they moved was 68 percent African American. Families who were displaced to other public housing presumably moved to even more racially segregated neighborhoods.[62]

In general, our knowledge of how displaced families fare after being moved out of public housing depends on "tracking" studies that follow the families relocated by PHAs. Most of these studies focus on HOPE VI projects and most report the outcomes for displaced families who receive relocation assistance— either financial assistance or help with the housing search, or both. In fact, this gives us an incomplete picture of the displacement process. Families who leave without assistance, who vacate their units and therefore forfeit their relocation assistance, or those who leave their units while the PHA is slowly emptying the building through a process of de facto demolition are not tracked by our studies. If these families who move without assistance do so because they have more resources than others and do not require support in moving, then the outcomes for displaced families overall might be better than the picture that emerges from the research. If on the other hand families who slip through the cracks do so because they are more troubled, or perhaps have language barriers that interfered with their understanding of their relocation rights, then they are less likely to relocate to "neighborhoods of opportunity" than are those who receive PHA assistance, and the overall picture of displaced public housing residents is likely to be worse than we know.

In the end, the fact that most displaced public housing residents do not significantly upgrade or change their neighborhood environments is not surprising. Low-income minority families may voluntarily restrict their housing search to other racially segregated neighborhoods because they anticipate opposition and a negative reaction from neighbors should they relocate to predominantly white areas, or because they simply wish to avoid standing out in their new neighborhoods.[63] Researchers from Memphis, on the other hand, found that Memphis residents did choose their new housing "based on potential neighborhood improvements."[64] For those who do want to upgrade, the barriers to their upward mobility in neighborhood terms are many. The spatial distribution of resources upon which low-income families depend, most notably affordable housing, public transportation, affordable childcare, and other services, focuses and limits housing searches to certain neighborhoods. This is especially the case if the family moves to another public housing development or receives a Housing Choice Voucher—housing units with rents that meet the program eligibility requirements, and that have landlords willing to accept HCVs, are clustered in low-income neighborhoods.[65] Middle class suburban neighborhoods may often lack the infrastructure utilized by low-income families.[66] In some cases, neighborhood characteristics may be of secondary importance to families who are most interested in finding a unit large enough and one that is well maintained, especially if they have experienced poor maintenance and management in their public housing units.[67] Attachment to place and the desire to preserve informal support networks upon which they rely may also limit housing searches to nearby neighborhoods. Relocation choices, furthermore, can be affected by the quality of the relocation assistance that families receive and whether they are made aware of housing opportunities in unfamiliar neighborhoods.[68] The demolition of public housing in one neighborhood does nothing to increase the availability or quality of housing for very low income families in another neighborhood, so the housing market itself and the spatial distribution of affordable housing will also constrain mobility choices.

The prospect of finding adequate housing for low-income families in many U.S. cities is daunting. Facing significant income constraints, needing to balance transportation, childcare, and other considerations, and searching in local housing markets that steer them toward existing concentrations of low-cost units, real economic or racial deconcentration becomes a relatively rare outcome for families displaced from public housing. The difficulties of relocation are magnified for "hard to house" families who may have many children, physical or mental disabilities, or criminal backgrounds.[69]

Resident Reactions

Two years after they were displaced, the former residents of Harbor View were asked to provide a summary judgment of whether the move was good for them or bad. Thirty-seven percent had a positive view of the move, and 17 percent a negative one. The most common response, however, was a mixed one in which residents could identify both positive and negative outcomes associated with their forced relocation.[70] Cynthia Barker, for her part, is bitter about what happened to her as a result of the demolition of Harbor View. For her, displacement has been a major life disruption. Though she had her issues with the DHA about conditions at Harbor View, displacement and demolition were not the solutions to the problems she saw. In fact, she thinks displacement has brought her down. Cynthia had been employed at the community center located in the heart of the Harbor View complex. After the HOPE VI grant was announced and families began to move out in 2004, Cynthia and others lost their jobs as the center downsized. Though the HOPE VI office offered to pay for school, Cynthia said, "I got to find a job. School won't pay the bills. What I need is a job. I won't go on welfare again. I have been off welfare since 1998 when I got this job, and I won't do it again." She complains that the HOPE VI project ignores the fact that people at Harbor View have families, they have bills to pay, and that all of that is disrupted by displacement. She named the DHA HOPE VI coordinator and said, "he's getting paid to put us out. He's getting paid every day and he's getting paid to put us out, and I'm not happy about that at all."

"That move put me through a bunch of changes," she said. She kept coming back to the job she lost: "I'm unemployed because of HOPE VI." Cynthia also feels lonely in her new community one year into it. Of her old friends and acquaintances from Harbor View she says, "We don't hang out like we used to. They all on the west side, so far away now. I don't really have friends around here, just my children. I feel like I went from 'something' to 'nothing.' I went from helping my kids out to them helping me. That is not a good feeling," she says quietly.

John and Rochelle Quinn love the space they have in a large five-bedroom home on the city's near-east side: "it's beautiful here, ceilings are high, oak stairs, nice basement." They also love the neighborhood, which they feel is quiet and safe. Their children on the other hand are not so happy because they miss the community center at Harbor View and all the friends they used to play with there. But John did not like Harbor View for his kids; he felt that there were too many bad influences and that he had to worry too much about his kids' safety and behavior. John also felt that things were getting worse at Harbor View and he was glad to leave. "I like this neighborhood—not for the fact that it's secluded, but for the fact that it gives them more opportunity, more leeway to make a better decision. Over there [Harbor View], there's a very thin line....Around here at least I can monitor our kids, see what's going on and where they're at, and keep them in line, keep them out of trouble." Their children changed schools as a result of the move and John reports that they are doing "fine" in the new one.

Neither he nor Rochelle misses Harbor View much. They only see a couple of people they used to know there, "but we didn't have a lot of close friends there, anyway," he adds. They both think that the move has been largely good for them. Despite a generally positive experience with relocation, and despite not reporting much disruption in their lives, neither John nor Rochelle thinks much of the redevelopment process in general. They do not want to move back to the completed site because they need a larger unit than the homes going up at Harbor View. They are also suspicious of how well Harbor View will serve the needs of any of the original residents. When asked what she thinks of the new development, Rochelle says, "I think it's crap. Because I don't think they're going to make it affordable for low income people to go back there, and I really don't think they're going by their word. They're not making it accessible for lower income people to go back there. There was a single lady who wanted to go back up there, but she can't because they aren't making any single units." They regard themselves as having ended up better than most. "For the most part everyone that we know didn't make it out as well as we did," says Rochelle. "We worked to get a place that suited our family. Everybody else just wanted the [relocation] money. Then they just [moved to] a hole in the wall." The Quinns' view of being displaced is informed by a sense of injustice. Though the family has not experienced anything negative in the move, Rochelle questioned being made to move and the presumption that the redevelopment was supposed to be for her benefit. The entire experience seemed to her like some kind of experiment: "I think that's the true reason they call them the 'projects.'—it's a project to see how people act. It was like we were lab rats....I think that I'm being put in a maze to run around and find the cheese."

Deborah Stefanovich was fleeing an abusive husband when she moved to Harbor View from Michigan with her three daughters in 1998. Without an income, Deborah and the girls lived with relatives for a few months before getting into Harbor View. She lived there only four years before the DHA received the HOPE VI grant and began moving people out. Although Deborah moved into a scattered site public housing unit that she likes perfectly well, she is critical of the redevelopment. Her worst fear from the redevelopment is ending up homeless again. She is participating in a self-sufficiency program in which a portion of her rent goes into an escrow account that she can use for a home purchase after five years. But she must remain in public housing the entire time in order to receive the benefits, so she worries that if she is made to relocate she will forfeit her savings.

She is also worried about the girls' school: "We moved a lot since they were little. They've been to a lot of different elementary schools. I think Angie was in like five different schools. Donna [the eldest] has probably gone through three or four....I think this is probably the longest we've lived in one place since they were babies. So, you know, that's why I didn't want to disrupt the school. I was like, 'Oh, I can't do that again, we've been through that so many times.'"

Deborah's main misgivings about HOPE VI, however, are not about what will happen to her; it is about what has happened to the community she used to be a part of. Her girls used to socialize at the community center, and they return there even now after they have moved. But the girls feel disconnected in their new neighborhood: "My kids said once you move out of here, you come back up and it's almost painful. It's kind of nice, but it's almost painful....They took away a community. I saw a lot of old neighbors at the grand opening [of Phase I at Harbor View]. I got lots of hugs, a lot of cheers, a lot of tears. People who have lived here were really sad. Most of the ones who were sad were those that never got out of this neighborhood. Now they're lonely. They're not adjusting to the new neighborhood."

The Llewellyns story is different. Elderly and with Ross significantly disabled, the couple faced moving away from Harbor View for the first time in thirty years. Because of the lateness of their decision they had little time to move or to search. They went from being protected in this process, by being allowed to move directly into one of the first newly completed units, to having only a couple of weeks at most to try their hand in a housing market they had not engaged in for three decades, and with the constraints of their income, age, and Ross's disability. The stress of the situation was clear on Alice's face and demeanor. They had not counted on this. If anyone had a right to complain about displacement it might have been the Llewellyns.

But with their new roommate the couple found a unit in the bottom floor of a duplex on the city's West Side and moved in. In one week they went from near panic and uncertainty to a new place they love: "Here I have a basement and can use my own stove. I have a sun porch....I like old houses. We can put our knick-knacks around the dining room there. It's just the way I like it." The landlords are a young couple who live in the unit upstairs and so the Llewellyns expect that they will be responsive and careful with the building. As for the neighborhood, Alice says, "we haven't gone through a summer [with kids out of school and more of everyday life occurring outside], so we don't know yet." When asked about how they are adjusting, Alice worries about how they will fit into the neighborhood. But the concerns she expresses are practical ones: "The lady next door, she says that she gets over one hundred kids for Halloween, so I'm going to have to get candy to be ready for that."

THE TRACKING STUDIES

Studies of families displaced by public housing demolition typically involve interviews or surveys to compare their experiences in the new neighborhood with life in the old public housing project. Residents are asked about their health, their economic situation, their children, and various other dimensions of life.

The researchers are interested in how these things have changed in their new neighborhoods compared to life in the old public housing project. There is, of course, no way to compare the hypothetical third possibility—life in a renovated and upgraded public housing project. But if the hopes and theories of public housing transformers are correct, one would expect the families relocated from public housing to report improvements on a range of items from employment and economic self-sufficiency to physical and mental health. The evidence, unfortunately, tells a largely different story.

The biggest disappointment in the experience of displaced families is the fact that they do not seem to benefit with better employment or increased economic security. The research evidence is clear and consistent that displacement from public housing has no demonstrable positive effect on the employment, earnings, or income of individuals.[71] Even where public housing families voluntarily move out and are obliged to move to low-poverty neighborhoods as in the Moving to Opportunity (MTO) and Gautreaux programs, there have been no employment benefits.[72] First, a forced relocation can be disruptive to families, interrupting established routines and presenting new challenges in terms of child care and transportation.[73] The sudden inability to cover child care needs or to get to and from places where there are jobs may actually impede efforts to find or maintain employment. Health problems, too, are a significant obstacle for a large percentage of public housing residents, and moving from one place to another does nothing to reduce that barrier.[74] Racial and ethnic discrimination in the job market may disadvantage job seekers, too, regardless of where they live.[75] Whatever the reasons, mere mobility is not the answer to problems of chronic joblessness and poverty. Urban Institute researchers, summarizing the findings from a national study of HOPE VI residents, conclude that "relocation and voluntary supportive services are unlikely to affect employment or address the many factors that keep disadvantaged residents out of the labor force."[76] In fact, there is evidence that forced displacement is disruptive and may actually increase economic insecurity. Studies from several cities have found that a significant percentage of displaced families report difficulties paying rent and utilities in their new accommodations.[77]

In contrast to the outcomes related to economic self-sufficiency, the best results have been in residents' sense of safety for themselves and their children. The research findings here are consistent and positive; families that have been relocated from public housing typically report feeling safer in their new environments. The effect is strong in some places where public housing communities were notoriously crime-ridden and weaker in places where residents felt less threatened, such as the Columbia Villa project in Portland, Oregon.[78] Families feel safer because they typically see less drug- and gang-related activity, and fewer outward signs of social disorder in their new neighborhoods. Displacees' new sense of safety, of course, is partially dependent on what kind of neighborhood they find themselves in after relocation. Families that are displaced into other public housing projects report fewer benefits than others who move with Section 8 assistance.[79] Young people moved out of public housing in one neighborhood may move from one gang territory to another, putting them at some risk in their new communities.[80] Susan Clampet-Lundquist finds that displacement may increase the sense of vulnerability for young people who are displaced because they face a "different threat environment" in their new neighborhoods without the security and predictability provided by their familiar social ties.[81] Despite these exceptions, displaced families in general report a greater sense of safety in their new neighborhoods.

Unfortunately, according to the largest national tracking study, the greater sense of safety felt by relocatees is not linked to any secondary benefits such as improved mental or physical health, or greater economic security.[82] Nevertheless, the peace of mind and the reduction of fear associated with relocation is a consistent and significant benefit in itself for families displaced from public housing.

Facilitating the movement of low-income families out of high-poverty neighborhoods is also expected to produce health benefits, both physical and psychological. Relocation from distressed public housing projects may reduce exposure to harmful environments and reduce the stress of living in unsafe and disadvantaged neighborhoods. Relatively few studies have explored the issue, however, for families involuntarily displaced by public housing.[83] The main evidence comes from the Urban Institute's five-city Panel Study. Residents at those sites had many health problems prior to relocation; more than one-third of adults reported having a chronic illness or health condition, asthma was reported by over 20 percent of adults, and the rate of children's asthma was over three times the national average. Mental health problems, including depression, stress, fear, and anxiety, were also common, and occurred at a rate nearly 50 percent higher than the national average.[84]

Unfortunately, these poor health conditions did not improve as a result of HOPE VI relocation. Three-fourths of the Panel Study subjects reported no change or a decline in their health over time. In fact, the percentage of those reporting a need for ongoing care rose steadily over the study period. Similarly, children of HOPE VI families also showed no health improvements over a five-year period.[85] In some cases, the stress of moving to new environments can actually contribute to health problems, especially where residents are stigmatized or isolated in their new communities.[86]

Similarly, there is no evidence that children of displaced public housing families show improvements in school outcomes as a result of their relocation.[87]

In many cases, families forced to move because of public housing demolition or transformation move to other schools "within the same, underperforming urban school systems."[88]

When asked to evaluate their new living conditions, residents displaced from public housing generally report high levels of satisfaction with their new housing and neighborhood conditions.[89] Some report less crime, better housing conditions, and neighborhood improvement.[90] But better housing conditions do not always translate into greater neighborhood satisfaction among displaced residents. Factors such as proximity to bus lines, or places to buy necessities, or proximity to family and friends may be more problematic in the new neighborhood. This leads to situations in which families can identify their new neighborhoods as safer, their new homes as better, they can report fewer signs of neighborhood problems and social disorder, and yet not report greater satisfaction in their new neighborhoods.[91] In fact, one study of displaced families in Seattle found that most felt that their former public housing residence was a better place to live than their new neighborhoods.[92]

Though transportation and convenience play a role, much of the ambivalence that displaced families show toward their new neighborhoods is based on their social experiences and the degree to which they miss social networks from their old communities. To date, the research has shown little in the way of successful social integration of displaced families. In most cases, residents report fewer neighboring behaviors and less-supportive social relationships in their new neighborhoods.[93] Very few adults report that they have rebuilt social ties in their new neighborhoods, regardless of neighborhood poverty levels.[94] There is some evidence that youth among these families were more likely to rebuild friendship networks than the adults.[95]

The hope of mixed-income communities is that social mix will lead to the adoption of more middle-class behaviors and attitudes among the chronically poor.[96] But the studies of displaced public housing families echo earlier studies of other mixed-income communities that show little social interaction between higher and lower-income residents.[97] Youth in particular were unlikely to look at their new neighbors as role models, or to interact with other adults in their new neighborhoods.[98]

Many involuntarily displaced families are not ready or entirely willing to move out of their existing public housing communities. Those who have lived in public housing the longest are the least willing to move because most regarded their particular development as home, they had put down roots, and they were attached to the community.[99] In one study of the Columbia Villa HOPE VI project in Portland, many residents reminisced about the community; they mourned the loss of their neighbors, the open space, and the level of comfort they felt, and thought their new neighborhoods did not measure up to the community that they felt and benefited from at Columbia Villa. Only one-third felt their new neighborhood had a better sense of community than their original public housing site.[100] Public housing residents' attachment to place is especially important because there is evidence that families with the greatest place attachment show fewer beneficial outcomes from displacement and relocation.[101]

The Complexity of Resident Outcomes

Those who advocate the demolition of public housing and the displacement of its residents make a number of simplifying assumptions about how the move will affect low-income people. The displaced residents are assumed to have negative feelings about their public housing units, to welcome the chance to move out and into different and "better" neighborhoods, and to benefit from these moves. First, as we have seen, none of these assumptions apply across the board, and in fact none of them apply even to a majority of public housing residents. At the same time, critics of public housing demolition are incorrect when they assume the opposite, that all residents oppose displacement, that none welcome the move away from public housing, and than none report benefits from the move. What the evidence shows is a much more complex picture in which all assumptions apply in varying degrees across sites and to varying degrees across residents within a site.

Second, it should be noted that the summary judgments of displaced families regarding their condition and experience may be at odds with their thoughts about their previous homes and their subsequent homes. Negative feelings about one's public housing home do not inevitably lead to eager acceptance of displacement. The desire to stay in or leave public housing, as we have seen, is not perfectly correlated with a sense of prior well-being in public housing. Residents can simultaneously be highly critical of the public housing in which they live, have elevated concerns for their safety and for the safety of their children, and identify specific and sometimes numerous problems with the conditions of their housing and environment, while still wishing to remain in public housing. In the postdisplacement period, residents who are relocated to new housing and different neighborhoods can be quite satisfied with the housing (indeed even more satisfied with it than they were with their previous public housing accommodations) and with the neighborhood, and still regard themselves as worse off for having been removed from their previous community or housing unit. Neither does a positive evaluation of one's new, postrelocation home invariably lead to a positive assessment of the displacement event. As John and Rochelle Quinn and Deborah Stefanovich illustrate, one's assessment of displacement is sometimes unrelated to one's own experience but is instead based on what has happened to friends and acquaintances.

Third, the positive or negative outcomes associated with displacement are not cumulative.[102] Residents are likely to experience and feel a range of different outcomes. That is, residents who report being more satisfied with their housing postdisplacement are not more likely than others to report greater satisfaction with their neighborhoods. Those who report neighborhood benefits are no more likely than others to report benefits to their children's education or to their own economic security. Those who report feeling safer do not report being healthier or more economically self-sufficient. Benefitting in one area is not correlated with benefits in other areas. Because of their limited means, people of very low incomes are forced to make trade-offs in their housing and mobility decisions. Displacement from public housing does not eliminate this basic fact of life for such families. Housing accommodations may provide advantages in some respects while presenting significant challenges and disadvantages on other dimensions. For low-income families with very little purchasing power in the marketplace and sometimes with additional and significant constraints, housing accommodations are frequently a mix of good and bad.[103] Displacement from public housing simply imposes a new set of trade-offs to low-income families. The record of displacement is not, however, a record in which the predominant impact on families has been beneficial.

Making Sense of the Record

The demolition of public housing has for the most part not produced significant or consistent benefits for the very low income families displaced. The argument behind public housing demolition is that conditions were so desperate there that *any* move away would benefit the families. In fact, the evidence to date suggests that while some of the intended outcomes have been produced, others have not. In some areas, residents are as a whole arguably worse off than before. Families feel safer and in most places they report greater satisfaction with their new housing. But there are conspicuously no benefits in employment, income, welfare dependency, or physical health. Further, many of the families suffer significant disruptions in the systems of social supports they construct to get by on very limited incomes.

There seems then to be a fundamental contradiction to the existing efforts to help public housing families by displacing them from presumably harmful environments: concentrations of poverty are detrimental to their residents, but dispersal has not been an effective solution.[104] The lack of benefits from such moves is problematic at best, and it is even more profound and more consistent for the most disadvantaged families living in public housing.[105] The most vulnerable populations, those with significant human capital deficiencies or significant health challenges, are the least likely to see any benefits from being displaced from public housing.

Some of the reasons for this pattern are apparent enough. Perhaps foremost among them is that the record of displacement and relocation in the current period of public housing demolition has mirrored the patterns seen in previous episodes of mass urban displacement. Among the involuntarily displaced, there seems to be little appetite overall for moves to socially and geographically distant neighborhoods. The dispersal pattern in HOPE VI and other examples of forced relocation indicate that residents typically move from public housing to other segregated, higher-poverty neighborhoods. This is a pattern that urban planners have known about for decades, at least since the large-scale displacement of residents during urban renewal and the construction of the interstate highway system.[106] In the HOPE VI program and others like it in which families are involuntarily displaced due to government action, residents are entitled to assistance in moving but they are not obligated to move to any particular neighborhood.[107] The result is that the degree of geographic dispersal is not very great. The extent to which displaced families disperse throughout an area is limited both by the preferences of families and by the workings of local housing markets.[108] Although studies have shown that HOPE VI families and other public housing displacees do, in fact, move to neighborhoods with less poverty and fewer signs of distress,[109] the *degree* of neighborhood improvement, at least according to more objective indicators from the census, is not very great. Moving from a concentrated poverty neighborhood (more than 40% of the population below the poverty line) to a high-poverty neighborhood (more than 30% below poverty) does not significantly alter the microlevel processes shaping poverty, either exogenous to the neighborhood (such as the quality of public services) or endogenous (such as social support and stigmatization).

Even were families to successfully relocate to more distant, middle-class neighborhoods, relocation alone may not be sufficient to induce significant changes in economic self-sufficiency. Most observers now feel that dispersal needs to be accompanied by social service supports for families.[110] These service supports could range from those that would aid in the development of human capital resources to those that might ameliorate some of the financial hardship associated with being relocated out of public housing. Even so, there are no comprehensive studies of whether social service delivery to displacees provides an increment in benefits above the provision of social services without the forced mobility.

The displacement and relocation model of poverty amelioration also seriously underestimates the complexity of poverty. A focus on neighborhood conditions and their role in conditioning the life chances of the poor is a simplification if it excludes a range of other potentially determinative factors. The macro- and meso-level processes that operate on neighborhoods, that mediate job availability, structural economic shifts, the accumulation of human capital, and migration and mobility patterns, suggest that it is possible to overestimate the role of neighborhood, and to consequently overestimate the importance of changing neighborhood environments for the poor.[111] The overestimation of the impact of neighborhood is compounded by an incomplete understanding of the neighborhood dynamics themselves. The expectations of benefits are based on the argument that high concentrations of poverty result in community decline and poor socioeconomic outcomes for individuals, yet the exact nature of the link between environment and poverty remains unspecified. Though there is a compelling body of evidence that neighborhood context affects poverty, it is less clear which factors matter most and which, if addressed, will improve community and individual outcomes most effectively.[112]

Similarly, there is no certainty that "better" neighborhoods, as we generally have operationalized the term, produce the types of benefits expected. The uncertainty here is twofold. First, our statistical studies measure neighborhood deprivation in terms of poverty, the degree of racial segregation, rate of welfare dependency, or some other indicator of economic or social marginality. But we are not certain that the types of neighborhood benefits pursued in the HOPE VI program are produced by or correlated with reductions in such conditions. In fact, recent studies suggest little to no correlation between census indicators of neighborhood quality and the subjective ratings of neighborhoods offered by subsidized household members.[113] Further, we don't really even know what the important thresholds are that would trigger the changes we seek.[114] Voluntary mobility programs, for example, are set to specific metrics of poverty rate or rate of racial/ethnic segregation. MTO directs the relocation of low-income families into neighborhoods with less than a 10 percent poverty rate. The Gautreaux program directed families into neighborhoods with less than 30 percent African American population. Quite apart from the question as to whether such measures are appropriate indicators, it is not clear that the thresholds that drive our programs are the critical ones necessary to generate benefits. This issue is even more germane in the case of public housing demolition where neighborhood improvements in terms of poverty rate reduction and decreased rates of racial/ethnic segregation experienced by displaced families are much more modest than what is seen in voluntary programs.

An equally important factor in all of this is the way in which planners and policy advocates have underestimated the importance of supportive social networks and attachment to place for the low-income residents of public housing. Attachment to place goes well beyond mere nostalgia for buildings or people.

Very low income people are obliged to create often complex informal systems of support to compensate for their lack of economic resources.[115] These systems are frequently, by necessity, grounded in particular places or neighborhoods. From the development of informal work, to the establishment of reciprocal arrangements for child care and transportation, very low income persons improvise a variety of means for paying rent, feeding children, buying clothes, and acquiring the necessary services that middle-class people acquire by purchase. The development of intricate survival systems is based on social and everyday connections.[116] Because daily activity patterns for the poor occur mostly within a local area, social networks based in place may help the disadvantaged access "spur of the moment" job opportunities.[117] Forced displacement from public housing directly disrupts if not completely destroys these social networks. Displacees are forced to reconstruct the networks in their new environments, but in the meantime carefully constructed and negotiated means of making ends meet are shattered. Movers thus understandably miss their old social contacts and acutely feel isolated in their new communities.[118]

The Contingency of Benefits

It is no accident or mystery why a sense of safety and satisfaction with the quality of the housing are the only consistent benefits reported by displaced public housing residents. These factors vary considerably between neighborhoods, and reflect environmental conditions most directly. The benefits of greater safety and reduced social disorder, for example, are enjoyed passively. Residents need not take any action nor engage institutions or social structures in order to feel safer or to notice the lack of broken windows or to enjoy a newer and better-maintained apartment. Thus, we would expect displaced families to be more likely to identify these particular benefits resulting from relocation; they are universally accessible and passively enjoyed. And this pattern is exactly what the studies of HOPE VI (and even the studies of voluntary mobility) reveal.[119]

Other expected neighborhood advantages of relocation (rates of employment and self-sufficiency, better schools and educational experiences, better health, and higher levels of social capital) are not experienced passively. For these benefits to be manifest to new residents, relocatees must take active steps, and must engage public and private institutions and social structures that may remain biased in ways that make it difficult for residents to realize benefits. To take but one example, dispersal, according to one study,

> will improve education outcomes for the children ... *provided* families successfully relocate, children accompany their parents to the

new neighborhoods, the educational opportunities experienced by children are higher in their new environments, and…parents and children react to these changes in ways that translate into improved educational outcomes.[120]

One might add to that the caution that any unforeseen crisis in health or family stability, conditioned by the child's (or family's) previous residence in a high-poverty neighborhood, could also prevent the expected positive outcomes from materializing. Employment is another good example. Displacement from distressed public housing may well eliminate problems of spatial mismatch and put residents into closer proximity to a greater number of job opportunities. For that to benefit the resident, however, a series of additional preconditions must be met. The job openings that exist must match or be appropriate to the training, education, or experience of the resident. The resident must become aware of the appropriate job openings. The hiring process must be free of discrimination so that the resident is not unfairly treated due to skin color or ethnicity. The resident must be healthy enough to be able to pursue the employment, must have the necessary child care in place, and the means to get to and from the interview and the job site. Many of the expected benefits of relocation could be extended in a similar manner to expose fairly lengthy chains of events that need to occur for each of the individual benefits anticipated by policy makers. In general, the more contingent and indirect the benefit, the less likely it is to occur for displaced public housing families.

EFFECTS AND PROSPECTS IN REVITALIZED COMMUNITIES

> When HOPE VI was launched...the notion that public housing redevel-
> opment could help turn around whole neighborhoods and strengthen
> cities' fiscal health seemed naively optimistic. But in a significant
> number of cities, HOPE VI investments—imaginatively planned, well
> designed, and competently implemented—have coincided with posi-
> tive market and demographic forces to accomplish just that.
>
> —Margery Austin Turner, "HOPE VI, Neighborhood Recovery, and the Health of
> Cities"

August Wilson's *Radio Golf*, the last of his plays set in the Hill District of
Pittsburgh, revolves around a pair of black real estate developers looking to
build an upscale apartment building in the neighborhood who are confronted
by the longtime residents whom their development will displace. The play is
set in 1997 and takes as its subject the gentrification actually occurring in the
neighborhood at the time. Wilson himself is one among many black artists
who lived and worked in the neighborhood during its heyday when "the Hill"
was the heart of the African American community in Pittsburgh and a vibrant
cultural center—"the crossroads of the world," according to Harlem Renaissance poet Claude McKay.[1] But urban renewal projects displaced thousands
of residents in the 1950s, and riots tore at the community in the 1960s. By the
1990s, the area was largely depopulated (only 30 percent of the peak level of
1950) and almost exclusively poor.

Set between downtown to the west and the Oakland neighborhood, home to
the University of Pittsburgh and Carnegie-Mellon University to the east, the Hill
did retain at least one important asset, its location. During the 1990s, more
than $300 million in public and private investment poured into the neighbor-
hood, including the Bedford Additions HOPE VI revitalization, the city's third
HOPE VI grant. A generation earlier, the residents of the Hill had organized to
stop displacement from spreading beyond the urban renewal projects in the lower
Hill area. During the 1990s they organized again to force the Pittsburgh Housing
Authority to build replacement housing first, before demolishing the 460 units

of Bedford Addition. It was well that they did, because the neighborhood has seen "a slow brewing residential shift" that is bringing in the black middle class and professionals to the neighborhood.[2] As black professionals enter (or in some cases return to) the neighborhood and housing prices increase, tensions between long-term residents and the newcomers arise, just as depicted by Wilson in the last of his Pittsburgh decalogy.

A Community Intervention

In addition to being an intervention into the lives of very low income families, the dismantling of public housing is a community intervention, a place-based revitalization strategy that is meant to turn around the fortunes of declining or distressed communities. The revitalization approach rests on two strategies, the complete physical upgrading of the area and the introduction of market-rate housing through mixed-income development.

The physical changes produced by public housing transformation are often startling. The neglected buildings and grounds of older public housing developments with their expanses of patchy grass and dirt strewn with broken glass and debris, and their broken play areas that more often than not serve as the unpoliced territory of local gangs, are swept away. In their place are typically put two- and three-story townhomes, with siding unworn and paint fresh, each with a quaint-looking front porch and a small patch of thick grass connecting to the newly built sidewalk that runs the length of streets that have been redesigned to connect to the existing grid so that the new homes become a seamless part of the local environment. The design objective is to produce a completely different image of the space—to change its social meaning and to eliminate the stigma attached to it. The old visual associations with decline, concentrated poverty, and disadvantage are removed. For this purpose, full-scale demolition is often necessary to make way for the New Urbanist designs calculated to produce visions of middle class urbanity. The new visual prompts suggest personal safety, more accepted middle class values, and investment security.

The other element of public housing transformation is the mixed-income nature of the rebuilt communities. Affordable and public housing units are mixed with market-rate homes. The attraction of middle income households, who presumably have many options in the local housing market, is the real challenge and innovation in most public housing transformations. The locational attributes of the site and the physical upgrading of the site and the surrounding infrastructure—streets, parks, and public areas—are crucial in this respect. Proximity to downtowns or to cultural centers or to physical amenities helps attract investors and middle class residents. These factors have long been under-stood to underpin processes of gentrification in cities. The mixed-income model, of course, brings more affluent people into the neighborhood, but it also reduces the concentration of poor people in the area. The removal of such concentrations and the displacement of gangs are an equally important element of the trans-formation pursued by city officials in these cases. Indeed, where mixed-income developments are not part of the process, that is, where the demolition, sale, or conversion of public housing occurs without redevelopment, the community intervention is simply the removal of the stigmatized habitat and its low-income population.

Generating Spillover Effects

In many cases it is not just the public housing that gets a face-lift. To generate the secondary physical and social changes that will spread throughout the neighbor-hood surrounding the old public housing site, the demolition is often part of larger, publicly funded redevelopment efforts or, if not part of a larger plan, it is at least accompanied by secondary investments by the public sector. Many HOPE VI projects are part of larger redevelopment efforts that include new school buildings and commercial redevelopment. The Holly Park HOPE VI in Seattle, for example, featured public investments in a community center, library, and parks.[3] In Memphis, the city plans a $77 million Hilton hotel as part of Triangle Noir, a ten-year, $1 billion redevelopment effort that will replace the Cleaborn Homes and Foote Homes public housing projects.[4] Similarly, Memphis's Lamar Terrace HOPE VI redevelopment was part of a larger redevel-opment effort that also targeted nearby commercial and industrial structures.[5] As Margery Austin Turner summarizes, public housing redevelopment in some cities "has engaged mayors, community development officials, state housing agencies, and private sector investors in sustained partnerships."[6]

Although the experience of public housing transformation across the county has frequently borne out the expectations of spillover impacts, there are occa-sions when larger neighborhood transformation has not taken place. The Park Du Valle development in Louisville, Kentucky, replaced the Cotter and Lang Homes in the southwest part of the city. Home values increased in the neighbor-hood, crime went down significantly, but the project has been unsuccessful in attracting commercial investment and the neighborhood surrounding the devel-opment remains highly segregated.[7] Ten years after the Lafayette Courts high-rises were demolished in Baltimore, residents of the new Pleasant View Gardens were worried about rising crime and deteriorating conditions in the new housing itself. Pleasant View Gardens has not triggered a more general turnaround in its East Baltimore neighborhood.[8]

The lack of spillover effects from public housing transformation may be due to a number of reasons. First, neighborhoods that are more remote or locationally disadvantaged may not be attractive to private investors. There may be little or no latent market value in such places, remote as they are from downtown or the center of metropolitan areas, or significantly isolated by industrial land uses or by barriers such as railways and highways. Just as important, however, such neighborhoods are much less likely to be the subject of more comprehensive redevelopment efforts that combine public housing demolition with other public sector revitalization initiatives. Without secondary investments and infrastructure improvements, neighborhoods surrounding transformed public housing may remain unattractive to investors and to homebuyers or renters with choice in the private market.

In those cases where larger neighborhood change does accompany public housing demolition it is frequently difficult to establish that the public housing transformation is responsible for the wider neighborhood changes. Sometimes the larger neighborhood change predates or anticipates the public housing transformation; in other cases it occurs as the result of concurrent public and private sector investment. Indeed both of these scenarios are likely. Elvin Wyly and Daniel Hammel's study showed that many HOPE VI projects follow the path of revitalization that has already been established, with such projects often part of larger redevelopment efforts.[9] In other cases, neighborhood changes are spillover effects generated by the public housing transformation, or represent increased investment and land use changes that would not have occurred but for the transformation of public housing.

Spillover and Displacement Effects

The impact of public housing transformation on the housing market is a frequently researched question. The findings of this research are generally supportive of the notion that public housing transformation enhances nearby property values. Edward Bair and John Fitzgerald, for example, found that for six public housing redevelopments completed during the 1990s, property values around the sites decreased 8 to 10 percent for each quarter mile in distance away from the redevelopment.[10] Property values around a Tampa, Florida, HOPE VI redevelopment increased significantly faster than citywide values in the years during and after redevelopment.[11] A study of three redevelopments in Baltimore, however, found a positive impact on property values in only one; no effects were found for two projects that were located in highly distressed neighborhoods and which were somewhat isolated within those neighborhoods.[12] Another study of public housing redevelopment projects in Boston and Washington, D.C., showed positive property value effects in three of four cases.[13] The U.S. General Accounting Office studied twenty HOPE VI sites that received grants in 1996; housing values increased in thirteen neighborhoods and housing costs in fifteen.[14] One-half of the neighborhoods experienced an increase in mortgage lending, though significant decreases in lending were evident in seven of the neighborhoods. The authors of these studies suggest that the housing market impacts of public housing transformation on the surrounding neighborhood is dependent on a number of factors, including the degree to which the project is integrated into the community, the strength of the neighborhood housing market, and the degree of distress in the surrounding area.

Researchers have looked at other dimensions of neighborhood change as well. Sean Zielenbach, for example, found a great deal of neighborhood improvement taking place in the eight HOPE VI areas he investigated.[15] Seven of the eight neighborhoods increased their education levels, five gained white population (and thus became more integrated), and six increased their per capita income relative to the city. Crime declined significantly at each site.[16] Mindy Turbov and Valerie Piper found generally positive impacts on crime and nearby housing markets in the four neighborhoods they examined.[17] Mary Joel Holin et al. found significant reductions in crime, poverty, and unemployment in HOPE VI neighborhoods relative to citywide changes.[18] Other studies from cities across the country reinforce these findings.[19] Survey results generally indicate that neighbors of the HOPE VI sites perceived their areas as improving, though the magnitude of the improvement varied from site to site. In the GAO study, average household income increased in fifteen of the twenty sites, and the percentage of the population with a high school diploma increased in eighteen of the sites.

Most of the community-level changes accompanying public housing transformation are associated with population turnover rather than upward mobility of original residents. This is certainly true in the short term. Poverty is reduced in these neighborhoods because poor households move out and are replaced by the nonpoor, not because poor residents have improved their incomes. Education levels rise in the neighborhood not because of greater educational progress by the incumbent residents, but through an influx of more highly educated people to the neighborhood. Private investment in the community is attracted by the prospect of a new set of consumers with the buying power to sustain businesses. Crime is reduced in part through the displacement of gangs and low-income residents upon whom criminals prey. Property values increase in response to more upscale housing, inhabited by those paying market-rate prices in the mixed-income communities that replace demolished public housing development. Thus, these generally impressive spillover effects are best understood as "displacement effects" in that the changes are measures of demographic turnover due to the replacement of one population with another.

Despite occasionally contrary evidence, there is, according to Urban Institute researchers, "little doubt that HOPE VI redevelopments have unleashed impressive market and other improvement in their broader communities."[20] Frequently, public housing transformation is credited with "unleashing the latent potential" of neighborhoods by removing the last or largest obstacle to private sector investment. HUD notes a number of projects in which redevelopment has spurred private investment, including Earle Village in Charlotte, Mission Main in Boston, Hillside Terrace in Milwaukee, and the Manchester Homes project in Pittsburgh.[21] Manchester is called a "textbook example of how HOPE VI spurs private investment. People are coming back to the neighborhood, moving into rehabilitated 1840s row houses and stabilizing the market rate sector of the housing stock."[22] In Columbus, Ohio, the redevelopment of the Windsor Terrace project "convinced a paint manufacturer in an adjacent neighborhood to spend $32 million to upgrade its facility instead of moving to the suburbs."[23] In neighborhood after neighborhood the removal or redevelopment of public housing is generating investment in neighborhoods that otherwise have been shunned by private capital.

In Philadelphia the high-rise towers of the Martin Luther King public housing project were blown up in October 1999, a year after the city's Housing Authority had received a $25.2 million HOPE VI grant. Since then, millions of dollars of public and private investment have spurred a fast revitalization of the area. The housing market, which for all intents and purposes used to end two blocks away from the high-rises, soon featured condominiums and townhouses that sold quickly. While units on the site of the old projects went for $300,000, the redevelopment created a bridge to other parts of the Center City District that had already gentrified. For-profit developers jumped in to take advantage of the new opportunities in the neighborhood. "I am not certain I would have had the vision to develop...if all the demolition had not been done, and if I hadn't seen those homes going up a few blocks away," said one developer who was selling condos for as much as $1.5 million in the area. "Razing the Martin Luther King towers 'lifted a 400-pound weight from an entire region of the city,'" said another. "'The result has been a transformation that no one really had anticipated.'"[24]

HOPE VI sites near downtowns have generally seen a swift improvement in nearby conditions and even significant gentrification. For example, the Earle Village project in Charlotte, North Carolina, is one in which the "public housing

FIGURE 8. City West near downtown Cincinnati, a HOPE VI redevelopment. Laurel Homes, the second oldest public housing project in the nation, stood on the site and was removed from the National Register of Historic Places in order to be demolished for the HOPE VI project.

project has been a significant blighting influence, holding back an otherwise promising market environment in the surrounding area".[25] The Techwood and Clark-Howell projects in Atlanta were located on valuable land adjacent to downtown, Georgia Tech University, and Coca-Cola headquarters. Similarly, Allen Parkway Village in Houston, a project of over one thousand units originally built in the early 1940s, occupied a desirable location on the western edge of Houston's central business district and was demolished in 1996.[26] The St. Thomas project in New Orleans, over 1,350 units demolished in 2000, sat on land with "extraordinary latent market value" where the pressures to gentrify were intense.[27] The Capitol Hill neighborhood of Washington, D.C., has also experienced gentrification both before and after the demolition of the Ellen Wilson Dwellings in 1995.[28] Just east of downtown Louisville, the redevelopment of the Clarksdale public housing development has resulted in "an amazing number of developments going on there now."[29] Chicago's public housing demolition, the largest effort in the country, has resulted in significant gentrification both on the North Side and in the city's Bronzeville community on the South Side.[30]

The issue in these places is whether too much market activity has been unleashed. Harvey Newman found evidence of gentrification at the Techwood development in Atlanta.[31] In Chicago, the transformation of the neighborhood surrounding the Cabrini HOPE VI project is often cited as an example of gentrification triggered by public housing redevelopment. The Cabrini area went from being one of the most notoriously dangerous places in Chicago to "a largely mixed-income community of well-maintained townhouses located next to a new shopping center with a Starbucks café."[32] In New Orleans, property values in the neighborhood around the St. Thomas HOPE VI redevelopment increased by over 80 percent in the twelve months following the project's demolition, and the Earle Village project in Charlotte triggered a tenfold increase in property values in the First Ward Place neighborhood.[33] This type of gentrification, also noted for the Knoxville neighborhood surrounding the College Hill Homes, is called "a troubling impact" of the program by HUD because of the degree to which it reduces housing affordability and forces the indirect displacement of lower-income households who cannot afford increasing housing costs.[34]

Such an impact may be "troubling," but it is rarely unintentional. Leveraging private investment is one of the main objectives of HOPE VI redevelopments. In fact, over time HUD has put greater emphasis on the potential for additional investment and neighborhood change when evaluating HOPE VI proposals, looking for projects that could catalyze significant neighborhood transformation.[35] The emphasis on leveraging private capital that HUD introduced in 1995 is in practice an incentive for projects located in neighborhoods ripe for private investment. By fiscal year 2002, local housing authorities were required to demonstrate how their proposed HOPE VI redevelopment would "result in outside investment in the surrounding community."[36] Part of the emphasis on the neighborhood impacts of HOPE VI is driven by the belief among HUD officials that the program *must* generate spillover effects to succeed: "If the HOPE VI process," according to one HUD document, "does not help to solidify and revitalize the neighborhoods that surround each development, then the sustainability of these developments is thrown into question."[37] Thus, HUD attempted to choose projects that they felt had the greatest potential to spur additional public and private investment in the form of new or rehabilitated housing, commercial investment, new jobs, and improved public infrastructure. Calibrating the amount of that new investment so that it is sufficient to produce neighborhood improvement but modest enough to avoid triggering wholesale gentrification is difficult when the attempt is made. Wyly and Hammel document the ways in which HOPE VI redevelopment plans attempt to take advantage of local housing markets poised to take off, awaiting only the removal of worn-down public housing to set tremendous neighborhood changes in motion. In these locations, HOPE VI becomes one more element in a strategy of public and private investment that is aimed at removing "islands of decay in seas of renewal."[38] The direct displacement of public housing residents via demolition is in these cases supplemented by the indirect displacement of their neighbors via the market.

There is some evidence that HOPE VI projects selected between 2000 and 2005 were set in neighborhoods already experiencing declines in poverty since 1990. Thirty percent of the grants in those years went to projects that were located in areas that had dropped at least 10 percentage points in poverty during the 1990s.[39] Nineteen percent of the grants went to projects in neighborhoods with increased poverty (by more than 3 percentage points) over the previous decade. Because some of the poverty reduction might be accounted for by secular trends in the city over the course of the 1990s, a measure of relative decline in poverty is more appropriate. Twenty-three percent of the HOPE VI grants made in the first years of the new century went to projects located in neighborhoods where poverty had declined by at least 10 percentage points more than it had declined citywide. This suggests a significant targeting of program grants to neighborhoods that were *already experiencing* large reductions in poverty.

These include the McDaniel Glen project in the Mechanicsburg neighborhood just south of downtown Atlanta, and Piedmont Courts, within a mile of downtown Charlotte, North Carolina, both of which were beginning to feel development pressures and experience some demographic change prior to the demolition and redevelopment of public housing within the neighborhood. Often these neighborhoods are located near downtowns and thus have the locational advantage of being near amenity-rich areas or activity centers. In these and other cases it is likely that the neighborhood change led to public housing transformation, not the other way around.

In the Five Points neighborhood of Denver, situated just northeast of downtown, five public housing projects stood in the 1980s. As in most places where such a concentration of public housing occurred, the neighborhood suffered from disinvestment and high poverty rates. Things changed, however, during the 1990s. The construction of a baseball stadium just north of downtown helped breathe some life into the area and began a renaissance that included new commercial development and upscale housing. The neighborhood was well situated to ride the real estate wave of the 1990s that brought significant changes and upgrading to this neighborhood located so close to the city's economic hub. Despite a "a steady trend of revitalization," the public housing developments were the source of crime complaints and redevelopers declared "the long, blocky residential buildings" to be out of scale with the rest of the neighborhood. The availability of federal funds through the HOPE VI program, then only a couple of years old, provided the resources necessary to clear away two of the old projects, Curtis Park and Arapahoe Courts, and hasten the full renewal of the neighborhood.

Indirect Displacement

The process of neighborhood change involves considerable turnover in the population as lower-income families are displaced when property values rise and the market shifts to more upscale housing and commercial land uses. Redevelopment projects such as public housing transformation induce two types of displacement. The residents of public housing who are forced to move because their housing is being demolished or sold are *directly* displaced. Lower-income residents of the surrounding communities who are forced to move because of market changes in the neighborhood as the result of public housing transformation are *indirectly* displaced.

The extent of indirect displacement induced by public housing demolition depends on the degree of neighborhood change leveraged by redevelopment activities. In demolition-only projects where little or no additional investment takes place there is less likelihood of indirect displacement. This is especially true for public housing communities located in depressed land and housing markets, underserved by public services and by private enterprises. Improving neighborhood conditions beyond the borders of the redevelopment site requires inducing additional private and public sector investment. Redevelopment projects that go beyond demolition to transform public housing communities into attractive, mixed-income, mixed-use neighborhoods therefore have a much greater potential to generate the additional investment and thus induce indirect displacement.

The concentration of most public housing in heavily black neighborhoods means that indirect displacement, should it occur, will probably have a disproportionate impact on African Americans. Of the first 180 HOPE VI projects in cities with populations of more than one hundred thousand, 59 percent were located in neighborhoods that were predominantly (more than 50 percent) black. Sometimes the significant reduction in poverty that results from large-scale demolition of public housing is matched by racial turnover as neighborhood changes take on both racial and class dimensions. Indeed, for much of its relatively short history in American cities, gentrification has involved both racial and class turnover. More recent experience, however, indicates that the racial turnover is not inevitable. In an increasing number of cases, gentrification is being driven by the black middle class.[40] The basic dynamics of black gentrification are no different than the generic case: the neighborhood is physically upgraded, property values increase, retail businesses that cater to a more upscale market open, and middle-class and affluent households displace and replace the incumbent low-income residents. Often a shift from rental to homeownership housing will also take place. Similarly, there can be, and often is, tension between the gentrifiers and the incumbents as they compete to claim the place. In cases of black gentrification, however, there is a deeper level of conflict shaped by the political economy of race in the United States. Specifically, because black gentrifiers typically have fewer investment choices, they are forced to make investments in neighborhoods that are higher risk, and thus they are relieved and supportive to see gentrifying patterns around them. Second, black gentrifiers often claim their own rightful place in the neighborhood; they do not see themselves as interlopers, poaching new territory for investment opportunities, but rather the inheritors of a historic identity that recalls a time when these neighborhoods were centers for African American culture in their respective cities.

Such communities are riven by class, claimed on the one hand by long-term residents with low-incomes who endured years of public and private neglect, and the physical and social deterioration of the community, and on the other by a black middle class working to revitalize the area and protective of the personal investments they have made.[41] The black middle class, which "fiercely wants to 'restore' these communities to safe, prosperous, and tranquil places," sees the concentration of subsidized low-income housing, including and especially public housing, as a manifestation of discriminatory practices from which they and their communities have suffered for years.[42] They contend that their potential for wealth generation is limited by public policy decisions that concentrate subsidized housing in predominantly minority neighborhoods. They argue, with some justification, for a "fair share" approach to public and subsidized housing that would locate fewer such units in black neighborhoods and more in middle class white neighborhoods that are largely free of such housing. As a result, members of the black middle class support the demolition of public housing as a necessary step in creating livable communities. On the other hand, displacees see themselves as members of the same community that the black middle class is investing in. In many cases, black public housing residents have been in the community longer than members of the middle class who might be more recent residents. To public housing residents forced out of their neighborhoods, black gentrification is no better than white gentrification. Indeed, in many ways, black gentrification is seen as a greater betrayal.[43]

It is possible then to conceptualize the neighborhood change generated by public housing displacement as taking place along two dimensions defined by poverty and by race (see figure 9). In neighborhoods with little or no reduction in the poverty rate and in racial profile (the area near the intersection of the two axes), the neighborhood remains largely static despite the public housing demolition.

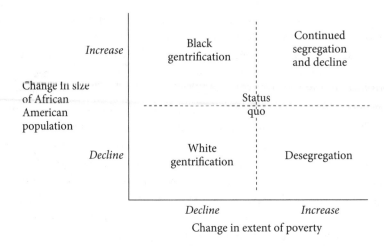

FIGURE 9.   Potential neighborhood changes in race and poverty.

Where racial turnover (black to white) has taken place, without a reduction in poverty (lower right quadrant), then the neighborhood has desegregated. When both racial turnover occurs and a significant reduction in poverty takes place (lower left), neighborhoods can be said to be experiencing white gentrification. When poverty is significantly reduced without racial change (upper left), black gentrification has occurred. Neighborhoods that continue to segregate and concentrate poverty are located in the upper right quadrant.

By looking at public housing redevelopments that began before 2000, one can estimate the degree of neighborhood change that has accompanied public housing transformation by looking at census data from 1990 and again from 2000. The difficulty in this approach is that very few HOPE VI projects were completed during the 1990s, limiting studies of completed projects to case studies or small-n comparative studies. By including projects that began during the 1990s and progressed to the point of relocation or demolition, we can expand the sample size and look at dozens of projects across the country. In the following section I look at HOPE VI projects that proceeded to demolition by 1999 (n = 64), and at projects that began relocating residents in 1999 or earlier (n = 100). It can be assumed that neighborhood change will be more extensive or further along for projects that have completed the redevelopment process, and thus the examination of projects that are only partially done in all likelihood underestimates the changes being induced by public housing transformation.

More than one-third of the HOPE VI projects in this sample are from cities in the South, while cities in the West only account for 15 percent of the projects. The rest are evenly divided between the Midwest and Northeast. The projects are generally in larger cities; half of the HOPE VI projects that went as far as demolition during the 1990s were in cities of five hundred thousand people or more. The larger sample of projects that progressed as far as relocation includes more projects in smaller cities. Most of this is the result of the early targeting objectives of the HOPE VI program, which limited grants to the most distressed and troubled public housing agencies, and these tended to be located in larger cities. Over the years, the bias toward larger cities declined as smaller agencies became more involved in the program, but this wider distribution is not fully represented in the samples analyzed here.

The average HOPE VI neighborhoods were 60 percent African American and 13 percent Hispanic. The HOPE VI neighborhoods were characterized by high poverty rates (45 percent), lower levels of owner-occupancy (less than 30 percent), and vacancy rates of close to 15 percent.

Poverty Reduction in HOPE VI Neighborhoods

The commonly accepted threshold for "concentrated poverty" is an area in which more than 40 percent of the population is below the poverty line.[44] Twenty-five of the one hundred neighborhoods in the larger sample (25% of the total) met the threshold for concentrated poverty in 1990 and then saw a reduction in poverty to a level below the 40 percent threshold by 2000. Most of the neighborhoods (72%) either remained above the 40 percent threshold or began the decade below it and remained there. Three of the HOPE VI neighborhoods actually began the decade with less than a 40 percent poverty rate and climbed above that threshold by the time of the 2000 census.

On average, the one hundred HOPE VI neighborhoods that progressed as far as the relocation stage of redevelopment had poverty rates that stood around 44 percent when the decade began. By 2000, these same neighborhoods averaged 36.1 percent poverty, a reduction of more than 8 percentage points over the ten-year period. However, some of this change may reflect larger trends occurring in the each of the cities with HOPE VI projects. Thus, a more appropriate number to look at is the poverty rate change net of larger changes taking place citywide.[45] The average decline in poverty, relative to changes taking place at the city level for the one hundred projects in which relocation took place, was 7.6 percentage points. That is, the average HOPE VI neighborhood saw a decline in poverty that was 7.6 percentage points greater than their respective citywide changes during the 1990s.

Some HOPE VI projects were associated with dramatic reductions in neighborhood poverty from 1990 to 2000. For example, the Ponce de Leon Courts project located in the College Hill neighborhood on the east side of Tampa received a HOPE VI grant of $32.5 million in 1997. The project resulted in the demolition of thirteen hundred units in two contiguous developments. Between 1990 and 2000 the neighborhood that included the project saw a reduction in poverty of 33.6 percentage points. Poverty in the city during this decade only declined a couple of percentage points. The difference between the citywide reduction in poverty and the neighborhood reduction is called the indirect displacement effect; it was a 32.29 percentage point reduction in poverty for the Ponce de Leon HOPE VI project. The neighborhood containing the Ida Barbour Homes HOPE VI project in Portsmouth, Virginia, saw a decline in poverty that was 44 percentage points greater than the citywide reduction. In all, nine HOPE VI projects that began before 2000 saw a drop in neighborhood poverty at least 25 percentage points more than their respective citywide changes, including Connie Chambers in Tucson, Holly Park in Seattle, Techwood in Atlanta, Vine Hill Homes in Nashville, Guinotte Manor in Kansas City, and Schuylkill Falls in Philadelphia.

Among the HOPE VI redevelopment projects in the two samples analyzed, most were located in neighborhoods that saw a decline in the poverty rate that was significantly greater than the secular trends taking place citywide (see table 6.1). Projects that moved to relocation during the 1990s are located in the middle column of the data table. In 46 percent of the cases, the HOPE VI neighborhoods saw a reduction in poverty that was at least 10 percentage points greater than what was happening citywide. In 13 percent the reduction in neighborhood poverty was between 5 and 10 percentage points more than what occurred citywide, and in 15 percent the neighborhood reduction in poverty was only slightly greater (less than 5 percentage points) than what was experienced citywide. Only one in four HOPE VI neighborhoods saw a reduction in poverty that did not exceed the citywide reduction. The pattern is even more extreme for neighborhoods in which the HOPE VI projects moved to the demolition stage, suggesting that as these projects moved toward completion during the 2000s, the impacts grew even larger.

Racial Turnover

Early HOPE VI projects were associated with less dramatic reductions in African American residents relative to citywide trends (see table 6.1). Only 23 percent of the HOPE VI neighborhoods saw a reduction in black population that was more than 10 percentage points greater than the citywide rate of change. At the other extreme, 25 percent of the HOPE VI neighborhoods that moved to the

TABLE 6.1 Changes in poverty and African American population in HOPE VI neighborhoods relative to changes taking place citywide, 1990–2000 (%)

	CHANGES IN POVERTY RATE		CHANGES IN AFRICAN AMERICAN POPULATION	
	PROJECTS THAT RELOCATED FAMILIES IN 1990S	PROJECTS THAT WERE DEMOLISHED IN THE 1990S	PROJECTS THAT RELOCATED FAMILIES IN 1990S	PROJECTS THAT WERE DEMOLISHED IN THE 1990S
Decline of more than 10 percentage points greater than citywide	46 (46)	33 (52)	23 (23)	15 (23)
Decline from 5 to 10 percentage points greater than citywide decline	13 (13)	7 (10)	27 (27)	15 (23)
Decline that exceeded the citywide rate by less than 5 percentage points	15 (15)	12 (19)	25 (25)	19 (30)
Neighborhood reduction that trailed the citywide rate of reduction	25 (25)	12 (19)	25 (25)	15 (23)
N	100	64	100	64

Source: Author's calculations.

Note: Figures in parentheses are column percentages.

relocation stage during the 1990s saw a reduction in black population that was less than the citywide reduction. In some of these neighborhoods there were in fact increases in the black population. In comparison to poverty reduction, the impact of HOPE VI on the racial profile of neighborhoods is more moderate.

For the most part, HOPE VI redevelopment projects that received funding in the 1990s were located in cities that were experiencing a slight decline in their African American populations. Among the one hundred projects that completed relocation during the 1990s, 57 percent were located in cities that saw a reduction in the proportion of residents who were African American (the figure is 55 percent for the sixty-four projects that went to demolition during the 1990s). The mean reduction in percentage black was less than 1 percentage point, however.

The neighborhoods in which these projects were located saw a greater decline in black population, on average, than did their cities. For projects that proceeded as far as relocation by 1999, their neighborhoods were 61.1 percent black in 1990 and 56.1 percent black in 2000. The per project displacement effect is 217; that is, the average project displaced 217 more African Americans from the neighborhood than would have been expected given citywide trends. For projects in which demolition took place in the 1990s, the neighborhoods fell from 60.3 percent black to 55 percent black. Among both groups of projects, the reduction in black population in these neighborhoods was greater, on average, than what took place in the rest of the city.

Some portion of the neighborhood-wide reduction in black population is due directly to the relocation/demolition of the public housing site while the rest is the spillover, or indirect displacement, effect. The extent of the direct and indirect displacement effects is impossible to determine because some of those displaced from the demolished public housing project may have moved elsewhere within the neighborhood; indeed, the research reviewed in chapter 5 shows that HOPE VI displacees tend not to move very far. Thus, we can expect that a portion of the reduction in black population within HOPE VI neighborhood areas is due to the direct displacement of blacks from the demolished project. Based on best estimates, it appears that, on average, HOPE VI redevelopment projects have *overall* generated little indirect displacement of African Americans at the neighborhood level.

These national averages, however, obscure significant variation across cities and across projects. As with poverty, there are some examples of HOPE VI neighborhoods that saw a dramatic reduction in African American population during the 1990s (net of changes taking place citywide). The most extreme case is the Schuylkill Falls project in Philadelphia, a city that saw a 2 percentage point increase in the black population between 1990 and 2000. The neighborhood of the Schuylkill Falls project saw a 27.95 percentage point decrease in the proportion of its population that is African American. Thus, the citywide trend and the neighborhood trend diverged by 30 percentage points. In this and other cases, such as the Earle Village project in Charlotte and the Ponce de Leon project in Tampa, the displacement estimate was greater than the actual level of decline in the neighborhoods because overall city trends were moving in the opposite direction. These two neighborhoods saw a drop in black population that was at least 15 percentage points greater than the citywide reduction. In five cases, Schuylkill Falls in Philadelphia, Techwood in Atlanta, the Ida Barbour Homes in Portsmouth, Virginia, Ponce de Leon in Tampa, and Holly Park in Seattle, significant racial change and poverty deconcentration have gone hand in hand.

At the same time there are a number of HOPE VI projects that have produced opposite effects or no racial change at all. For example, the three HOPE VI projects in Albany, New York, a city that experienced a decline in the African American population of 6.25 percentage points between 1990 and 2000, all saw increases in the black population in the neighborhoods surrounding the project sites. The Fairfield Homes project in Baltimore saw an increase in the black population of 4.12 percentage points, while the black population declined in the city as a whole by 4.88 percentage points. Similar patterns were seen in Hartford, Connecticut, and in single projects in Pittsburgh and Milwaukee.

Taken together, the data suggests that while significant secondary or indirect displacement of African Americans occurs in some cases, there are offsetting examples where no such pattern has occurred or where African American populations have actually increased in the neighborhoods surrounding redeveloped public housing. HOPE VI projects seem to be generating a range of neighborhood racial changes that are not easily summarized.

HOPE VI Displacement in Predominantly Black Neighborhoods

Looking only at predominantly black neighborhoods allows a more direct focus on the issue of black displacement. Sixty-two percent of the HOPE VI neighborhoods in the overall sample were predominantly black in 1990. In these neighborhoods blacks constituted on average 84 percent of the population in 1990 (see table 6.2). For projects that relocated public housing residents before 2000, the black population in the neighborhood surrounding the projects declined 5.5 percentage points (84.2 to 78.7). For projects that went as far as demolition the decline was 6 percentage points (84.7 to 78.8). The analysis shows that the average reduction in

TABLE 6.2 Indirect displacement of African Americans in predominantly black HOPE VI neighborhoods

NEIGHBORHOOD CHARACTERISTICS	RELOCATION IN THE 1990S	DEMOLITION IN THE 1990S
Mean black population, 1990	4,927	5,232
Mean percentage black, 1990	84.2	84.7
Mean black population, 2000	3,486	3,539
Mean percentage black, 2000	78.7	78.8
Mean reduction in black population	1441	1,694
Mean expected reduction in black population[a]	1,175	1,372
Per project displacement effect[b]	256	322
Excessive reduction in black population[c]	11,155	12,524
N	62	39

Source: Author's calculations.

[a] The reduction in the neighborhood black population if the neighborhood change had matched the overall city change.
[b] Actual reduction in neighborhood black population minus the expected reduction.
[c] Sum of per-project displacement effects.

black population over the decade was 1,175 persons for projects that completed relocation. For HOPE VI projects that went to relocation in the 1990s in predominantly black neighborhoods, the average reduction in the black population was 256 above what would be expected given citywide trends. For HOPE VI projects demolished during the 1990s the displacement effect was 322 persons.

Again, national averages on racial change hide a great deal of variation. Figure 10 provides a graphic look at all of the predominantly African American neighborhoods (in 1990) that were the location of HOPE VI projects and arrays them along two dimensions, change in poverty and change in African American population.[46] There are a number of neighborhoods that cluster in the area showing a sizable reduction in poverty with little to no racial change. This area, outlined in the figure, shows neighborhoods that experienced black gentrification. Many of the HOPE VI projects in these neighborhoods were begun in the late 1990s and thus the reduction in poverty probably reflects only the displacement of public housing residents from the neighborhood. Whether these residents were ultimately replaced by more affluent residents and whether the racial makeup of the neighborhood remained predominantly black has played out since the 2000 Census and is not reflected in this figure. Thus, not all of the projects that cluster within the blue box have undergone black gentrification. Projects that fit into the black gentrification area include LeMoyne Gardens (renamed College Hill) in Memphis, the Bronzeville neighborhood surrounding the Robert Taylor Homes on the South Side of Chicago (and the subject of three different books about black gentrification), and the Manchester public housing redevelopment in Pittsburgh. The data reveal that HOPE VI neighborhoods in Charlotte, Columbus, Louisville, and Wilmington (North Carolina) are also exhibiting these patterns.

Another set of neighborhoods appear in an area labeled "white gentrification." These are neighborhoods with HOPE VI projects that saw both a sizable reduction in poverty and a sizable reduction in the black population during the 1990s. White gentrification has taken place around the Techwood project adjacent to downtown Atlanta, on Chicago's Near North Side surrounding the old Cabrini-Green complex, and in Charlotte's First Ward area that used to be the home of the Earle Village public housing development.

Neighborhoods that are near the intersection of the two axes have not experienced significant change in either poverty or racial profile. In these neighborhoods the HOPE VI project had not triggered any larger neighborhood change by the time of the 2000 census. Finally, the smallest number of neighborhoods sees a sizable decline in African American residents but no change in poverty (desegregating neighborhoods) or sees an increase in poverty with little racial change.

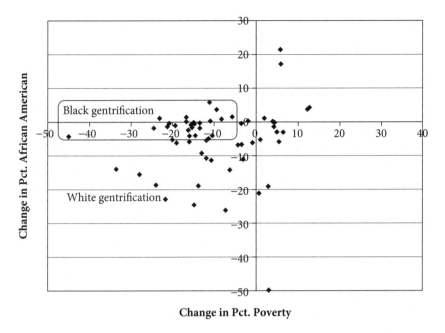

FIGURE 10.   Changes in race and poverty in predominantly black HOPE VI neighborhoods.

Inconsistency of Neighborhood Change

The neighborhood change induced by or accompanying public housing redevelopment in the United States does not follow a single model. In some cases considerable population change has occurred along with public housing redevelopment; some neighborhoods have experienced racial transition, more have experienced a significant reduction in and deconcentration of poverty. The experience of HOPE VI neighborhoods is varied; some show strong patterns of black or white gentrification, while others show little change. Comparative case studies have shown a variety of other changes occurring around public housing transformation from increasing property values to reduced crime.

The dismantling of public housing in U.S. cities does not, of course, occur in a vacuum. The demolition of public housing is rarely the only change taking place in the neighborhoods where it once stood. Very early in the HOPE VI program, HUD made larger neighborhood change one of the objectives of the program, and the likelihood of such change one of the factors on which they rated competing HOPE VI applications. In general, the scale of public housing redevelopment is large enough that there is a reasonable expectation that it will trigger spillover neighborhood changes. Although the question of whether the demographic changes described here were induced by HOPE VI or merely accompanied HOPE VI is an open one, there is a sense in which the question is moot. In many cases, HOPE VI public housing demolition is part of a larger public/private neighborhood revitalization effort. We know that in some cities public housing redevelopment occurred in neighborhoods that were already experiencing demographic and economic changes, or that were the target of other, public redevelopment investments that were not related to HOPE VI. In other cases, the demolition of public housing was necessary for the private sector to step forward and make sizable investments in previously neglected neighborhoods. All of these factors provide ample explanation for the neighborhood changes seen in many HOPE VI neighborhoods.

Conclusion

THE FUTURE OF PUBLIC HOUSING

When they're gone, we're gone.

—Wardell Yotaghan of the Coalition to Protect Public Housing, pointing to a drawing of the Cabrini-Green buildings

The record of public housing redevelopment in delivering benefits to the original residents is a critical context for any summary judgment of transformation policy since 1990. The demolition of public housing projects has significantly altered the urban landscape in cities across the United States, whether or not the teardown was accompanied by a HOPE VI-like redevelopment. High concentrations of poverty have been eliminated when residents are forced to move, and research shows the changes have frequently spilled over into the surrounding communities; property values have increased and crime has declined. In this respect the program has succeeded in the ways HUD and the Congress desired. The program has activated nascent land markets or swept away the last remaining obstacles to gentrification in many neighborhoods. Community-level benefits of an enhanced tax base and reduced service demands have been realized. In some places, the redevelopment promise of public housing transformation is so great that it has been made the foundation for large-scale urban redevelopment efforts. Its architects have, from the beginning, recognized that public housing transformation can be the foundation of much larger redevelopment outcomes. It is in many respects the equivalent of urban renewal in the 1950s and 1960s, providing the basis for a fundamental reconfiguration of the urban landscape.

At the same time, however, the outcomes for the residents of public housing have been more disappointing. Most simply move to other high-poverty and racially segregated neighborhoods that are unlikely to provide them with significantly greater opportunities than those from which they came.[1] The research to date shows that the benefits for original residents are limited and inconsistent. Their moves to marginally better neighborhoods leave them feeling safer on average, and they reduce the acute levels of fear and anxiety associated with crime and social disorder. But other hoped-for benefits, such as health improvements, enhanced economic self-sufficiency, or educational improvements among children, have not been seen. Expectations of economic benefits from relocation, or improved health, rest on an often complicated and extensive chain of events and circumstances. The mere act of relocating to a new neighborhood does little, if anything, to address the basic conditions that affect employability and health. Not only is there an absence of some expected benefits, but most research indicates that forced relocation upsets carefully constructed support networks and survival strategies employed by the very low income residents of public housing.

Whether relocated families are able to re-create social networks over time and overcome the short-term disruption of displacement remains to be seen. The question suggests changes that might be made to the program of transformation to minimize the disruption to public housing families and to connect them more directly to the community-level benefits produced by redevelopment. Phased redevelopment approaches that allow residents to stay on-site while work is done would avoid displacement and relocation, as would more tolerance for renovation over demolition. Ironically, a return to urban renewal era concerns about the adverse impacts of displacement seems a precondition for such changes.

Assessing Public Housing Transformation

One can summarize the dismantling of public housing by noting that place-based benefits are typical, but individual-level benefits for residents are not. There is a point, of course, at which these two patterns of outcomes converge. Very few residents find their way back to the redeveloped and improved sites. Most do not share in the place-based benefits because they have been removed, largely to other disadvantaged communities to carry on much as they have in the past. Although in some cases residents will "choose" not to move back to the redeveloped site, that choice can be induced by the long lead time between their initial displacement and the completion of redevelopment, which can easily be three to five years and in a significant number of cases is longer than that. For others, however, there is in fact no opportunity to return. The number of public housing units in most redevelopment projects is a fraction of the number demolished, and even if there were capacity to bring back all who wanted to return, new tenant screening criteria freeze out many. Since 1995 the community-level benefits of public housing transformation have been privileged over individual benefits. Demolition is the standard means of proceeding in HOPE VI even in the face of significant resident opposition. Only in rare cases (and often as the result of legal action) do residents prevail in their efforts to minimize displacement by phasing in construction. In the early years, relocation services were haphazard and hundreds of residents were lost in the redevelopment processes taking place.[2]

The dismantling of public housing makes little sense as housing policy. The policy constitutes a retrenchment in housing assistance that most directly affects very low income families. The loss of public housing and its deep subsidies is occurring at a time when the need for such subsidies is increasing. In 2010 Congress received a report from HUD on "Worst Case Housing Needs" in the country. Worst case needs are defined as households who have very low incomes (defined as below 50 percent of the area median income adjusted for household size), do not receive any form of housing assistance, and either pay more than 50 percent of their incomes on housing or live in "severely inadequate housing conditions" (defined by any of a range of physical deficiencies in the housing related to "heating, plumbing, electric, or maintenance").[3] Three findings from that report are especially important for the current rollback of public housing policy. First, the report indicates that there are close to six million families with worst case housing needs in the United States, an 18 percent increase since 2000. Second, "there is an insufficient supply of affordable and available rental housing for the lowest income groups," a deficit that grows with each additional unit demolished.[4] Interestingly, the report finds a surplus of units in the United States affordable to people at 60 percent and 80 percent of area median incomes (the market targeted by shallow-subsidy programs such as the Low-Income Housing Tax Credit), though not all of those units are actually occupied by people with those incomes. In contrast, the income stratum served by public housing faces an absolute shortage of units. Third, households with worst case needs living in urban areas are concentrated in high poverty neighborhoods, the types of neighborhoods in which most public housing is located, and the types of neighborhoods where it is being torn down or converted. A reduction in the number of public housing units in the face of growing need and in the very places where the need is greatest is difficult to justify in housing policy terms.

Chicago will demolish more than twenty thousand units of public housing over a fifteen-year period. Yet, in September 2010 the waiting list was opened and more than two hundred thousand families applied for Chicago public housing. That is roughly the number of family households in the entire city of Milwaukee, and more than in St. Louis, or Minneapolis, or Kansas City. Minneapolis, for its own part, recently received eight thousand applications for its public housing. The Minneapolis public housing authority reports that roughly 120 openings occur each year in its housing; thus the current waiting list provides roughly 66 years' worth of names. Since 1995 the Minneapolis Public Housing Authority has demolished one thousand units of public housing. In Waterbury, Connecticut, the housing authority has 2,394 people on its waiting list but plans to demolish fifty-two units of public housing in the near future.[5] On August 11, 2010, thirty thousand people showed up in East Point, Georgia, a suburb of Atlanta, simply to get applications for the Section 8 voucher waiting list. Police dressed in riot gear attempted to control the crowd. According to the *Atlanta Journal-Constitution*, "people collapsed in the heat. Emergency personnel drove up in a pickup truck and handed out bottled water. People were carried off on stretchers. A baby went into a seizure and was taken to a hospital."[6] In all, sixty-two people were injured and twenty were taken to a nearby hospital, some injured in the chaos that resulted when the door opened to take applications. In July 2011, five thousand applicants rushed to apply for housing assistance with Dallas County in what officials characterized as a "stampede." Months earlier the city of Dallas had accepted twenty-one thousand applications for their waiting list, and the city of Plano, Texas, received eight thousand applicants for one hundred available slots.[7] The systematic dismantling of the public housing system in the United States bears no relation to the scope of the need for very low cost housing in the country which is as acute as it has ever been.

Other evidence presented in earlier pages suggests an intentional rollback of social welfare policy in service to neoliberal policy initiatives to reduce government, privatize, and facilitate investment growth in cities. The pattern of demolition further suggests a race-based strategy for reclaiming central city space. Though nominally a policy aimed at the deconcentration of poverty, HOPE VI has proceeded in a manner that has disproportionately displaced African Americans. The analysis presented in the previous pages shows that demolition has targeted projects with disproportionately high percentages of African American residents. It has also shown that since 2000 public housing demolition has been more aggressive in cities in which the overall resident profile of public housing is disproportionately African American in comparison to the rest of the city.

The disparate impacts of demolitions, and its prevalence in cities where public housing is most identified with blacks, suggests a number of possible dynamics. There could be the conscious targeting of black residents, a greater tolerance of demolition if the victims are black, that blacks are living in the worst public housing, or that blacks are disproportionately represented within the family public housing that is being lost at greater rates than senior public housing. The statistical analysis discounts the latter two explanations, because race is a significant predictor even controlling for the age distribution of public housing residents and for the quality of the housing. This leaves the fact that in cities where public housing is most associated with black tenants, it is most likely to be demolished. Whether this is a surprise, given the racial history of public housing, the continued problems of residential segregation and housing discrimination in the United States, is beside the point. Our efforts to dismantle public housing seem to be proceeding in the same discriminatory manner in which the program has been operated for most of its existence. It is, of course, the fact that the constituents for public housing, its residents, are very low income and mostly of color, that the program enjoys little political support in the first place. It is an added injury that its dismantling should proceed in a way that has the effect of targeting blacks specifically.

The Commission's Recommendations

In 1992 the National Commission on Severely Distressed Public Housing was clear in its suggestions about how to deal with the nation's worst public housing. The public housing program, the Commission said, "continues to provide an important rental housing resource for many low-income families and others."[8] Therefore, the Commission recommended an approach that would preserve public housing assets. According to the Commission, the effort should be large enough to meet the existing need for improving the public housing stock, a need estimated at eighty-six thousand units, and it should reflect the preferences of the residents of public housing. The Commission envisioned an approach that would combine physical upgrading with resources to address the human needs of residents. "Traditional approaches to revitalizing seriously distressed public housing," noted the Commission, "have too often emphasized the physical condition of the developments without addressing the human condition of the residents."[9] As the research evidence has shown, this type of "traditional response" is exactly what we have gotten with the HOPE VI program.

The Commission was equally clear in its focus on modernizing and improving the existing stock. The recommendations focus on the rehabilitation of units wherever possible and the replacement of units lost to demolition or disposition. In fact, the commitment to the public housing stock was so strong that the Commission noted:

> In planning to replace units to be demolished or disposed of as a part of a comprehensive treatment program for severely distressed public housing, the Commission believes that PHAs must be exempted from impact restrictions in neighborhoods. That is, PHAs should be allowed to construct or rehabilitate the replacement units in the same neighborhood that contained the original units, even if there are "anti-impaction" restrictions.[10]

In the Commission's view, maintenance of the public housing stock was more important than the deconcentration or dispersal of subsidized units and poor households. A short four years later, HUD and PHAs across the country were devising plans to demolish public housing projects altogether, replacing them on a limited basis with fewer units mixed in with other subsidized and market-rate units in entirely new communities to be privately managed, and public housing residents were being displaced on a massive scale. The effort to reform public housing that had begun with the Commission's report had been transformed rapidly into an effort to dismantle the program. One might ask why the original estimate of eighty-six thousand units has been ignored and demolition extended to more than three times that number. Or why the Commission's preference for rehabilitation has given way to an almost universal reliance on demolition. Or why the Commission's preference for preserving the public housing stock over the deconcentration of poverty has given way to a reverse formula in which the deconcentration of poverty is pursued through the demolition of public housing and the dispersal of its residents.

The nature and the scale of the problem had not changed in those four years between the Commission's report in 1992 and the evolution of the HOPE VI

FIGURE 11. Mt. Airy Homes public housing complex in Saint Paul, Minnesota, which was rehabilitated in 1997.

program by 1996. What *had* changed were the national political environment and the economic conditions in many U.S. cities. The election of Bill Clinton and his administration's orientation toward redefining social welfare policy signaled a new willingness to consider radical changes in public housing policy. One year into his term, Henry Cisneros, Clinton's choice for secretary of HUD, was beginning to consider demolition as a solution to the worst problems of public housing. He was speaking openly about demolition by 1994.

The 1994 midterm elections ushered in a new Republican majority in Congress, and HUD became one of its targets. Public housing, never strongly supported by Republicans, was one of the first sacrificial lambs offered up by the Clinton administration to congressional Republicans. Cisneros, attempting to save the agency, proposed a complete remaking of the program to include the demolition of obsolete public housing projects. Cisneros's proposal mollified the Republicans and cleared the way for fundamental changes that would introduce new public/private partnerships and mixed financing and ownership to public housing.

On the economic front, coming out of the 1990–91 recession, urban areas were beginning to experience significant development pressure and investment interest that fueled a so-called third wave of gentrification. By the end of the decade a prolonged period of prosperity would lead to significant repopulation of many American downtowns. In the postrecession 1990s, local officials in many cities recognized the redevelopment potential of removing large public housing estates from critical parts of the urban landscape. Public housing demolition offered city officials the classic benefits of slum clearance (the elimination of blight and the fiscal burdens associated with it), and the preparation of strategic parcels of land to capitalize on private-sector development interest.

The belief that public housing was an albatross in too many urban land markets was widespread. As Renee Glover has written about her city, Atlanta, "the public housing projects were going downhill fast and dragging everything else in the city along with them."[11] Even in some of the toughest public housing communities there was the sense that a latent market demand existed, one that could be activated once the public housing buildings and residents were removed. Thus it was that the Commission's recommendations, which amounted to a call for improving the living conditions of very low income public housing residents, was in a short period of time hijacked to serve a development agenda that had a different set of objectives, objectives focused on the dispersal of low-income residents, the elimination of public housing communities, and the facilitation of private-sector reinvestment in urban areas that had been in that respect neglected for decades. Public housing demolition in the 1990s was greatest in cities that were experiencing the greatest development pressures.

The program shifted in the way it did because it became an effort to remake the landscape of American cities. The development agenda that focused on attracting private-sector investment, dispersing poverty, and facilitating the gentrification of inner-city neighborhoods necessitated the large-scale demolition of public housing estates. If the objectives of transformation had been different, and had been focused primarily on improving the lives of very low income residents, then the effort would have taken a different form than it has. For one, the shift to demolition would not have had to occur. From the standpoint of fixing the physical and design problems with public housing, rehabilitation would have sufficed in most cases. Physical upgrading and architectural and design enhancements could have created defensible space and reintegrated projects into their surroundings. The rehabilitation of the Commonwealth public housing development in Boston, for example, was a demonstration that, in fact, a careful rehabilitation could produce startling improvements in living conditions and achieve a significant redesign of the public housing environment.[12] The difference between the experience of Commonwealth and the way in which HOPE VI evolved is the community redevelopment component of HOPE VI. Rehabilitation, which might produce a much more tolerable living condition for public housing residents, would not have had the same redevelopment impact that total demolition has had. By making these communities, many of which were advantageously sited near downtowns and in the path of revitalization pressures, ready for private investment, HOPE VI expands the policy target and creates constituencies that would not have existed for a rehabilitation-based program. By contrast, a program of public housing rehabilitation would have been in many respects simply another welfare and antipoverty program. HOPE VI-style redevelopment could be sold as that and much more. The evolution of HOPE VI into a dispersal and demolition program created a constituency for the antipoverty element of public housing transformation.

The difference between the MTO and HOPE VI programs is instructive on this point. Poverty programs by themselves are chronically neglected and sometimes quickly abandoned. MTO was designed to facilitate the mobility of very low income families who wanted to move into low-poverty neighborhoods. No other benefits were forecast as a result of the program other than the improvements to the lives of the public housing families who participated. As a result, there was no constituency for the program other than the very low income families themselves. The MTO program was defunded in only its second year, abandoned by its liberal supporters in Congress because of the opposition of middle income communities who felt that they might be harmed by it. HOPE VI, on the other hand, was critically different than MTO in two important ways. First, public housing residents displaced by the program were not guaranteed a move to a low-poverty neighborhood. Indeed, as the research shows, just the

FIGURE 12.   Lauderdale Courts public housing in Memphis, which was built in 1938 by the WPA, was rehabilitated in 2003 and reopened as a mixed-income community called Uptown Square.

opposite has occurred—most families have moved to other segregated and poor neighborhoods. Thus, HOPE VI avoided generating the same backlash from middle income communities that MTO produced. Second, HOPE VI incorporated physical redevelopment of public housing communities, generating a supportive constituency for the program by spreading benefits to nearby property owners, investors, place-based entrepreneurs, large developers, and local officials. Property owners and investors could capitalize on the latent land value that had been suppressed by the existence of public housing, and local officials appreciated the increased property values and decreased service needs in the community postredevelopment. A more limited program of public housing rehabilitation similar to the one recommended by the Commission, a program that avoided displacement whenever possible and resulted in merely an improved public housing environment, would not have generated the same core constituency.

In some cases, the disinvestment in public housing over the years had progressed to the point that rehabilitation was not feasible. Similarly, in some cases the massive high-rise model required more extensive changes than rehabilitation would offer. Yet, even in those situations in which demolition, for one reason or another, could not be avoided, a program that focused on the benefits to residents would have looked different than what has ultimately transpired. As envisioned by the Commission, demolition, when unavoidable, would have been accompanied by full replacement of lost units, quickly and in the same neighborhoods where original units had stood.

What gives the lie most directly to the proposition that public housing transformation is about improving the lives of public housing residents is that it has been used only to downsize the public housing program. If, as the advocates for HOPE VI argue, we as a nation have found a way of producing public housing in mixed-income communities, well designed in ways that will foster the development of social capital and provide safe environments, then the model could be employed to rehouse all public housing residents who have been displaced. In fact, the model could also be used to expand public housing in the United States in a way that, in the words of HOPE VI advocates, ensures that we do not repeat the mistakes of the past. This has not been done, of course. Nor has it ever been advocated by those pushing the transformation of public housing. Instead, the new model of public housing is in almost all cases employed in the service of retrenchment, and in shrinking the stock of public housing in the United States.

False Choices

It is impossible to overstate the dysfunctional state of some public housing communities in the late 1980s and 1990s. The worst projects in our largest cities were, as Susan Popkin and her colleagues aver, humanitarian disasters.[13] In these conditions public housing tenants coped as well as they could, creating internal economic exchange systems even as they were systematically marginalized from mainstream economy.[14] They fought with their PHA landlords, trying to bring accountability to property management. They attempted to police themselves when no one else would provide them with security. In short, they attempted to change as much as they could about the environments in which they were living. The advocates of displacement, demolition, and dispersal often confuse criticism of demolition with defense of the status quo in public housing circa 1995. To resist displacement, to them, must be an acceptance of concentrated poverty or complacency about the conditions in the nation's worst public housing. Again, Renee Glover of Atlanta provides the paradigmatic example:

> Rather than address the real issues, many would prefer to debate whether the projects are really communities and these "incapable" poor people would be better off in the project because as bad and destructive as they are, these are their "communities."... I find it incredible that so many people don't comprehend the awful, corrosive impact of intensely

concentrated poverty and de-humanizing low standards and expectations.…We can do better than allow the horrible conditions at housing
projects to go unchallenged.[15]

The straw-man approach of this particular quote is of course a common rhetorical device used frequently to put one set of ideas in the best relief. But as a
means of dealing with the complex issues of poverty and community among
public housing residents, it is not of much use. The status quo is not the only
alternative to displacement, demolition, and dispersal. The Commission's recommendations highlight an alternative—rehabilitation and replacement—that
has been so neglected since 1995 that it is no longer even acknowledged by those
in the transformation movement.

One might also be tempted to give a pass to the dismantling of public
housing based only on the impressive neighborhood changes that frequently
accompany HOPE VI redevelopments. The eyesores of neglected public housing estates are replaced with new streets and infrastructure, new schools and
community centers flanking brand-new housing, built in a style that is for the
most part aesthetically pleasant. Crime and criminals are chased away to other
parts of the city, and private investment returns to the neighborhood. The
advocates point to these successes as proof of the superiority of the mixed-
income, HOPE VI model. This, too, implies that we face but two choices: on the
one hand we could have public housing, underfunded by Congress, poorly run
by HUD, at times utterly mismanaged by local housing authorities, in neighborhoods abandoned by the local government and by private investment, and
ceded to gangs. Or we can displace thousands of very low income families and
insert new occupants into mixed-income communities with new schools, better property management, collaboration with wider redevelopment efforts,
and better public services.[16] Off the table altogether, it seems, is the possibility
of public housing with excellent property management, good schools nearby,
high quality public services, engaged and informed public-sector supervision
of housing authorities, and private-sector investment providing jobs and retail
opportunities for residents. A mix of incomes is not the critical element in
these scenarios. The critical elements are the quality of public services, the
management of the properties, the collaboration with private and public investors to build a community that is attractive to a range of households, and the
public-sector commitment to support the community through important
infrastructure investments. There is very little inherent in the public housing
model that precludes these outcomes; it is how our public and private institutions respond to public housing that has produced the negative outcomes we
have seen in American public housing.

The advocates of HOPE VI and the dismantling of public housing have thus presented us with a pair of false choices. First, we can accept displacement and demolition or we can accept public housing as it was at its worst. Second, we can accept mixed-income developments supported by hundreds of millions of dollars of public and private investment, or we can continue to have public housing with crumbling public infrastructure, isolated from private reinvestment efforts and with poor to nonexistent public services. Choices like these are easy when the options are so limited. In fact, of course, our options should not be so constrained.

Alternative Options

The current solution being applied to public housing in communities across the country is disproportionate to the problem in two ways. First, we are demolishing more public housing than is necessary, and second, demolition itself is more than is required to address the issues of public housing. There are opportunities for a more measured approach. Architecturally distinctive and structurally sound projects, such as Iberville in New Orleans,[17] presented distinctive landscapes that already incorporated most of the New Urbanist prescriptions that HUD and local PHAs have been imposing on redeveloped sites. Successful models of rehabilitation, such as Commonwealth in Boston, provide a template for how to turn around public housing short of total demolition and redevelopment.[18] Yet, in city after city HUD and local PHAs have adopted a one-size-fits-all strategy of mass displacement, demolition, and redevelopment. In some cases they settle simply for the mass displacement and demolition.

A number of reasonable policy options are available and could and should be initiated immediately. The new direction for public housing policy should be to put resident concerns at the forefront. This would mean protecting the remaining units of public housing from demolition, eliminating or strictly minimizing the forced displacement of very low income residents, expanding the size of the public housing stock through new construction using the development model created through HOPE VI, and ensuring the mobility of those who wish to move out of public housing.

End the Demolition of Public Housing

The first step is to end the demolition of public housing. Given that HOPE VI has already far exceeded its mandate in terms of the number of units affected, and given that PHAs have demolished almost two hundred thousand other units on their own, outside of HOPE VI, we can be reasonably sure that the worst public housing projects have already been "dealt with." The number of units affected so far is roughly three times the number estimated by the Commission, and unless the Commission was incompetent in making its estimation, the job is done. Although there may be cases in which demolition is made necessary by the physical deterioration of the structure in the future, decisions about upgrading resident environments should return to the pre-HOPE VI presumption that the housing should be preserved.

Phase In the Redevelopment

Where demolition is absolutely necessary (and only after more rigorous over-sight and review from HUD), then it should be done in phases so that residents can stay in the community and so that the disruption of displacement is mini-mized. Phased redevelopment through HOPE VI has been accomplished in a few places. The courts mandated it in the case of the Henry Horner Homes in Chicago. In Pittsburgh, the PHA managed a phased redevelopment of Bedford Additions that allowed people to stay in the community. Phased redevelopment should be a mandatory element of any future limited program of public housing redevelopment.

The "Right to Remain"

Provisions should be made to honor the desire of some residents to remain in their communities. Attorneys for the residents of the Henry Horner Homes in Chicago negotiated such a right for their clients. All residents who wished to move into the redeveloped site could do so, provided they met basic requirements that the tenants themselves devised. Tenant would be screened for criminal behavior and rental history, but "importantly, residents are screened only on their behav-ior on or after...the date that the consent decree was entered....Accordingly, all Horner families were aware that they themselves controlled whether they would be eligible for a replacement unit. Knowing the eligibility requirements, each family knew what it had to do or not do to remain eligible."[19] A similar effort has been initiated in San Francisco by the Housing Rights Committee.[20]

One-for-One Replacement

The provision for one-for-one replacement of lost public housing units should be reinstated and enforced. Given the nationwide need for housing affordable to very low income families, estimated at close to six million units by HUD, all units that are lost to demolition should be replaced. The Obama administration's Choice Neighborhoods Initiative (CNI) reinstates one-for-one replacement. HUD should enforce this provision strictly.

Preserve Affordable Housing in Redevelopment Areas

HOPE VI has generated significant neighborhood turnover in many cities, and the Obama administration's CNI has been designed to spread these changes to the neighborhoods surrounding other forms of federally subsidized housing. These efforts should incorporate the preservation of affordable housing within the neighborhood. In this way, a greater mix of incomes can be achieved and the incumbent low-income residents have the opportunity to benefit from the neighborhood upgrading that takes place.

Build More

The proponents of public housing redevelopment are excited about the neighborhood improvements that have been associated with the development of new mixed-income communities. Supporters claim that mixed-income developments will attract private-sector investment in the form of new residential and commercial development. They argue that public housing developed in this way—as part of a larger mixed-income community—will have a better chance to persist over time, will avoid stigmatization, and will provide benefits to the residents. Proponents of the traditional neighborhood design utilized in HOPE VI projects claim that the new communities fit better into the neighborhoods in which they are placed, provide "eyes on the streets" and "defensible space" that will make the communities safer, and will enhance the creation of social capital. If these claims are correct, the HOPE VI program should be expanded with one important change: it should move from being a *re*development program to a development program. If, as Henry Cisneros and Renee Glover and Richard Baron and Andrew Cuomo and President Obama's HUD secretary, Shaun Donovan, contend, the HOPE VI model of public housing solves the problems associated with public housing, then the program should begin to build new public housing immediately. Long waiting lists exist in virtually every major city and most midsized cities. The amount of housing affordable to very low income families is inadequate everywhere. To date, HOPE VI has been enlisted only in the cause of diminishing the stock of public housing; it is time to use the HOPE VI development model to expand public housing.

Monitor the Racial Impact of Public Housing Policies

Given the consistent and sizable disproportionate impact on African American families that the demolition of public housing has produced, HUD should summarize the demographics of displaced households pursuant to any public housing redevelopment that takes place. The summary should include, but not be limited to, an analysis of the possible disparate impact on people of color.

Expand Voluntary Mobility Programs

Ebony Thomas, who lives in the Fort Hill public housing complex in Marietta, Georgia, says of her time in public housing, "I have been trying to move out since I moved in…life kept me here."[21] Ebony Thomas and others like her should be given the chance to move out of public housing. As the Poverty and Race Research Action Council notes, "advocates and policymakers must also recognize that the interests of residents are not 'monolithic.' In any given development, some residents may wish to return to the original site, while others may wish to leave."[22] The advocates of dispersal are right to the extent that they argue that too many public housing residents have been trapped in communities that they do not like, and that they would leave if they could. A voluntary program that helps people to move away from public housing neighborhoods if they want to should be a central part of public housing policy moving forward. In 1993, Congress created such a program—the Moving to Opportunity (MTO) program. MTO, however, was cut by Congress when it generated controversy in working class suburban areas that erroneously thought they would receive an influx of low-income black, former public housing residents. The ready retreat of liberal Democrats on this issue, and their willingness to kill MTO, is an especially disappointing aspect of this history. Giving people who want to leave the means of doing so should be a policy goal in and of itself. Careful, controlled experimental studies have been carried out on the effects of MTO, and they have shown quite modest program outcomes. But, the fact is, the studies should be irrelevant in this case. The benefits of MTO are the ability of residents to *exercise greater choice* about where to live and the ability to move to a neighborhood that they perceive is safer and more accommodating. There is no need to demonstrate that it improves health, self-sufficiency, education levels, or social integration. These outcomes are only important when the dispersal is forced upon residents and only as a means of justifying the disruption to lives, the breaking up of community, and the remarkable government intrusion represented by forced eviction. It is in this context that the limited benefits of displacement are so important. MTO needs to be restored and made a nationwide program. Residents who desire to move out of public housing should be supported in doing so. This would make room for the thousands of others who clog the waiting lists for public housing in city after city.

A New Legacy

The legacy of public housing in the United States is a complex one. Its failures have been terrible and widely heralded; its successes, which are much more the norm, are mostly overlooked. First enacted to serve multiple agendas that included economic recovery and slum clearance, public housing's dismantling now serves the cause of urban economic revitalization and, again, slum clearance.

Often lost in these dynamics are the struggles of very low income families living in public housing. Their experiences in the dismantling of public housing should have more bearing on events and on the course of policy than has been the case. The proponents of public housing transformation persist in the face of consistent evidence that resident benefits are quite limited and in any case balanced by measurable harm. Proponents also maintain their argument even in the face of resident opposition to displacement and demolition. It is the discourse of disaster, and the widespread understanding of public housing as a social intervention gone awry, that allows advocates to assert that any move away from public housing is almost by definition a benefit to a resident. It is the belief that public housing is irredeemable that leads public officials to dismiss resident opposition as ill-informed or shortsighted. Thus, former HUD secretary Henry Cisneros acknowledges tenant dissatisfaction but concludes that in the end he and the other architects of transformation knew better:

> Although even residents living in horrible conditions had mixed feelings about leaving neighborhoods where they had developed bonds of friendship and mutual support, it was *our judgment* that conditions in the most distressed public housing developments were so bad that replacement was the only reasonable course.[23]

Resident opposition, though vocal in some places, has been for the most part uneven. Though residents filed lawsuits to stop the demolitions, crowded city council meetings, met the bulldozers with pickets, and organized themselves to tell stories of communities being torn apart, there was in every city a portion of the public housing population that wanted to leave and that supported demolition. The support of these residents, whose concerns for their own well-being and desire for different living accommodations are as strong as the opinions of those who opposed demolition, undercut the political cause of their neighbors and reinforced the belief among officials that demolition was appropriate. As long as local housing authorities, HUD officials, and policy analysts could point to residents who wanted to leave and who welcomed demolition and relocation, the opposition of other residents could be set aside. In fact, of course, it should have been the other way around: as long as a sizable number of residents wished to remain and expressed concern about the loss of informal support networks upon which they relied, then the desire to demolish and set off universal displacement should have been set aside. Those who wanted to leave should have had their moves facilitated, but not at the expense of those who wished to remain.

Appendix

TABLE A.1 Variables used in multivariate analysis

EXPLANATION	VARIABLE AND EXPECTED DIRECTION OF RELATIONSHIP WITH THE DEGREE OF PUBLIC HOUSING REMOVAL	SOURCE
PHA quality	HUD PHMAP score average 1991–95 (–)	HUD
Concentrated poverty	Central city poverty rate 1990, 2000 (+)	U.S. Census, SOCDS[a],
	Concentrated poverty rate, 1990, 2000 (+)	and Jargowsky 2003
	Black concentrated poverty, 1990, 2000 (+)	
Social control / violent crime	Murder rate 1992, 1999 (+)	FBI data, SOCDS
	Robbery rate 1992, 1999 (+)	
	Assault rate 1992, 1999 (+)	
	Rape rate 1992, 1999 (+)	
Housing market	Median rent 1990, 2000 (+)	U.S. Census
	Median home value 1990, 2000 (+)	U.S. Census
	Vacancy rate 1990, 2000 (–)	U.S. Census
Gentrification pressure	Ratio of median public housing rent to median rent citywide, 1996, 2000 (–)	HUD *Picture of Subsidized Housing* and U.S. Census
Politics—progressive / labor strength	Unionization rate, 1995 (+/–)	www.unionstats.com
	Index of progressive policy approaches (+/–)	author's compilation[b]
Race	Size of African American middle class, 1990 (+)	U.S. Census, SOCDS
	African American pct. homeowner, 1990 (+)	
	Index of dissimilarity (black/white), 1990 (+)	
	Ratio of pct. black in public housing to pct. black citywide	
Control variables	City population (logged), 1990, 2000	U.S. Census
	Median household income, 1990, 2000	

[a] State of the Cities Data System, www.HUDUSER.org.
[b] Sources are Living Wage Resources Center, http://laborcenter.berkeley.edu/livingwage/resources.shtml; Kent Portnoy (2005), "Civic Engagement and Sustainable Cities in the United States," *Public Administration Review* 65 (5): 579–91, and the Center for Community Change, http://www.communitychange.org/.

TABLE A.2 Factors associated with removal of public housing units in large U.S. cities: A Poisson regression

DEPENDENT VARIABLE	1990–2000			2001–2007	
	PH UNITS REMOVED	P		PH UNITS REMOVED	P
Population 1990 logged	−.018	.929	Population 2000 logged	−.090	.597
West Region	.991	.013	West Region	1.514	.006
Midwest Region	.393	.263	Midwest Region	1.675	.021
Northeast Region	.430	.207	Northeast Region	1.524	.016
PHA Management Assessment Score	−.010	.183	PHA Management Assessment Score	−.003	.659
Concentrated Poverty 1990	−.026	.077	Concentrated Poverty 2000	.024	.122
Crime-Robbery with Gun 1992	.001	.002	Crime-Robbery with Gun 1999	.003	.015
Median Housing Value 1990	−6.43e−06	.045	Median Housing Value 2000	7.73e−07	.829
Residential Vacancy Rate 1990	−.013	.716	Residential Vacancy Rate 2000	.126	.044
Ratio of Public Housing Rent to Citywide Rent 1996	−5.531	.031	Ratio of Public Housing Rent to Citywide Rent 2000	−5.002	.059
Union Strength	−.016	.380	Union Strength	−.085	.014
Progressive Policy	−.002	.988	Progressive Policy	−.372	.043
Racial Segregation 1990	−.065	.976	Racial Segregation 2000	.788	.618
Black Middle Class 1990	1.524	.444	Black Middle Class 2000	−.721	.537
Ratio of pct. Black in PH to pct. Black in City 1990	−.128	.551	Ratio of pct. Black in PH to pct. Black in City 2000	.349	.015
			Pct. of PH units removed 1990–1999	.018	.057
Public Housing Units 1996	exposure		Public Housing Units 2000	exposure	
Log pseudo-likelihood	−19787			−19823	
Pseudo R2	.502			.610	
N	110			109	

TABLE A.3   Characteristics of public housing projects associated with demolition: Logistic regression results

	ODDS RATIO	P
Number of units	1.004	.000
Percent occupied	.960	.000
Median rent	.980	.000
Percent very low income	.997	.789
Percent female headed household	.988	.165
Percent under 25	.990	.250
Percent over 62	.966	.000
Percent black	1.011	.001

Notes: Odds ratios and p value not shown for city dummy variables.
Unit of analysis is "public housing project," n = 1,773.
LR chi-square = 433.85, p < .001
Pseudo R-square = 0.309.

Notes

INTRODUCTION

1. See Hunt (2009).

2. ABLA is an acronym that stands for four different public housing projects that sat on adjacent land on the city's near South Side: the Jane Addams Homes, the Robert Brooks Homes, Loomis Courts, and the Grace Abbott Homes.

3. This quote is on the home page of the Museum's web-site: http://www.public housingmuseum.org/.

4. National Commission on Severely Distressed Public Housing (NCSDPH) (1992, 2).

5. Quoted in Feldman and Stall (2004, 84). Beverley and Harris are hardly alone in their views of public housing. Typically, whenever asked by researchers, a significant number—sometimes half or more—of residents forcibly displaced by public housing demolition indicate a preference to stay in the community rather than move out. See also Goetz (2009), Gibson (2007), and Kleit and Manzo (2006).

6. HOPE VI is the sixth program in a series first created in the 1990 National Affordable Housing Act. HOPE stands for Homeownership Opportunities for People Everywhere.

7. This information is available at HUD's website http://www.hud.gov/offices/pih/systems/pic/sac/.

8. Dries (2009).

9. Pratt (2008).

10. "Shallow" and "deep" in this instance refer to the level of affordability achieved by a subsidy. Public housing is a deep subsidy because it provides affordability to extremely low income families (incomes less than 30% of the area median). Shallow subsidies are able to produce affordability only for those with relatively higher incomes, typically 50% to 80% of the area median.

11. Calthorpe (2009, 53–54).

12. Polikoff (2009, 77).

13. The same argument is made about 'social housing' in Europe. As Hall and Rowlands (2005, 47) argue, the large public housing estates of Europe "were planned, developed, and allocated during a socioeconomic paradigm that characterized the four decades following the Second World War, the basic tenets of which no longer apply."

14. From the speech by Franklin Delano Roosevelt on the dedication of Techwood Homes, Atlanta. November 29, 1935. http://georgiainfo.galileo.usg.edu/FDRspeeches/FDRspeech35-2.htm.

15. It should be noted that FDR came late to the public housing bandwagon. Advocates for the program worked for years in the face of indifference from FDR and even opposition from some of his cabinet members. See Friedman (1968).

16. See Hunt (2009) for a description of this process in Chicago.

17. See, e.g., Vale (2002), Williams (2004).

18. Al Gore, quoted in Williams (2004, 238).

19. Comment made by Secretary of HUD Henry Cisneros about Chicago public housing, "Cisneros Urges Demolition of High-rise Projects" (1994).

20. Massey and Kanauaipuni (1993).

21. See, e.g., the description in Goering (2003) of the decision by HUD to focus the Moving To Opportunity (MTO) mobility program on poverty deconcentration instead of racial desegregation.

22. See Hall and Rowlands (2005) for the European parallel.

23. See, e.g., Skutch (2010) and Seidel (2010)

24. Brenner and Theodore (2002).

25. Williams (2004).

26. Regan (2001).

27. Glover (2009b, 152).

28. Emphasis in the original. Atlanta Housing Authority (2010), "About Us: Our President and CEO" http://www.atlantahousing.org/profile/index.cfm?fuseaction = ceo.

29. Glover (2009a).

30. Hackworth (2007, 51) and Wilen and Nayak (2006).

31. Vale (2000).

32. National Housing Law Project (2002).

33. Jones and Popke (2010, 125).

34. Bloom (2008).

35. Spence (1993).

36. See Tonrys (1995) and Gordon (1994).

37. Neil Smith (2002, 92).

38. See Hackworth (2007); Moore (2009); Hackworth and Smith (2001).

39. This argument is contained in Hackworth and Smith (2001).

40. Wyly and Hammel (1999). This phrase itself is a reversal of the one used by geographer Brian Berry (1985) who, in the 1980s, lamented the limited impact of urban redevelopment efforts, calling them mere islands of renewal amid seas of decay.

41. Newman (2002).

42. Reichl (1999).

43. "New Urbanists Urge Uncle Sam: 'Don't Abandon HOPE.'" Similarly, Margery Austin Turner of the Urban Institute argues that it simply "makes sense to think of public housing redevelopment as an essential ingredient of a larger revitalization." Turner (2009, 181).

44. See, e.g., Boyd (2008).

45. Pfeiffer's (2006) study focuses on Cabrini-Green on Chicago's Near North Side and, in part, depicts a naming war between the developers of the new mixed-income developments who erected signposts and name plates advertising the new housing being built. Residents responded by spray-painting "Cabrini" onto buildings and signs in prominent areas.

46. See Moore (2009) on black gentrification.

47. As Wilson (2004, 773) argues, neoliberalism is "now anything but a brute economic and political imposition."

48. These quotes, in order, are from Katz (2009, 17), Williams (2004, 238, quoting Al Gore), and Popkin, Gwiasda, et al. (2000).

49. Polikoff (2009, 77).

50. Jarvie (2008).

51. Calthorpe (2009, 61).

52. The coalescence of these policy streams led to the emergence of what Imbroscio (2008, 2010) calls the "dispersal consensus."

53. Hackworth (2007, 183).

54. See, e.g., Frost (2010), Hackworth (2007), Seattle Displacement Coalition (http://www.zipcon.net/~jvf4119/#Activities%20and%20issues%20the%20Coalition), Goetz (2003), Cardinale (2007a), Hogarth 2007.

55. Regan (2001).

56. Pfeiffer (2006, 49) quotes a Chicago public housing resident as saying about the redevelopment of the Cabrini-Green project, "I've been here my whole life, I don't want to leave, especially now, just as it's cleaning up."

1. THE QUIET SUCCESSES AND LOUD FAILURES OF PUBLIC HOUSING

1. Macek (2006).

2. Friedman (1968), Bloom (2008), Hunt (2009).

3. See Hunt (2009), especially chapter 1, for a fuller discussion of the uneasy alliance between the Progressives and the housing reformers in the campaign to create the public housing program in the United States.

4. Friedman (1968).

5. Gelfand (1976, 60).

6. See Friedman (1968, 119–20), and Wright (1981, 230).

7. Ouroussoff (2006).

8. Vale (2000) and Franck (1998).

9. Bailey, Milligan, and Persce (1996).

10. See, e.g., Vale (2002) and Fuerst (2005).

11. McCarthy (1987).

12. *United States v. Certain Lands in the City of Louisville*, 78 F. 2d 684 (6th Cir. 1935).

13. Fisher (1959).

14. Fisher (1959), Friedman (1968).

15. Hunt (2009, 31).

16. Bloom (2008).

17. This quote is taken from an excerpt from the legislative hearings for the Housing Act of 1936, in Mitchell (1985, 247). Hunt (2009) argues that the impulse to keep public housing from competing with the private sector was the overriding cause of its problems.

18. Quoted in Keith (1973, 98).

19. Friedman (1968, 115).

20. This leaflet, from Lubbock, Texas, declares public housing to be socialism and urges voters to vote no on a public housing referendum, "unless you want Lubbock to sell its birthright for the Mess of Public Housing Potage." Quoted in Baxandall and Ewen (2001, 94).

21. Davies (1966, 127); see also Wright (1981).

22. Gelfand (1976).

23. Quoted in Vale (2000, 239).

24. Weiss (1985).

25. Keith (1973, 99).

26. See Keith (1973), Friedman (1968), and Gelfand (1976).

27. Freedman (1969, 38).

28. Parson (2005).

29. Freedman (1969, 53).

30. Hunt (2009).

31. In contrast, Vale (2000) reports that in Boston, white politicians maneuvered to have public housing placed in their wards into the 1950s. This reflected the occupancy rules of the BHA at the time and the generally better construction and design characteristics of the earliest public housing in that city. This dynamic ended, of course, as the quality of the new projects declined and as occupancy shifted from white to black.

32. Goldstein and Yancey (1986).

33. Robinson (1994).

34. The black middle class also frequently resisted the placement of public housing in their communities. See, e.g., Hunt (2009).

35. Hunt (2009).

36. Radford (2000).

37. See, e.g., Vale (2000, 174).

38. Williams (2004, 97).

39. See Bloom (2008) and Hunt (2009) on how this affected the development strategies of local housing authorities, and the quality and nature of the projects they produced.

40. Friedman (1968, 113).

41. Lewis Mumford, quoted in Radford (2000, 113).

42. See Franck (1998) on the design advantages of superblocks, and Hunt (2009) on the cost-containment origins of the strategy.

43. Hunt (2009, 46).

44. Catherine Bauer, quoted in Biles (2000, 147).

45. Gentry (2009, 206).

46. Newman (1972).

47. Mandelker (1973).

48. Ibid.

49. Vale (2000, 337).

50. See Meehan (1979, 37).

51. Hunt (2009).

52. Biles (2000, 149).

53. Hunt (2009), see esp. chapter 6.

54. Vale (2000), Bloom (2008).

55. Vale (2000, 256). See also Williams (2004).

56. Williams (2004, 44).

57. Vale (2000).

58. Bloom (2008).

59. Vale (2000, 181).

60. Mandelker (1973)

61. Hunt (2009, 52).

62. Feldman and Stall (2004).

63. Williams (2004, 98).

64. Vale (2000, 270), Williams (2004), and Hartman (1964) quoted in Vale (2000, 281).

65. Bloom (2008).

66. Spence (1993).

67. Stegman (1991, 52).

68. Feldman and Stall (2004) and Epp (1998) reports public housing incomes averaging 16 percent of area medians by 1995.

69. See, e.g., Kolodny (1985).

70. Hunt (2009, 223).

71. Williams (2004, 67).

72. Simmons (1993a).

73. Simmons (1993b).

74. Bratt (1986). See also Vale (2000).

75. Landis and McClure (2010, 332).

76. Hartman and Carr (1969) as cited in Bratt (1986, 346).

77. Connerly (1986).

78. Schill (1993).

79. Struyk (1980, 136).

80. Williams (2004, 145).

81. Baron (2009, 43).

82. Henderson (1995).

83. Ibid., 42.

84. Friedman (1968, 142).

85. Montgomery and Bristol (1987).

86. Ibid.

87. Macek (2006, 167).

88. McCarthy (1987).

89. Dries (2010a).

90. Currie and Yelowitz (2000).

91. Gibson (2007, 17)

92. Stockard (1998, 245).

93. Stegman (1991, 51).

94. Cuomo (1999).

95. Ibid.

96. Rabushka and Weissert (1977), quoted in Bratt (1986).

97. Feldman and Stall (2004).

98. Venkatesh (2000).

99. See, e.g., Kleit and Manzo (2006), Gibson (2007), Vale (1997).

100. Bratt (1986, 344).

101. Connerly (1986).

102. Quoted in Bratt (1986, 343).

103. Popkin, Gwiasda, et al. (2000, 189).

104. See, e.g., Salisbury (1958).

105. Bauer (1957).

106. This is the argument of Eugene Meehan (1979).

107. See, e.g., ibid.

108. Hunt's (2009) argument is that the political fear of opposition based on cost led administrators at the federal level to stress cost containment in construction to such an extent that it produced inferior project designs, ultimately leading to the deterioration and decline of projects; see esp. 44–47.

2. DISMANTLING PUBLIC HOUSING

1. Gutzmann (2004).

2. Pratt (2008).

3. National Housing Law Project (NHLP) (1990).

4. Codified as §1437(p) of 42. U.S.C. entitled "Demolition and Disposition of Public Housing."

5. NHLP (1990).

6. Schill (1993, 500, n. 23).

7. The Public Housing Management Assessment Program (PHMAP) is a system created by HUD in accordance with the National Affordable Housing Act (NAHA) of 1990. The system is intended to provide an objective means of measuring the performance of local public housing authorities. The specific indicators of performance are spelled out in the NAHA and include vacancy rates, unexpended modernization funds, rents collection rates, energy consumption, average length of time required to rerent vacant units, percentage of work orders outstanding, percentage of units failing annual inspection, tenants' accounts receivable, operating reserves, and balance of operating expenses to operating income and subsidies. Source: chapters 1 and 6 of the PHMAP handbook, at http://hud.gov/offices/adm/hudclips/handbooks/pihh/74605/index.cfm.

8. NHLP (1990).

9. *Edwards v. District of Columbia*, 628 F. Supp. 333 (D.D.C. 1985).

10. Ibid.

11. Ibid., 11.

12. NHLP (1990, 72–73).

13. *Edwards v. District of Columbia*, 8.

14. H.R. Conference Report No. 426, 100th Congress, First Session, 1987.

15. *Concerned Tenants Association of Father Panik Village v. Pierce*, 685 F. Supp. 316 (D.C. Conn. 1988).

16. *Concerned Tenants Association*, 318.

17. NHLP (1990, 43).

18. *Tillman v. Housing Authority of Pittsburgh*, No. 88–0311 (W.D. Pa. filed Feb. 17, 1988), in Krislov (1988). See also *Clearinghouse Review* 173 (1988, 22).

19. *Dessin v. City of Fort Myers*, 783 F. Supp. 587 (M.D. Fla.1990). This is the only case since the congressional amendments of 1987 to disallow a suit on the basis of a de facto demolition claim. The court, despite the well-known legislative history of the 1987 amendment, found the congressional language ambiguous and not expressly granting tenants a right to sue. The decision in the case remains an aberration.

20. *Tinsley v. Kemp*, 750 F. Supp. 1001 (W.D. Mo. 1990).

21. *Boles v. Kemp*, No. 92–056 CV-W-9 (W.D. Mo.) filed July 7, 1992.

22. Levin and Levin (2007).

23. *Gomez v. El Paso Housing Authority*, 805 F. Supp. 1363 (W.D. Tex. 1992).

24. Powell (1995).

25. *Velez v. Chester Housing Authority*, 850 F. Supp. 1257 (E.D. Pa. 1994). *Henry Horner Mothers Guild v. Chicago Housing Authority and the U.S. Department of Housing and Urban Development*, 780 F. Supp. 511 (N.D. Ill. 1991).

26. NHLP (1990).

27. Ibid., 49, in the case of Newark, New Jersey.

28. Ibid., 79.

29. NHLP (1990).

30. Ibid., 79.

31. Konkoly (2008).

32. Tuttle (2008).

33. *Anderson v. Jackson*, 556 F. 3d 351 (5th Cir. 2009).

34. Massey and Kanaiaupuni (1993).

35. Cisneros (1995) and Hartman (1995).

36. Hartman (1995).

37. Goering (2003).

38. In 1990, the National Affordable Housing Act included a series of HOPE (Homeowner for People Everywhere) programs that reflected HUD Secretary Jack Kemp's focus on ownership and public housing reform. The program that became HOPE VI was added to the series during the 1992 congressional session in order to "encourage the [Bush] administration's acceptance" of it. See Katz (2009, 25).

39. All of these quotes are from the Commission report (NCSDPH 1992, 2).

40. NCSDPH (1992, 2).

41. Ibid., 2.

42. The first quote is from page 3 of the Commission report (ibid.) the second is from page 5.

43. NCSDPH (1992).

44. Ibid., 17, emphasis added.

45. Ibid., 87.

46. Ibid., 85.

47. U.S. HUD (2002b), Popkin et al. (2004), Wexler (2001).

48. These categories were developed by the NCSDPH, whose recommendations led to the HOPE VI program.

49. See Zhang and Weismann (2006).

50. U.S. GAO (2002).

51. From a memo by Baron to HUD officials, quoted in Baron (2009, 31).

52. Cisneros (2009, 6); emphasis added.

53. Quoted in Jones and Popke (2010, 118).

54. Smith (2006a).

55. Fosburg, Popkin, and Locke (1996).

56. U.S. GAO (2003).

57. Fischer (2006).

58. Ibid.

59. "Asset management" is a management approach that stresses the viability of individual projects, eliminating cross-subsidization of projects within agencies. This approach and the formula for supporting "well-run" public housing are contained in the so-called *Harvard Cost Study* (Harvard University GSD, 2009), which provided the basis for the HUD policy changes.

60. Miller (2007), Brown (2006), Fischer (2006), Silva (2008), and Burt (2008).

61. See, e.g., Andreatta (2010).

62. Olivio (2010).

63. The record of demolitions and removals from HUD public housing inventory come from HUD, including information on the means by which units were removed (either sale or demolition) and the date of removal for all public housing in the United States through the middle of 2007 (Freedom of Information Act Request, FOIA Control Number FI-459986, response from HUD dated September 18, 2008). For a small number of cases in a small number of cities, the HUD data did not distinguish between demolition and "disposition" (sale of the unit). There were sixty-three cases of this, accounting for 5,489 units, or 4.5 percent of the database total. In these cases, I distributed the units evenly between demolition and disposition.

64. The sample of large cities was chosen by creating a list of the 150 most populous cities in the United States according to the 1990 census and then again by the 2000 census. These steps produced a list of 169 cities in total. Several of these places, however, are not central cities and have no history of involvement in the public housing program. The analysis that follows focuses only on the 137 central cities on the list. The data for this analysis were compiled from several sources. The record of demolitions and removals from HUD public housing inventory come from HUD (see note 64 above). Information on public housing in these cities was gathered from HUD's online database of assisted housing (HUD, *A Picture of Subsidized Households—1996*, http://www.huduser.org/datasets/assthsg/statedata96/index.htm). Information on the citywide characteristics of public housing was gathered for 1996, the earliest date available from this source. These data were supplemented by information from the 1990 census on housing, population, and economic characteristics of the city, FBI data on crime rates, and public finance data from the *Census of Governments* available through the "State of the Cities Data System" (http://socds.huduser.org/index.html).

65. "Poisson" regression techniques are appropriate when the dependent variable is a count, that is, a variable that cannot have a negative value—in this case the number of public housing units demolished in a given city.

66. See, e.g., Wyly and Hamel (1999), Smith (2006a), and Bennett and Reed (1999).

67. Powell (1995).

68. Reichl (1999).

69. Hackworth (2007) and others have suggested that public housing demolition is reminiscent of urban renewal for its role in downtown or near-downtown revitalization. Urban renewal was used by cities to physically clear the way for greater capital accumulation in cities. Friedland (1980), for example, found that urban renewal activity was related to downtown economic change and growth. The greatest reductions in public housing might be occurring in those cities that are most rapidly adapting to postindustrial economic environments. Wyly and Hamel (1999) identify HOPE VI redevelopment activity as central to contemporary patterns of gentrification in many cities. They argue that HOPE VI plans in cities with "vibrant housing market" activity incorporate new, mixed-income designs aimed at leveraging class transformations taking place nearby.

70. Newman (2004), Wyly and Hammel (1999).

3. DEMOLITION IN CHICAGO, NEW ORLEANS, AND ATLANTA

1. Hunt (2009, 230).

2. Ibid.

3. Studies documenting CHA's misdeeds and the extreme conditions of Chicago public housing are almost too numerous to count, but include Meyerson and Banfield's (1955) account of the early years of the program, and more recent updates by Hirsch (1998) and Hunt (2009), Popkin, Gwiasda, et al.'s (2000) study of the gang war and violence in CHA properties, and Venkatesh's (2000) ethnographic account of life in the Robert Taylor Homes.

4. Quoted in Hunt (2009, 261).

5. Quoted in Smith (2006b).

6. Business and Professional People for the Public Interest (2009, 12).

7. Hunt (2009).

8. Ibid.

9. Biles (2000, 149).

10. Remarks of Jack Markowski, commissioner of the Chicago Department of Housing, 1999 to 2007, at the symposium for "The Plan for Transformation at 10" held at the University of Illinois at Chicago, December 10–11, 2009 (personal notes of the author). These remarks were echoed at the same event by Doug Guthrie, a former CHA official, who talked about the "complete disconnect between CHA and other city departments." Former HUD secretary Henry Cisneros, at the same event, noted that PHAs were often the backwaters of city administration; posts were handed out as patronage and then ignored.

11. Kotlowitz (1992). See also Popkin, Gwiasda, et al. (2000).

12. A federal district court in *Pratt v. Chicago Housing Authority*, 848 F. Supp. 792 (N.D. Ill., 1994) suspended Lane's crime sweeps as a violation of the Fourth Amendment rights against warrantless searches.

13. Popkin, Gwiasda, et al. (2000).

14. Schill (1997).

15. *Henry Horner Mother's Guild v. CHA*, 824 F. Supp. 810 (N.D. Ill. 1993).

16. Hunt (2009, 277). This scene is reminiscent of Boston's Mayor Kevin White who in 1980 reacted to news of the Boston Housing Authority being put into receivership by saying, "that's all right. If they want it, they can have it." Quoted in Vale (2000, 348).

17. Smith (2006b) and Hunt (2009).

18. Smith (2006b).

19. Ibid. Prior to the announcement of the Plan for Transformation, the City of Chicago had received ten HOPE VI grants (including demolition-only grants) for six separate public housing sites (Cabrini-Green, Henry Horner Homes, ABLA, Robert Taylor Homes, Madden/Wells, and Washington Park). This activity was folded into the Plan and included as part of the Plan's goals.

20. Ibid.

21. The exact number of buildings and units to be demolished and the targeted number of replacement units have varied over time as redevelopment plans at individual sites have changed and as the PFT as a whole has evolved.

22. Wright (2006, 141).

23. Public remarks by Jack Markowski at "The Plan for Transformation at 10: The Symposium," December 10, 2009 (author's notes from the event).

24. Halasz (2008).

25. Wright et al. (1997).

26. Fisher (2003) and Illinois Assisted Housing Action Research Project (IHARP) (n.d.).

27. Fisher (2003).

28. *Wallace v. Chicago Housing Authority*, 298 F. Supp. 2d 710 (N.D. Ill. 2004). The independent monitor's report is Sullivan (2004).

29. IHARP (n.d.).

30. Lowenstein (2008).

31. Boyd (2008).

32. See ibid., Patillo (2007), and Hyra (2008).

33. See, e.g., Zielenbach (2003) and Turbov and Piper (2005).

34. Popkin, Rich, et al. (2012).

35. A similar process has been documented for Louisville, Kentucky. The Park-Duvalle HOPE VI project produced a significant reduction in crime in the neighborhood that encompasses the redevelopment. However, crime hot spots reemerged shortly after the redevelopment in other public housing developments across the city (see Suresh 2000).

36. Halasz (2008).

37. Ibid.

38. Rogal and Turner (2004).

39. Bloom (2008, 215).

40. Feldman and Stall (2004).

41. Smith (2006b, 109–10).

42. Wright (2006).

43. There had always been some tension between CPPH and the formal means of resident involvement in CHA management, the Local Advisory Committee (LAC) and CAC process. Resident representatives on LAC and CAC may have felt that CPPH was ignoring the established channels by which residents provided feedback and input to CHA activities. They may have felt that the leaders of CPPH were attempting to build rival constituencies. CPPH leaders attempted to minimize those tensions as much as possible, but the undeniable reality is that by its mere existence, CPPH was questioning the leadership of LAC and CAC representatives. See Wright (2006).

44. At the CHA's celebratory ten-year anniversary symposium for the Plan for Transformation, CAC member and CHA board member Myra King called for the moratorium. CHA officials in attendance did not respond to the call, nor was it mentioned in press reports of the event.

45. Ouroussoff (2006).

46. Mahoney (1990).

47. Ibid., 1280.

48. Reichl (1999).

49. Smith and Keller (1983).

50. NHLP (1990).

51. U.S. GAO (1996).

52. Reichl (1999, 172).

53. Ibid.

54. Cook and Lauria (1995).

55. NHLP (1990).

56. Arena (2012).

57. Ibid.

58. Washington et al. (n.d.).

59. Advancement Project (n.d.). Fair market rents define which private-sector apartments are eligible for occupancy with a housing choice voucher. If the FMR is too low there aren't enough rental units available for voucher holders to lease up.

60. Filosa and Russell (2005).

61. Ibid.

62. Pyles (2009, 109).

63. Cass and Whoriskey (2006).

64. Ibid.

65. Pyles (2009).

66. Jervis (2007).

67. Weaver (2007).

68. "Pelosi, Reid Ask Bush to Halt Demolition" (2007).

69. Wilbert (2007).

70. Filosa (2007a).

71. Filosa (2007b).

72. Filosa (2007a).

73. Hernandez (2008).

74. Foster (2008).

75. Associated Press (2011).

76. Cohen (2010).

77. See the account in Brinkley (2006).

78. See Seicshnaydre (2007) and Ratner (2008).

79. The Preston quote is from Filosa (2008).

80. Reckdahl (2009).

81. Reed and Steinberg (2006).

82. Brooks (2005).

83. Testimony of Yusef Freeman of McCormack Baron Salazar, before the Subcommittee on Housing and Community Opportunity Field Hearing, August 21, 2009, New Orleans, Louisiana. financialservices.house.gov/media/file/hearings/111/freeman.pdf.

84. Reckdahl (2008).

85. Reckdahl (2011).

86. Quoted in Keating and Flores (2000, 277).

87. Newman (2002).

88. Keating and Flores (2000, 277).

89. State of the Cities Data Systems, http://www.huduser.org/portal/datasets/socds.html.

90. Newman (2002).

91. Quoted in Keating and Flores (2000, 289).

92. Centre on Housing Rights and Evictions (2007).

93. Both quotes are taken from the website blog of Renee Glover, August 17, 2009. ahalessonslearned.blogspot.com/2009_08_01_archive.html.

94. "Federal Government Gives Approval for Demolition." Atlanta Housing Authority, News Release, July 3, 2008. http://www.atlantahousing.org/pressroom/index.cfm?Fuseaction=pressreleases_full&ID=24 Emphasis added.

95. Keating and Flores (2000).

96. Stirgus (2008).

97. Glover (2009a).
98. Newman (2002, 16).
99. Newman (2002).
100. Dries (2010b).
101. Newman (2002, 16).
102. Ibid., 17.
103. Oakley, Ruel, Reid, and Sims (2010).
104. Springston (2007).
105. Rich et al. (2010).
106. Testimony of Renee Glover before the United States House of Representatives Subcommittee for Housing and Community Opportunity, April 29, 2003, page 2. archives. financialservices.house.gov/media/pdf/042903rg.pdf.
107. Oakley, Ruel, and Wilson (n.d.).
108. Springston and Cardinale (2007).
109. Cardinale (2007a).
110. Cardinale (2007b).
111. Cardinale (2008).
112. Brown (2009, 16).
113. Massey and Denton (2003, 57).
114. Meyer (2000).
115. See Meyerson and Banfield (1955) and Hirsch (1998) for an early history of the city of Chicago's placement of public housing.

4. "NEGRO REMOVAL" REVISITED

1. Oakes and Pelton (1999).
2. Anderson (1964).
3. Mohl (2000).
4. Hunt (2009).
5. See Williams (2004) for an example of this dynamic in Baltimore, Maryland.
6. I estimate the racial impact of displacement by looking at the racial breakdown of public housing units prior to their demolition. HUD's *Picture of Subsidized Households* database (at http://www.huduser.org/portal/datasets/assthsg.html) provides the racial breakdown of public housing residents for the years 1996, 1997, 1998, and 2000. In general, I use the dataset that corresponds to the year prior to the demolition of a given project. Thus, for projects demolished in 1997, the 1996 database provides information on the resident mix in the project. No resident information is available for projects demolished prior to 1997. For all projects demolished after 2000 I use the most recently available database, the 2000 version.
7. In cases of partial demolition (e.g., a project with three high-rise towers in which only one is demolished), I assume that the racial breakdown of tenants in the demolished building is identical to that of the overall public housing development.
8. The first year of the analysis is because 1996 is the first year for which data on the racial occupancy of individual projects is available through the HUD database. For some cities in some years, no racial occupancy data are reported for any units.
9. The number of residents displaced is estimated by multiplying the average household size in each project by the number of occupied units.
10. This difference is statistically significant at $p < .05$.
11. This is a reasonable assumption, given that HOPE VI initially was limited to the largest and most troubled PHAs. Critics of the program have also argued that it has overreached its initial objective to redevelop the worst 6 percent of the public housing stock.

12. For this analysis the dependent variable is dichotomous, and I employ a fixed-effects logistic regression technique to assess the importance of various characteristics of the project for its ultimate status in 2007, either demolished or still standing. See the appendix for details.

13. NCSDPH (1992),

14. Olivio (2010).

15. See Weiss (1985).

16. Winslow (2010).

5. THE FATE OF DISPLACED PERSONS AND FAMILIES

1. Goetz (2010a).

2. The quotes used in this chapter come from interviews with Harbor View residents conducted between August 2004 and January 2006.

3. Varady and Walker's (2000) study of vouchering out is an exception to that, although the families displaced had been living in public housing.

4. Goetz (2009).

5. McCraven (1996).

6. These figures come from respondents to a survey taken two years after relocation. Twenty-two percent of residents indicated that they had wanted to move prior to the redevelopment, 55 percent said they did not want to move, and 23 percent said they were unsure.

7. Hilson Jr. (1995).

8. Fried (1963).

9. Fried and Bleicher (1961).

10. Fried (1963, 167).

11. Jones (2009).

12. Gans (1962, 309).

13. Fullilove (2005).

14. Ibid., 10.

15. Venkatech's description of social ties in the Robert Taylor Homes is an example. See also, Keene, Padilla, and Geronimus (2010).

16. Kleit and Manzo (2006); Manzo, Kleit, and Couch (2008); and Gibson (2007).

17. Trudeau (2006) makes this argument for families moved out of public housing in Buffalo who generally relocated nearby. See also Reed (2006).

18. Curley (2010a, 47).

19. Keene and Geronimus (2011).

20. Curley (2009).

21. This was written on a questionnaire given to former residents of Harbor View by the author.

22. Duluth Housing Authority (2002), attachment A, page 1, and attachment C, pages 42 and 43.

23. Fonger (2010).

24. "City Plans to Demolish Prospect Plaza Housing Complex in Brooklyn" (2010).

25. Weisel and Meagher (1996, 23).

26. Keene, Padilla, and Geronimus (2010, 278).

27. Dang (1996). See also Hilson Jr. (1995) quoting another resident saying, "I think it's not that bad living here, definitely not so bad where it's got to be torn down."

28. Wright (2006).

29. Feldman and Stall (2004). See also Pfeiffer (2006) on the belief of some Chicago residents that relocation would lead to homelessness.

30. Goetz (2003, 164).

31. Keating and Flores (2000).

32. Quoted in NHLP (2002, 7).

33. Keating and Flores (2000) argue that the residents of Techwood in Atlanta were told of homeownership options that were feasible for only a small number. The quote is from Lohr (2009).

34. Buron (2004).

35. Marquis and Ghosh (2008).

36. Engdahl (2009, 134).

37. Jones and Popke (2010, 126). The percentage varies from development to development, however. Curley (2010b) reports that almost half of the Maverick Gardens residents returned to the completed redevelopment.

38. Kohn (2003).

39. Olivo (2006).

40. See, e.g., Oakley, Reid, and Ruel (2011). See also Rich et al. (2010) and Harris et al. (2011).

41. See Comey (2007), Goetz (2003, 2010b), Gibson (2007), Clampet-Lundquist (2004), Varady and Walker (2000), Fisher (2003), Trudeau (2006).

42. See Comey (2007), Goetz (2003, 2010b), Johnson-Hart (2007), Gibson (2007), Clampet-Lundquist (2004), Varady and Walker (2000), Fisher (2003), Trudeau (2006), Robinson (2004). Overall, only 14 percent of relocatees in the five Urban Institute HOPE VI Panel Study cities moved outside of the central city.

43. Fisher (2003); see also Kataria and Johnson (2004).

44. Goetz (2003).

45. Trudeau (2006).

46. Kingsley et al. (2003).

47. An average of over five miles in Chicago; see Reed (2006).

48. Kleit and Galvez (2011, 400).

49. Stephens (2009).

50. Vogt (2009).

51. See Lowenstein (2008) and Patillo (2007).

52. Carson (1995).

53. This is one of the most consistent findings from all of the HOPE VI and public housing transformation literature; see, e.g., Curley (2010b), Buron et al. (2002), Clampet-Lundquist (2004), Fisher (2003), Goetz (2003, 2010b), Kingsley et al. (2003), Popkin et al. (2004), Fraser et al. (2005), Trudeau (2006), Boston (2005).

54. Kingsley et al. (2003).

55. See, e.g., Clampet-Lundquist (2004), Goetz (2010b).

56. Buron et al. (2002), Fraser et al. (2005), Boston (2005), Goetz (2003, 2010b), Clampet-Lundquist (2004).

57. Buron et al. (2002), Comey (2007).

58. See, for example, Goetz (2003).

59. Goetz (2003) finds that the subsequent moves of displaced families tended to be to neighborhoods with higher (and growing) poverty rates and higher (and growing) levels of racial segregation. Rich et al. (2010) find that the proportion of former residents living within a two-mile radius of the original McDaniel Glenn public housing site in Atlanta increased over time.

60. Comey (2007) finds that residents who have moved multiple times since being displaced by HOPE VI actually reduce their exposure to high poverty neighborhoods slightly.

61. Oakley and Burchfield (2009, 605). These findings echo the earlier work of Fisher (2003). Fisher reports only "slight improvements" in census-tract racial diversity among Chicago public housing relocates. Varady and Walker (2000) report the same for tenants vouchered out of HUD projects in four cities. Buron et al. (2002) find only modest

improvements in levels of racial segregation in receiving tracts for HOPE VI relocatees in the Panel Study sites.

62. Kingsley et al. (2003).

63. In a baseline study of households at a soon-to-be demolished HOPE VI site near Seattle, Manzo, Kleit, and Couch (2005, 20) found that residents expressed concerns about being accepted by neighbors in unfamiliar, white neighborhoods.

64. Harris et al. (2011, 21).

65. See Pendall (2000) on limits to the geographic distribution of vouchers.

66. Turner (1998), Smith (2002).

67. Manzo, Kleit, and Couch (2005).

68. Turner (1998), Goetz (2003), Smith (2002).

69. Popkin, Gwiasda, et al. (2000).

70. Respondents were asked whether the move from Harbor View was good or bad overall for the respondent and his or her family. The possible responses to this question were "very good for us," "mostly good for us," "both good and bad," "mostly bad," and "very bad for us." Descriptive analysis shows that the response most frequently selected was "both good and bad," which was selected by almost 46 percent of respondents. Slightly over 37 percent of respondents indicated that the move was either "very good" or "mostly good," while 9.5 percent indicated that the move was "mostly bad" and 7.6 percent indicated that the move was "very bad."

71. Levy and Woolley (2007) find no employment or earnings increases across all of the Urban Institute Panel Study sites for residents who were moved out of their old public housing projects due to HOPE VI redevelopment. Goetz (2002, 2010b) found no employment increases among public housing residents forced to moved in Minneapolis, or among HOPE VI relocatees in Duluth. Clampet-Lundquist (2004) found the same in Philadelphia, as did Curley (2010b) for Boston.

72. The lack of any effect on economic self-sufficiency is repeated for all forms of dispersal (see Kling, Liebman, and Katz 2007; Turney et al. 2006; Levy and Woolley 2007; Clampet-Lundquist 2004; Goetz 2002, 2010b; U.S. HUD 2004; Vigdor 2007). Across all five MTO cities, Kling, Liebman, and Katz (2007, 99) "found no significant evidence of treatment effects on earnings, welfare participation, or amount of government assistance after an average of five years since random assignment." Mobility seems not to be effective in increasing employment rates among low-income families in other contexts as well. Vigdor (2007) found that Hurricane Katrina displacees from New Orleans showed no employment, earnings, or income increases from their forced displacement, either.

73. HUD's own evaluation of the Welfare to Work Voucher program documented a negative impact on employment, an effect the evaluators attributed to the disruption caused by moving (U.S. HUD 2004).

74. Levy and Woolley (2007) point to the significant health problems (both physical and mental) of relocatees as the main barrier.

75. Various researchers have investigated the reasons for the lack of positive impact. Barret, Geisel, and Johnston (2006) found transportation and child care to be barriers to employment. Clampet-Lundquist (2004) suggests that the purported social capital benefits of dispersal, the argument that low-income families would benefit from a more diverse social network and one that is more integrated into the productive economy, simply do not occur. Individuals who had relied on friends or other local connections to gain employment when they lived in the pre-HOPE VI public housing development, did not report using the same techniques after moving to new neighborhoods. Involuntary displacement seems to have actually undermined the social capital strategies of the low-income families in her study. Other factors include the influence of family factors

(Oreopoulos 2003) and racial and ethnic discrimination in the job market (Carlson and Theodore 1997; Immergluck 1998).

76. Levy and Woolley (2007, 1). Kling, Liebman, and Katz (2007, 108) come to the same conclusion about MTO, a voluntary program that involves people who actively desire to move: "Housing mobility by itself does not appear to be an effective anti-poverty strategy, at least over a five-year horizon."

77. In Fort Worth, for example, Barrett, Geisel, and Johnston (2006) found that two-thirds of relocatees worry about having enough money for food, a large increase over predisplacement levels, and one-half reported fear of eviction due to their economic insecurity. Three out of five HOPE VI relocatees in the Urban Institute's Panel Study with vouchers reported difficulties paying rent or utilities within the previous year (Popkin 2006, 82). In Portland, one-third of HOPE VI displacees reported hardship making their rent payments and 60 percent reported difficulties paying for utilities (Gibson 2007). For many relocatees, utilities are a new expense and therefore a source of economic hardship. See also Curley (2010b).

78. Studies consistently show that families that move out of neighborhoods of concentrated poverty report benefits of increased sense of safety (see Popkin and Cove 2007; Kling, Liebman, and Katz 2007; Petit 2004; Gibson 2007; Goetz 2003, 2010b; Curley 2010b). The improved sense of safety is not universal; Gibson (2007) reports that 30 percent of displaced households in Portland's Columbia Villa HOPE VI project thought their new neighborhoods were safer while 18 percent felt they were less safe in their new neighborhoods.

79. Popkin and Cove (2007).

80. Rogal and Turner (2004). See also Jones (2009).

81. Clampet-Lundquist (2010).

82. Popkin and Cove (2007).

83. There is more evidence on this question from studies of voluntary relocation through the MTO program. Unfortunately, the evidence from MTO provides little support for the dispersal argument. Kling, Liebman, and Katz (2007) found no improvements for asthma, hypertension, physical limitations, or in general health among experimental group members five years after the program began. The only physical benefit that showed up among MTO movers was a reduction in obesity among experimental group members. Adults reported several mental health benefits from moving as did female youth. But the benefits experienced by female youth were matched by adverse effects on male youth. Clampet-Lundquist et al. (2006) find that among MTO movers, girls showed fewer high-risk behaviors than those in the control group, though there was no such effect among boys.

84. Popkin (2006).

85. Manjarrez, Popkin, and Guernsey (2007) for the findings on adult health, and Gallagher and Bajaj (2007) for the findings on children.

86. Keene and Padilla (2010).

87. Gallagher and Bajaj (2007) report no major changes in school engagement for children in five HOPE VI sites across the country. Jacob (2004) finds that children in households relocated due to HOPE VI-like public housing redevelopment in Chicago show no educational improvements relative to control group members on a range of academic achievement measures. Again, the news is no better for the MTO program (see, e.g., Kling, Liebman, and Katz 2007). In fact, Sanbonmatsu et al. (2006) found no significant effects on math or reading test scores, school behavior problems, or levels of engagement for any age grouping among MTO children aged six to twenty in 2002. This despite the fact that families in the experimental group moved to neighborhoods with "substantially less" poverty and they sent their children to higher-quality schools. The authors conclude that school achievement benefits from improved neighborhood environments "if they exist, are small" (686).

88. Popkin (2006, 82).

89. See Popkin (2006). For example, most Duluth respondents report a high level of satisfaction with most aspects of their housing; 73 percent were satisfied with the size of their housing unit (23 percent were dissatisfied), 92 percent were satisfied with the cost (and 6 percent dissatisfied), 72 percent were satisfied with the quality of their Harbor View apartment (22 percent dissatisfied). Residents were more likely to express satisfaction with the cost of the Harbor View apartments (92%) than with the quality (72%). Overall, 81 percent expressed satisfaction with their general housing situation. Interestingly, 68 percent of household heads were satisfied with the safety of the neighborhood, although this item registered the highest levels of dissatisfaction as well (28%). Eighty-eight percent were satisfied with the convenience of health care facilities, 68 percent were satisfied with the grocery stores in the neighborhood, and 68 percent were satisfied with the proximity of friends. When asked to give an overall assessment of the neighborhood, three-quarters of respondents said they were very satisfied or somewhat satisfied, while only 15 percent said they were dissatisfied. Most residents (65%) felt that they had moved to homes and neighborhoods to their liking, while 22 percent of respondents did not. Sixty-seven percent of the former residents stated that they had moved into the kind of home that they wanted.

90. Buron et al. (2002), Popkin et al. (2004, 30), Comey (2007). Brooks et al. (2005) find a similar outcome for HOPE VI relocatees in Atlanta, with families using Housing Choice Vouchers reporting higher levels of satisfaction. Goetz (2003) found that both voluntarily and involuntarily displaced residents of public housing in Minneapolis were more satisfied with the quality of their new housing than comparison groups. Satisfaction was greater among families who moved voluntarily.

91. Goetz (2003).

92. Manzo, Kleit, and Couch (2005).

93. Barrett, Geisel, and Johnston (2006) for Fort Worth, Texas. See similar findings from Seattle (Kleit and Manzo 2006); Minneapolis (Goetz 2003); Boston (Curley 2008); Philadelphia (Clampet-Lundquist 2010); and Tampa (Greenbaum et al. 2008).

94. Clampet-Lundquist (2004, 57), based on interviews with forty-one displaced Philadelphia HOPE VI families conducted two years after relocation

95. Clampet-Lundquist (2007).

96. See Joseph, Chaskin, and Webber (2007).

97. See Schwartz and Tajbakhsh (1997), Clark (2002), and Curley (2010a) for examples. There seems to be little in the record of forced displacement (or even in cases of voluntary displacement such as MTO) to suggest that relocated low-income families will fulfill the expectations of the dispersal model and form relationships with their (presumably higher-income) neighbors, thereby building "bridging" social capital critical to finding employment opportunities.

98. In a study of displaced families in Minneapolis, parents reported that their children were more socially isolated in their new neighborhoods (Goetz 2003), a finding repeated in the five-city HOPE VI Panel Study (Gallagher and Bajaj 2007). Petit (2004) finds no direct effects of moving on the social interactions of MTO families in Los Angeles. In fact, in findings that mirror those from HOPE VI, Petit finds that younger children are less socially connected in their new communities, and there are no differences for teenagers. Qualitative interviews suggest that financial hardships experienced by families who moved to low-poverty neighborhoods had a negative impact on the social connections of younger children.

99. Kleit and Manzo (2006) and Vale (1997). Families with greater place attachment in turn show fewer beneficial outcomes from relocation. Varady and Walker (2000) also note that residents in several older HUD projects were not pleased to have to move out when the conversion of subsidies to Housing Choice Vouchers resulted in their displacement.

100. Gibson (2007). The story is also told in the documentary *Imagining Home*, Hare in the Gate Productions, http://www.hareinthegate.com.

101. Goetz (2010b).

102. The evidence of the Duluth residents indicates that the likelihood of reporting positive outcomes in one area, such as a reduction in the fear of crime, is not associated with other positive outcomes (Goetz 2010b). The Urban Institute's Panel Study shows just this lack of correlation between a reduced fear of crime and employment gains. See Popkin and Cove (2007).

103. See Goetz, Skobba, and Yuen (2010).

104. Fauth (2004, 33).

105. Popkin et al. (2004).

106. Hartman (1964).

107. Goetz (2003). This is a major difference between HOPE VI and the voluntary mobility programs such as MTO and the Gautreaux program in Chicago. In the mobility programs, participants must move to neighborhoods below program-set thresholds for poverty or nonwhite population. In HOPE VI, displaced families move without such restrictions.

108. On the other hand, in Gautreaux and MTO, where participants *must* move away from such neighborhoods, families have had significant difficulties successfully leasing units. The dispersal impacts of voluntary programs are limited by the prevailing spatial distribution of fair market rents, the willingness of landlords to participate in the programs, and the difficulty of using housing vouchers in tight housing markets (see Ladd and Ludwig 1997). Fewer than half of the MTO experimental group members across the five cities were able to lease units (Kling, Liebman, and Katz 2007). In the Gautreaux program fewer than one-third of families were able to lease (Rubinowitz and Rosenbaum 2000).

109. Buron et al. (2002), Clampet-Lundquist (2004), and Trudeau (2006).

110. Fauth (2004), Clampet-Lundquist (2007), and Levy and Wooley (2007)

111. See Goetz and Chapple (2010) and Teitz and Chapple (1998).

112. Ellen and Turner (1997), Galster (2007), and Teitz and Chapple (1998).

113. Goetz (2010b) and Buron and Patrabansh (2008)

114. See Galster, Quercia, and Cortez (2000).

115. As Venkatesh and Celimli (2004) note, "nostalgia may be a factor, but the social supports they spent years, if not decades, building up are not easy to cast aside."

116. Edin and Lein (1997), Kelly (1994), Portes (1994).

117. Chapple (2001), Gilbert (1998), Hanson and Pratt (1995).

118. See Gibson (2007), Clampet-Lundquist (2004, 2007), and Kleit (2001, 2002). In Buffalo, families displaced from public housing actually chose to live in other segregated neighborhoods because of their support systems and space-time constraints in negotiating work and family obligations (Trudeau 2006).

119. Popkin and Cove (2007), Gibson (2007), Goetz (2003).

120. Ladd and Ludwig (1997), emphasis in the original.

6. EFFECTS AND PROSPECTS IN REVITALIZED COMMUNITIES

1. Clemetson (2002).

2. Ibid.

3. Epp (1998).

4. Dries (2010b).

5. Harris et al. (2011).

6. Turner (2009, 176).

7. Engdahl (2009).

8. Fenton and Daemmrich (2005). Castells (2010) found varying outcomes across Baltimore projects. The Heritage Crossing project, which replaced Murphy Homes, has not had a positive impact on the surrounding community, in part because of its physical isolation. But Broadway Terrace, which replaced Broadway Homes, has triggered price increases in the surrounding housing stock.

9. Wyly and Hammel (1999). See also Turner (2009) for the importance of more expansive public sector revitalization efforts accompanying public housing redevelopment.

10. Bair and Fitzgerald (2005).

11. University Partnership for Community and Economic Development (n.d.). See also Cloud and Roll (2011) for evidence of property value impact in Denver.

12. Castells (2010).

13. Zielenbach and Voith (2010).

14. U.S. General Accounting Office (2003).

15. Zielenbach (2003).

16. See also Zielenbach and Voith (2010), in which a decrease in crime is documented for three of four HOPE VI sites studied. Further, the University Partnership for Community and Economic Development's study of the Belmont Heights Estates (a HOPE VI redevelopment in Tampa, Florida) showed a decrease in crime in the neighborhood that exceeded the citywide reduction.

17. Turbov and Piper (2005).

18. Holin et al. (2003).

19. See Cloud and Roll (2011) and Cahill, Lowry, and Downey (2011).

20. Kingsley, Abravanel, et al. (2003, 33) and Turner (2009, 173).

21. U.S. HUD (2002b).

22. Ibid., 49.

23. Ibid., 6.

24. Heavens (2010).

25. Kingsley, Abravanel, et al. (2003, 37).

26. McGhee (2004).

27. Bagert (2002).

28. Fosburg, Popkin, and Locke (1996).

29. Eigelbach (2011).

30. Bennett and Reed (1999), Hyra (2008), and Patillo (2007).

31. Newman (2002).

32. Harvard Law Review (2003); see also Bennett and Reed (1999).

33. Bagart (2002), U.S. HUD (2002b).

34. U.S. HUD (2002b, 39).

35. Zielenbach (2002).

36. U.S. GAO (2003).

37. U.S. HUD (2002b, 36).

38. Wyly and Hammel (1999).

39. The analysis is based on the author's assembled data on HOPE VI redevelopment projects. Information on project characteristics was obtained from various sources, including HUD and local housing authorities. Address information was obtained from HUD and verified through direct observation, online sources, and from local housing authorities. The projects were geocoded and census data from the 1990 and 2000 decennial censuses were collected for the areas surrounding the projects. A HOPE VI project is defined as the full set of redevelopment-related activities that take place at spatially separate public housing developments. A single HOPE VI project may receive multiple HOPE VI grants (and several do). Different public housing developments that share physical space are deemed

to be a single project for the purposes of this analysis. So, for example, the ABLA projects in Chicago are four separate public housing developments, with thirty-six hundred apartments in a single contiguous location on the city's Near West Side. For this study, ABLA, which received eight separate HOPE VI grants, is considered a single project. In this study, "neighborhood" is defined as all the census block groups whose centroid is within a half-mile radius of the HOPE VI project address. These trapezoidal areas were truncated wherever significant manmade or natural boundaries occurred, such as rivers or major highways. Once the relevant block groups were identified, the Geolytics Neighborhood Census database was used to collect social, physical, and economic characteristics for the neighborhoods in 1990 and 2000. The Geolytics database standardizes census boundaries across the two census years, allowing for comparison of identical spatial areas.

40. See Patillo (2007), Hyra (2008), Boyd (2008), Moore (2009), and Weber (2002).

41. Hyra (2008) and Patillo (2007).

42. Hyra (2008, 130).

43. Patillo (2007, 207–8) quotes one public housing resident's reaction to the opposition of black middle class residents on Chicago's South Side to rebuilding public housing in the neighborhood: "It hurted me so bad because I never would think that our own people would feel that way. You know you look for different races to feel that way but not your own people. I've never seen anything like it before in my life, not amongst our own people anyway. It was horrible. And I took my daughter with me because I told her, I said, 'I want you to understand and see for yourself exactly how your own people will treat you when it comes to certain things.' And I told her, I say, 'especially when they feel that they are above you.'"

44. Jargowsky (1996).

45. Because I wish to detect the degree of neighborhood change that is induced by public housing redevelopment I control for changes taking place more broadly within the city. Thus, I look at the degree of neighborhood change relative to changes taking place at the city level. I measure displacement as a decline in the neighborhood of a given population (poverty households and the African American population) at a rate greater than is occurring in the city at large. A simple measure of the relative change in the African American population, for example, is computed as follows: (CB2K–CB90)–(NB2K–NB90), where CB2K=percentage of citywide population that is black in 2000; CB90=percentage of citywide population that is black in 1990; NB2K=percentage of neighborhood population that is black in 2000, and NB90=percentage of neighborhood population that is black in 1990. This produces a difference-in-difference score in which a positive value indicates greater decline in the black population at the neighborhood level than was experienced at the citywide scale.

46. The data are shown only for those projects that moved to relocation during the 1990s. The distribution of projects along these two dimensions is similar for projects that progressed as far as demolition in the 1990s.

7. CONCLUSION

1. The HOPE VI experience in the United States also provides support for Roisman's (2001) argument that a policy focus on economic desegregation is unlikely to produce a significant degree of racial desegregation.

2. See Engdahl (2009, 135) describing Louisville losing track of hundreds in the Cotter and Lang redevelopment, and Keating (2000) describing Atlanta and Techwood.

3. Hardiman et al. (2010).

4. Ibid., 5.

5. Overton (2010).

6. Schneider and Joyner (2010).

7. Horner (2011).

8. NCSDPH (1992, 2).

9. Ibid., 3.

10. Ibid., 16.

11. Glover (2009b, 146).

12. Vale (2000).

13. Popkin et al. (2000).

14. Venkatesh (2000), Williams (2004), Feldman and Stall (2004).

15. Glover (2009a).

16. Stacy Seischnaydre makes a similar argument in the context of post-Katrina New Orleans, suggesting that the public housing transformation movement has presented "a false dichotomy that would have us choose between affordable housing supplied on a segregated basis or none at all....In other words, this fallacy would require us to choose either to reopen public housing exactly as it existed before the storm...or adopt a redevelopment agenda that would result in drastic reductions in the number of affordable housing units available to low-income people" Seischnaydre (2007, 1268).

17. See Ouroussoff's (2006) architectural defense of Iberville.

18. Vale (2000).

19. Wilen and Nayak (2006).

20. Castaneda (2010).

21. Davis (2010).

22. Poverty and Race Research Action Council (2008).

23. Emphasis added. Cisneros (2009, 13).

References

Abrams, Charles. 1967. "Urban Renewal Realistically Reappraised." In *Urban Renewal: People, Politics and Planning*, edited by Jewel Bellush and Murray Hausknecht. New York: Anchor Books.

Advancement Project. N.d. "Primer on New Orleans Public Housing." www.advance mentproject.org.

Anderson, Martin. 1964. *The Federal Bulldozer*. Boston: MIT Press.

Andreatta, David. 2010. "Housing Authority Eyes Plan as a Private Landlord." *Democrat and Chronicle*, February 26. http://www.democratandchronical.com/fdcp/ !1267223072116.

Arena, Jay. 2012. *Driven from New Orleans: How Nonprofits Betray Public Housing and Promote Privatization*. Minneapolis: University of Minnesota Press.

Associated Press. 2011. "New Orleans Receives Money to Redevelop Iberville Housing Complex." *New Orleans City Business.com*, September 1. http:// neworleanscitybusiness.com/blog/2011/09/01new-orleans-receives-money-to-redevelop-iberville-housing-complex/.

Atlanta Housing Authority. 2010. "About Us: Our President and CEO." http://www.atlantahousing.org/profile/index.cfm?fuseaction=ceo.

Bagart, Brod, Jr. 2002. "HOPE VI and St. Thomas: Smoke, Mirrors and Urban Mercantilism." London: London School of Economics.

Bailey, Darlyne, Sharon Milligan, and Linda Persce. 1996. "HOPEVI Baseline Case Study: King Kennedy Estates and Outhwaite Homes, Cleveland, OH." In *An Historical and Baseline Assessment of HOPE VI: Volume II Case Studies*. Washington, D.C.: U.S. Department of Housing and Urban Development.

Bair, Edward, and John M. Fitzgerald. 2005. "Hedonic Estimation and Policy Significance of the Impact of HOPE VI on Neighborhood Property Values." *Review of Policy Research* 22 (6): 771–86.

Baron, Richard D. 2009. "The Evolution of HOPE VI as a Development Program." In *From Despair to Hope: HOPE VI and the New Promise of Public Housing in America's Cities*, edited by Henry G. Cisneros and Lora Engdahl, 31–48. Washington, D.C.: Brookings Institution.

Barrett, Edith J., Paul Geisel, and Jan Johnston. 2006. *The Ramona Utti Report: Impacts of the Ripley Arnold Relocation Program: Year 3 (2004–5)*. Paper prepared for the City of Fort Worth, Texas.

Bauer, Catherine. 1957. "The Dreary Deadlock of Public Housing." *Architectural Forum* 106 (5–6).

Baxandall, Rosalyn F., and Elizabeth Ewen. 2001. *Picture Windows: How the Suburbs Happened*. New York: Basic Books.

Bennett, Larry, and Adolph Reed Jr. 1999. "The New Face of Urban Renewal: The Near North Redevelopment Initiative and the Cabrini-Green Neighborhood." In *Without Justice for All: The New Liberalism and Our Retreat from Racial Equality*, edited by Adolph Reed Jr., 175–211. Boulder, CO: Westview Press.

Berry, Brian J. 1985. "Islands of Renewal in Seas of Decay." In *The New Urban Reality*, edited by Paul E. Peterson, 69–96. Washington, D.C.: Brookings Institute Press.

Biles, Roger. 2000. "Public Housing and the Post-War Urban Renaissance, 1949–1973."
   In *From Tenements to the Taylor Homes: In Search of an Urban Housing Policy in
   Twentieth Century America*, edited by John F. Bauman, Roger Biles, and Kristin
   M. Szylvian. University Park: Pennsylvania State University Press.
Bloom, Nicholas Dagen. 2008. *Public Housing That Worked: New York in the Twentieth
   Century*. Philadelphia: University of Pennsylvania Press.
Boston, Thomas D. 2005. "The Effects of Mixed-Income Revitalization and Residential
   Mobility on Public Housing Residents: A Case Study of the Atlanta Housing
   Authority." *Journal of the American Planning Association* 71 (4): 1–19.
Boyd, Michelle. 2008. *Jim Crow Nostalgia: Reconstructing Race in Bronzeville*.
   Minneapolis: University of Minnesota Press.
Bratt, Rachel. 1986. "Public Housing: The Controversy and Contribution." In *Critical
   Perspectives on Housing*, edited by Rachel G. Bratt, Chester Hartman, and Ann
   Meyerson. Philadelphia: Temple University Press.
Brenner, Neil, and Nik Theodore. 2002. *Spaces of Neoliberalism: Urban Restructuring in
   North America and Western Europe*. Malden, MA: Blackwell.
Brinkley, Douglas. 2006. *The Great Deluge: Hurricane Katrina, New Orleans, and the
   Mississippi Gulf Coast*. New York: Harper Collins.
Brooks, David. 2005. "Katrina's Silver Lining." *New York Times*, September 8. http://
   www.nytimes.com/2005/09/08/opinion/08brooks.html.
Brooks, Fred, Carole Zugazaga, James Wolk, and Mary A. Adams. 2005. "Resident Per-
   ceptions of Housing, Neighborhood, and Economic Conditions after Relocation
   from Public Housing Undergoing HOPE VI Redevelopment." *Research on Social
   Work Practice* 15 (6): 481–90.
Brown, Curt. 2006. "St. Paul Feels Affordable Housing Pinch." *Minneapolis Star
   Tribune*, September 28.
Brown, Robbie. 2009. "Atlanta Is Making Way for New Public Housing." *New York
   Times*, June 21, 16.
Buron, Larry. 2004. "An Improved Living Environment? Neighborhood Outcomes
   for HOPE VI Relocatees." Urban Institute Policy Brief No. 3, September.
   Washington, D.C.: Urban Institute.
Buron, Larry, and Satyendra Patrabansh. 2008. "Are Census Variables Highly Cor-
   related with Housing Choice Vouchers Holders' Perception of the Quality of
   Their Neighborhoods?" *Cityscape: A Journal of Policy Development and Research*
   10 (1): 157–83.
Buron, Larry, Susan Popkin, Diane Levy, Laura Harris, and Jill Khadduri. 2002. *The
   HOPE VI Resident Tracking Study*. Washington, D.C.: Urban Institute.
Burt, Cecily. 2008. "Oakland Housing Agency Reassures Tenants Who Fear Section 8
   Voucher Plans." *Oakland Tribune*, September 24. http://www.insidebayarea.
   com/localnews/ci_10551818.
Business and Professional People for the Public Interest. 2009. *The Third Side: A Mid-
   Course Report on Chicago's Transformation of Public Housing*. Chicago: BPPPI.
Cahill, Meagan, Samantha Lowry, and P. Mitchell Downey. 2011. *Movin' Out: Crime
   Displacement and HUD's HOPE VI Initiative*. Washington, D.C.: Urban Institute
   Justice Policy Center.
Calthorpe, Peter. 2009. "HOPE VI and New Urbanism." In *From Despair to Hope:
   HOPE VI and the New Promise of Public Housing in America's Cities*, edited by
   Henry G. Cisneros and Lora Engdahl, 49–64. Washington, D.C.: Brookings
   Institution Press.
Calthorpe Associates. N.d. "Curtis Park HOPE VI Revitalization Project." Unpublished
   manuscript. On file with author.

Cardinale, Matthew. 2007a. "AHA Quietly Passes Eviction Plan amidst Shouting, Public Unaware." *Atlanta Progressive News,* April 27. http://www.atlanta progressivenews.com/interspire/news/2007/04/29/aha-quietly-passes-eviction-plan-amidst-shouting-public-unaware.html.

———. 2007b. "AHA Deceives Residents, Prepares Evictions without HUD Approval." *Atlanta Progressive News,* December 16. http://www.atlantaprogressivenews. com/interspire/news/2007/12/16/aha-deceives-residents-prepares-evictions-without-hud-approval.html.

———. 2008. "Seniors, Resident Leaders Ask HUD to Postpone Demolition Review." *Atlanta Progressive News,* May 2. http://www.atlantaprogressivenews.com/ interspire/news/2008/05/02/seniors-resident-leaders-ask-hud-to-postpone-demolition-review.html.

Carlson, Virginia, and Nikolas Theodore. 1997. "Employment Availability for Entry-Level Workers: An Examination of the Spatial Mismatch Hypothesis in Chicago." *Urban Geography* 18 (3): 228–42.

Carson, Larry. 1995. "Ruppersberger's Outcry May Help Him Politically." *Baltimore Sun,* October 19. http://articles.baltimoresun.com/1995-10-19/ news/1995292129_1_ruppersberger-county-executive-baltimore-county.

Cass, Julia, and Peter Whoriskey. 2006. "New Orleans to Raze Public Housing." *Washington Post,* December 8, A03. http://www.washingtonpost.com/wp-dyn/ content/article/2006/12/07/AR2006120701482.html.

Castaneda, Adrian. 2010. "The State of Black SF." *San Francisco Bay Guardian,* February 4. http://www.sfbg.com/politics/2010/02/04/state-black-sf.

Castells, Nina. 2010. "HOPE VI Neighborhood Spillover Effects in Baltimore." *Cityscape: A Journal of Policy Development and Research* 12 (1): 65–99.

Centre on Housing Rights and Evictions (COHRE). 2007. *Fair Play for Housing Rights: Mega-events, Olympic Games and Housing Rights.* Geneva, Switzerland: COHRE.

Chapple, Karen. 2001. "Time to Work: Job Search Strategies and Commute Time for Women on Welfare in San Francisco." *Journal of Urban Affairs* 23 (2): 155–73.

Cisneros, Henry. 1995. *Regionalism: The New Geography of Opportunity.* Washington, D.C.: U.S. Department of Housing and Urban Development.

———. 2009. "A New Moment for People and Cities." In *From Despair to Hope: HOPE VI and the New Promise of Public Housing in America's Cities,* edited by Henry G. Cisneros and Lora Engdahl, 3–14. Washington, D.C.: Brookings Institution Press.

"Cisneros Urges Demolition of High-Rise Projects." 1994. *Baltimore Sun,* May 3. http://articles.baltimoresun.com/1994-05-03/news/1994123189_1_cisneros-projects-middle-class-neighborhoods.

"City Plans to Demolish Prospect Plaza Housing Complex in Brooklyn." 2010. http://blogs.villagevoice.com/runningscared/archives/2010/01/city_plans. February 7.

Clampet-Lundquist, Susan. 2004. "Moving Over or Moving Up? Short-Term Gains and Losses for Relocated HOPE VI Families." *Journal of Policy Development and Research* 7 (1): 57–80.

———. 2007. "No More 'Bois Ball: The Effect of Relocation from Public Housing on Adolescents." *Journal of Adolescent Research* 22 (3): 298–323.

———. 2010. "'Everyone Had Your Back': Social Ties, Perceived Safety, and Public Housing Relocation." *City & Community* 9 (1): 87–108.

Clampet-Lundquist, Susan, Kathryn Edin, Jeffrey R. Kling, and Greg J. Duncan. 2006. "Moving At-Risk Teenagers out of High-Risk Neighborhoods: Why Girls Fare Better Than Boys." Princeton IRS Working Paper 509.

218   **REFERENCES**

Clark, Sherri. 2002. "Where the Poor Live: How Federal Housing Policy Shapes
    Residential Communities." *Urban Anthropology* 31 (1): 69–92.
Clemetson, Lynette. 2002. "A Black Enclave in Pittsburgh Is Revived." *New York Times*,
    August 9. http://nytimes.com/2002/08/09/national09HILL.html?
    pagewanted=all.
Cloud, William, and Susan Roll. 2011. "Denver Housing Authority's Park Avenue
    HOPE VI Revitalization Project: Community Impact Results." *Housing Policy
    Debate* 21 (2): 191–214.
Cohen, Ariella. 2010. "Even with Plenty of Subsidized Housing, Most Still Clustered in
    Poorest Areas." *The Lens*, November 14. http://thelensnola.org/2010/11/
    11hano-vouchers-locations/.
Comey, Jennifer. 2007. *HOPE VI'd and On the Move.* Brief No. 1. Washington, D.C.:
    Metropolitan Housing and Communities Center, Urban Institute.
Connerly, Charles E. 1986. "What Should Be Done with the Public Housing Program?"
    Journal of the American Planning Association 52 (2): 142–55.
Cook, Christine, and Mickey Lauria. 1995. "Urban Regeneration and Public Housing
    in New Orleans." *Urban Affairs Review* 30 (4): 538–57.
Cove, Elizabeth, Margery Austin Turner, Xavier de Souza Briggs, and Cynthia
    Duarte. 2008. *Can Escaping from Poor Neighborhoods Increase Employment and
    Earnings?* Washington, D.C.: Urban Institute.
Cuomo, Andrew. 1999. "Remarks by Secretary Andrew Cuomo to the Public Housing
    Authorities Directors Association." September 17. http://archives.hud.gov/
    remarks/cuomo/speeches/phadasph.cfm.
Curley, Alexandra M. 2008. "A New Place, A New Network? Social Capital Effects of
    Residential Relocation for Poor Women." In *Networked Urbanism,* edited by
    T. Blokland and M. Savage. Aldershot: Ashgate.
———. 2009. "Draining or Gaining? The Social Networks of Public Housing Movers
    in Boston." *Journal of Social and Personal Relationships* 26 (2–3): 227–47.
———. 2010a. "Neighborhood Institutions, Facilities, and Public Space: A Miss-
    ing Link for HOPE VI Residents' Development of Social Capital?" *Cityscape:
    A Journal of Policy Development and Research* 12 (1): 33–63.
———. 2010b. "HOPE VI–A Viable Strategy for Improving Neighborhood Conditions
    and Resident Self-Sufficiency? The Case of Maverick Gardens in Boston."
    Housing Policy Debate 20 (2): 237–94.
Currie, Janet, and Aaron Yelowitz. 2000. "Are Public Housing Projects Good for Kids?"
    Journal of Public Economics 75: 99–124.
Dang, Dan Thanh. 1996. "Good, Bad Memories Tumble Down as Lexington Terrace High-
    Rises Implode." *Baltimore Sun,* July 28. http://articles.baltimoresun.com/1996-07-
    28/news/1996210098_1_lexington-terrace-demolition-terrace-residents.
Danziger, Sheldon, and Peter Gottschalk. 1987. "Earnings Inequality: The Spatial
    Concentration of Poverty, and the Underclass." *American Economic Review*
    77 (2): 211–15.
Davies, Richard O. 1966. *Housing Reform during the Truman Administration.*
    Columbia: University of Missouri Press.
Davis, Janel. 2010. "Last Marietta Housing Project to Be Demolished, Residents to Be
    Relocated with Vouchers." *Atlanta Journal-Constitution*, September 8. http://
    www.ajc.com/news/cobb/last-marietta-housing-project-609375.html.
Dries, Bill. 2009. "City Closer to Erasing Public Housing." *Memphis Daily News*,
    September 24. http://www.memphisdailynews.com/editorial/Article.
    aspx?id=44959.

———. 2010a. "Developer Calls for More HOPE VI Projects." *Memphis Daily News*, October 4. http://www.memphisdailynews.com/editorial/ArticleEmail. aspx?id=53227.

———. 2010b. "IDB Approves $45 Million for Downtown Hilton." *Memphis Daily News*, July 23. http://www.memphisdailynews.com/editorial/Article. aspx?id=5150.

Duluth Housing Authority. 2002. *Harbor View HOPE VI Grant Application*. Duluth, MN: Duluth Housing and Redevelopment Authority.

Edin, Kathryn, and Laura Lein. 1997. *Making Ends Meet: How Single Mothers Survive Welfare and Low-Wage Work*. New York: Russell Sage Foundation.

Eigelbach, Kevin. 2011. "Replacing Clarskdale Project with Liberty Green Has Been a Plus for East Market Neighborhood." *Business First*, January 21. http://www. bizjournals.com/louisville/print-edition/211/01/21/replacing-clarksdale-project-with.html?page=all.

Ellen, Ingrid Gould, and Margery Austin Turner. 1997. "Does Neighborhood Matter? Assessing Recent Evidence." *Housing Policy Debate* 8 (4): 833–66.

Engdahl, Lora. 2009. "The Villages of Park DuValle, Louisville." In *From Despair to Hope: HOPE VI and the New Promise of Public Housing in America's Cities*, edited by Henry G. Cisneros and Lora Engdahl, 121–41. Washington, D.C.: Brookings Institution Press.

Epp, Gayle. 1998. "Emerging Strategies for Revitalizing Public Housing Communities." In *New Directions in Urban Public Housing*, edited by David P. Varady, Wolfgang F. E. Preiser, and Francis P. Russell, 121–41. New Brunswick, N.J.: Center for Urban Policy Research.

Fauth, Rebecca C. 2004. "The Impacts of Neighborhood Poverty Deconcentration Efforts on Low-Income Children's and Adolescents' Well-Being." *Children, Youth, and Environments* 14 (1): 1–55.

Feldman, Roberta M., and Susan Stall. 2004. *The Dignity of Resistance: Women Residents' Activism in Chicago Public Housing*. Cambridge: Cambridge University Press.

Fenton, Justin, and JoAnna Daemmrich. 2005. "New Hopes for Public Housing Suffer as Old Woes Resurface." *Baltimore Sun*, August 19. http://articles.baltimoresun. com/2005-08-19/news/0508190012_1_slater-lafayette-pleasant-view-gardens.

Filosa, Gwen. 2007a. "Live Updates on Demolition Vote from Council Chambers." http://www.nola.com/news/index.ssf/2007/12/city_hall_girds_for_public_hou. html.

———. 2007b. "Mayor Applauds Council's Vote." *Times-Picayune*, December 20. http://www.nola.com/news/index.ssf/2007/12/mayor_applauds_councils_vote. html.

———. 2008. "New HUD Chief Says New Orleans Public Housing Is Back on Track." *Times-Picayune*, June 30. http://www.nola.com/news/index.ssf/2008/06/new_ hud_chief_says_new_orleans_2.html.

Filosa, Gwen, and Gordon Russell. 2005. "Public Housing Takes a Blow to the Gut." *Times-Picayune*, October 9.

Fischer, Will. 2006. "Public Housing Squeezed between Higher Utility Costs and Stagnant Funding." Washington, D.C.: Center on Budget and Policy Priorities.

Fisher, Paul. 2003. "Where Are the Public Housing Families Going? An Update." http:// www.viewfromtheground.com/view.cfm/stories/sullivanreports.html.

Fisher, Robert M. 1959. *Twenty Years of Public Housing: Economic Aspects of the Federal Program*. New York: Harper and Brothers.

Fonger, Ron. 2010. "Records Show Flint Housing Commission Complexes Failing to Meet Minimum Standards." *Flint Journal,* May 16. http://www.mlive.com/news/flint/index.ssf/2010/050records_show_flint_housing_com.html.

Fosburg, L. B., Susan J. Popkin, and G. Locke. 1996. *An Historical and Baseline Assessment of HOPE VI. Volume I: Cross-Site Report.* Washington, D.C.: U.S. Department of Housing and Urban Development.

Foster, Margaret. 2008. "In New Orleans, Demolition Begins on Public Housing." National Trust for Historic Preservation. March 13. http://www.preservationnation.org/magazine/2008/todays-news/in-ne.

Franck, Karen A. 1998. "Changing Values in U.S. Public Housing Policy and Design." In *New Directions in Urban Public Housing,* edited by David P. Varady, Wolfgang F. E. Preiser, and Francis P. Russell, 85–103. New Brunswick, N.J.: Center for Urban Policy Research.

Fraser, James, William Rohe, Shannon Van Zandt, and Chris Warren. 2005. *Few Gardens HOPE VI Evaluation: Baseline Values for Economic Development and Neighborhood Revitalization.* Report for the Durham Housing Authority. Chapel Hill: Center for Urban and Regional Studies, University of North Carolina.

Freedman, Leonard. 1969. *Public Housing: The Politics of Poverty.* New York: Holt, Rinehart and Winston.

Fried, Marc. 1963. "Grieving for a Lost Home: Psychological Costs of Relocation." In *The Urban Condition,* edited by Leonard J. Duhl. New York, Basic Books,.

Fried, Marc, and Peggy Bleicher. 1961. "Some Sources of Residential Satisfaction in an Urban Slum." *Journal of the American Institute of Planners* 27: 305–15.

Friedland, Roger. 1980. "Corporate Power and Urban Growth: The Case of Urban Renewal." *Politics and Society* 10 (2): 203–22.

Friedman, Lawrence M. 1968. *Government and Slum Housing.* Chicago: Rand McNally.

Frost, Janelle. 2010. "Forced Moves Anger Atlantic Beach Public Housing Residents." *Sun News,* July 8. http://www.thesunnews.com/2010/07/08/1575640/forced-moves-anger-ab.html.

Fuerst, J. S. 2005. *When Public Housing Was Paradise: Building Community in Chicago.* Champaign, IL: University of Illinois Press

Fullilove, Mindy T. 2005. *Root Shock: How Tearing Up City Neighborhoods Hurts America, and What We Can Do about It.* New York: Ballantine Books.

Gallagher, Megan, and Beata Bajaj. 2007. "Moving On: Benefits and Challenges of HOPE VI for Children." June. Brief No. 4. Washington, D.C.: Metropolitan Housing and Communities Center, Urban Institute.

Galster, George. 2007. "Neighbourhood Social Mix as a Goal of Housing Policy: A Theoretical Analysis." *European Journal of Housing Policy* 7 (1): 19–43.

Galster, George C., Roberto G. Quercia, and Alvaro Cortes. 2000. "Identifying Neighborhood Thresholds: An Empirical Exploration." *Housing Policy Debate* 11 (3): 701–32.

Gans, Herbert. 1962. *The Urban Villagers: Group and Class in the Life of Italian-Americans.* New York: Free Press.

Gelfand, Mark I. 1976. *A Nation of Cities: The Federal Government and Urban America, 1933–1965.* New York: Oxford University Press.

Gentry, Richard C. 2009. "How HOPE VI Has Helped Reshape Public Housing." In *From Despair to Hope: HOPE VI and the New Promise of Public Housing in America's Cities,* edited by Henry G. Cisneros and Lora Engdahl, 205–27. Washington, D.C.: Brookings Institution Press.

Gibson, Karen J. 2007. "The Relocation of the Columbia Villa Community: Views from Residents." *Journal of Planning Education and Research* 27 (1): 5–19.

Gilbert, M. 1998. "'Race,' Space, and Power: The Survival Strategies of Working Poor Women." *Annals of the Association of American Geographers* 88: 595–621.

Glover, Renee. 2009a. "The Toxic Impact of Concentrated Poverty." http://ahalessonslearned.blogspot.com/2009/08/toxic-impact-of-concentrated-poverty_17.html.

———. 2009b. "The Atlanta Blueprint: Transforming Public Housing Citywide." In *From Despair to Hope: HOPE VI and the New Promise of Public Housing in America's Cities*, edited by Henry G. Cisneros and Lora Engdahl, 145–68. Washington, D.C.: Brookings Institution Press.

Goering, John. 2003. "Political Origins and Opposition." In *Choosing a Better Life? Evaluating the Moving to Opportunity Social Experiment*, edited John Goering and Judith D. Feins, 37–57. Washington, D.C.: Urban Institute Press.

Goering, John, and Feins, J. 2003. *Choosing a Better Life? Evaluating the Moving to Opportunity Social Experiment*. Washington, D.C.: Urban Institute Press.

Goetz, Edward G. 2002. "Forced Relocation vs. Voluntary Mobility: The Effects of Dispersal Programmes on Households." *Housing Studies* 17 (1): 107–23.

———. 2003. *Clearing the Way: Deconcentrating the Poor in Urban America*. Washington, D.C.: Urban Institute Press.

———. 2009. *The Harbor View Hillside HOPE VI Revitalization Evaluation*. Submitted to the Housing and Redevelopment Authority of Duluth. Minneapolis: University of Minneapolis, Humphrey Institute of Public Affairs.

———. 2010a. "Desegregation in 3D: Displacement, Dispersal, and Development in American Public Housing." *Housing Studies* 25 (2):137-158.

———. 2010b. "Better Neighborhoods, Better Outcomes? Explaining Relocation Outcomes in HOPE VI." *Cityscape: A Journal of Policy Development and Research* 12 (1): 5–31.

Goetz, Edward G., and Karen Chapple. 2010. "'You Gotta Move': Advancing the Debate on the Record of Disposal." *Housing Policy Debate* 20 (2): 209–36.

Goetz, Edward G., Kimberly Skobba, and Cynthia Yuen. 2010. *The Impact of Subsidized Housing on Very Low Income Persons*. Report to the McKnight Foundation. Minneapolis: Humphrey Institute of Public Affairs, University of Minnesota.

Goldstein, Ira, and William L. Yancey. 1986. "Public Housing Projects, Blacks, and Public Policy: The Historical Ecology of Public Housing in Philadelphia." In *Housing Desegregation and Federal Policy*, edited by John M. Goering, 262–89. Chapel Hill: University of North Carolina Press.

Gordon, Diana R. 1994. *The Return of the Dangerous Classes: Drug Prohibition and Policy Politics*. New York: W. W. Norton.

Greenbaum, Susan, Wendy Hathaway, Cheryl Rodriguez, Ashley Spalding, and Beverly Ward. 2008. "Deconcentration and Social Capital: Contradictions of a Poverty Alleviation Policy." *Journal of Poverty* 12 (2): 201–28.

Gutzmann, Jon. 2004. Speech Accepting the Community Builders Award from Habitat for Humanity, April 13. http://www.stpaulpha.org/forms/issues_address_Habitat%20Award%202004.pdf.

Hackworth, Jason. 2002. "Post-Recession Gentrification in New York City." *Urban Affairs Review* 37: 815–43.

———. 2007. *The Neoliberal City: Governance, Ideology, and Development in American Urbanism*. Ithaca, N.Y.: Cornell University Press.

Hackworth, Jason, and Neil Smith. 2001. "The Changing State of Gentrification." *Tijdschrift voor Economische en Sociale Geografie* 92: 464–77.

Halasz, Erin. 2008. "As Murder Migrates, Neighbors Point to High-Rise Demolition." Medill Reports, Northwestern University. http://news.medill.northwestern.edu/chicago/news.aspx?id=89113.

Hall, Stephen, and Rob Rowlands. 2005. "Place Making and Large Estates: Theory and Practice." In *Restructuring Large Housing Estates in Europe*, edited by Ronald van Kempen, Karien Dekker, Stephen Hall, and Ivan Tosics. Bristol, U.K.: Policy Press.

Hanson, Susan, and Geraldine Pratt. 1995. *Gender, Work, and Space.* New York: Routledge.

Hardiman, David L. Carolyn Lynch, Marge Martin, Barry L. Steffen, David A. Vandenbroucke, and Yung Gann David Yao. 2010. *Worst Case Housing Needs 2007: A Report to Congress.* Washington, D.C.: U.S. Department of Housing and Urban Development.

Harris, Laura, Stanley Hyland, T. Buchanan, and Phyllis Betts. 2011. "Evaluation for Lamar Terrace/University Place HOPE VI: Final Report." Memphis, TN: School of Urban Affairs and Public Policy, University of Memphis.

Hartman, Chester. 1964. "The Housing of Relocated Families." *Journal of the American Institute of Planners* 30 (4): 266–86.

———. 1995. "Roberta Achtenberg: HUD Assistant Secretary for Fair Housing and Equal Opportunity." *Shelterforce* 17 (1): 7–11.

Hartman, Chester W., and Gregg Carr. 1969. "Housing Authorities Reconsidered." *Journal of the American Institute of Planners.* 35 (1): 10-21.

Harvard Law Review. 2003. "When Hope Falls Short: HOPE VI, Accountability, and the Privatization of Public Housing." *Harvard Law Review* 116: 1477–98.

Harvard University Graduate School of Design. 2003. *Public Housing Operating Cost Study Final Report.* Cambridge: Harvard University Graduate School of Design. http://www.gsd.harvard.edu/research/research_centers/phocs/documents/Final%206.11.pdf.

Heavens, Alan J. 2010. "An Urban Makeover." *Philadelphia Enquirer*, March 7. http://www.philly.com/philly/business/homepage/20100307_An_Urban_Makeover.html.

Henderson, A. Scott. 1995. "'Tarred with the Exceptional Image': Public Housing and Popular Discourse, 1950–1990." *American Studies* 36 (Spring): 31–52.

Hernandez, Eugenio, III. 2008. "Lafitte Demolition Permit Unsigned." *Times-Picayune*, March 12. http://blog.nola.com/updates/2008/03/katrinas_damage_to_lafitte_cal.html.

Hilson, Robert, Jr. 1995. "Demolition Plans Cause Mixed Feelings at High-rises." *Baltimore Sun*, September 27. http://articles.baltimoresun.com/1995-09-27/news/1995270012_1_lexington-terrace-lexington-st-rise.

Hirsch, Arnold R. 1998. *Making the Second Ghetto: Race and Housing in Chicago, 1940–1960.* Chicago: University of Chicago Press.

Hogarth, Paul. 2007. "Demolition of Alice Griffith Homes Dominates Newsom Forum." *BeyondChron*, February 12. http://www.beyondchron.org/news/index.php?itemid=4187.

Holin, Mary Joel, Larry Buron, Gretchen Locke, and Alvaro Cortes. 2003. *Interim Assessment of the HOPE VI Program: Cross-site Report.* Cambridge, MA: Abt Associates.

Horner, Kim. 2011. "Thousands Line Up, Stampede to Get on Wait List for Housing Vouchers in Dallas County." Dallasnews.com, *Dallas Morning News,* July 14. http://www.dallasnews.com/news/community-news/dallas/headlines/20110714-thousands-line-up-stampede-to-get-on-wait-list-for-hard-to-get-housing-vouchers-in-dallas-county.ece

Hunt, D. Bradford. 2009. *Blueprint for Disaster: The Unraveling of Chicago Public Housing.* Chicago: University of Chicago Press.

Hyra, Derek. 2008. *The New Urban Renewal: The Economic Transformation of Harlem and Bronzeville.* Chicago: University of Chicago Press.

Illinois Assisted Housing Action Research Project (IHARP). N.d. *Are We Home Yet? Creating Real Choice for Housing Choice Voucher Families in Chicago.* Chicago: Voorhees Center for Neighborhood and Community Improvement, University of Illinois at Chicago. http://www.uic.edu/cuppa/voorheesctr/Publications/IHARP%20HCV%20Report%202010.pdf.

Imbroscio, David L. 2008. "'United and Actuated by Some Common Impulse of Passion': Challenging the Dispersal Consensus in American Housing Policy Research." *Journal of Urban Affairs* 30 (2): 111–30.

Immergluck, Daniel. 1998. *Neighborhood Jobs, Race, and Skills: Urban Unemployment and Commuting.* New York: Garland.

Jacob, Brian. 2004. "Public Housing, Housing Vouchers, and Student Achievement: Evidence from Public Housing Demolitions in Chicago." *American Economic Review* 94 (1): 233–58.

Jargowsky, Paul A. 1996. *Poverty and Place: Ghettos, Barrios, and the American City.* New York: Russell Sage Foundation.

Jargowsky, Paul A., and Mary Jo Bane. 1991. "Ghetto Poverty in the United States, 1970–1980." In *The Urban Underclass*, edited by Christopher Jencks and Paul E. Peterson, 235–73. Washington, D.C.: Brookings Institution.

Jarvie, Jenny. 2008. "Atlanta Rethinks Housing Changes." *Los Angeles Times*, January 21. http://articles.latimes.com/2008/jan/21/nation/na-housing21.

Jervis, Rick. 2007. "Demolition of Public Housing in N.O. Draws Protest." *USA Today*, December 13. http://www.usatoday.com/news/nation/2007-12-13-no-public-housing_N.htm.

Joseph, Mark, Robert Chaskin, and H. Webber. 2007. "The Theoretical Basis for Addressing Poverty through Mixed-Income Development." *Urban Affairs Review* 42 (3): 369–409.

Johnson-Hart, Lallen T. 2007. "Residential Outcomes of HOPE VI Relocatees in Richmond, VA." Unpublished master's thesis, Virginia Commonwealth University.

Jones, Diana N. 2009. "Losing the Place They Call Home." *Pittsburgh Post-Gazette*, November 15. http://www.post-gazette.com/pg/09319/1013300-53.stm?cm pid=news.xml.

Jones, Katherine T., and Jeff Popke. 2010. "Re-envisioning the City: Lefebvre, HOPE VI, and the Neoliberalization of Urban Space." *Urban Geography* 31 (1): 114–33.

Kataria, Guarav, and Michael P. Johnson. 2004. "Neighborhood Selection of Public Housing Residents in the Housing Choice Voucher Program: Quasi-Experimental Results from Chicago." Unpublished manuscript, Carnegie Mellon University.

Katz, Bruce. 2009. "The Origins of HOPE VI." In *From Despair to Hope: HOPE VI and the New Promise of Public Housing in America's Cities*, edited by Henry G. Cisneros and Lora Engdahl, 15–30. Washington, D.C.: Brookings Institution Press.

Keating, Larry. 2000. "Redeveloping Public Housing: Relearning Immutable Lessons." *Journal of the American Planning Association* 66 (4): 384–99.

Keating, Larry, and Carol A. Flores. 2000. "Sixty and Out: Techwood Homes Transformed by Enemies and Friends." *Journal of Urban History* 26: 275–311.

Keene, Danya E., and Arline T. Geronimus. 2011. "Community-Based Support among African American Public Housing Residents." *Journal of Urban Health: Bulletin of the New York Academy of Medicine* 88 (1): 41–53.

Keene, Danya E., and Mark B. Padilla. 2010. "Race, Class and the Stigma of Place: Moving To 'Opportunity' in Eastern Iowa." *Health and Place* 16: 1216–23.

Keene, Danya E., Mark B. Padilla, and Arline T. Geronimus. 2010. "Leaving Chicago for Iowa's 'Fields of Opportunity': Community Dispossession, Rootlessness, and the Quest for Somewhere to 'Be OK.'" *Human Organization* 69 (3): 275–84.

Kegley, Josh. 2010. "New Neighborhood Rises from City's First Public Housing Community." http://www.scbarchitects.com/news/2010/06/07/new-neighborhood-rises-citys-first-public-housing-community.

Keith, Nathaniel S. 1973. *Politics and the Housing Crisis since 1930.* New York: Universe Books.

Kelly, M. Patricia Fernandez. 1994. "Towanda's Triumph–Social and Cultural Capital in the Transition to Adulthood in the Urban Ghetto." *International Journal of Urban and Regional Research* 18 (1): 88–111.

Kingsley, G. Thomas, Martin D. Abravanel, Mary Cunningham, Jeremy Gustafson, Arthur J. Naparstek, and Margery Austin Turner. 2003. "Lessons from HOPE VI for the Future of Public Housing." Washington, D.C.: Urban Institute.

Kingsley, G. Thomas, Jennifer Johnson, and Kathryn S. Pettit. 2003. "Patterns of Section 8 Relocation in the HOPE VI Program." *Journal of Urban Affairs* 25 (4): 427–47.

Kleit, Rachel Garshick. 2001. "The Role of Neighborhood Social Networks in Scattered-Site Public Housing Residents' Search for Jobs." *Housing Policy Debate* 12 (3): 541–73.

———. 2002. "Job Search Networks and Strategies in Scattered-Site Public Housing." *Housing Studies* 17 (1): 83–100.

Kleit, Rachel Garshick, Daniel Carlson, and Tam Kutzmark. 2003. *Holly Park and Roxbury HOPE VI Redevelopments.* Evaluation Report submitted to the Seattle Housing Authority, December. Seattle: Evans School of Public Affairs, University of Washington.

Kleit, Rachel, and Martha Galvez. 2011. "The Location Choices of Public Housing Residents Displaced by Redevelopment: Market Constraints, Personal Preferences, or Social Information?" *Journal of Urban Affairs* 33 (4): 375–407.

Kleit, Rachel Garshick, and Lynne Manzo. 2006. "To Move or Not to Move: Relationships to Place and Relocation Choices in HOPE VI." *Housing Policy Debate* 17 (2): 271–308.

Kling, Jeffrey R., Jeffrey B. Liebman, and Lawrence F. Katz. 2007. "Experimental Analysis of Neighborhood Effects." *Econometrica* 75 (1): 83–119.

Kohn, David. 2003. "Tearing Down Cabrini-Green." *CBS News*, July 23. http://www.cbsnews.com/stories/2002/12/11/6011/main532704.shtml.

Kolodny, Robert. 1985. "Management Problems in U.S. Public Housing and Possible Lessons for Abroad." In *Postwar Public Housing in Trouble*, edited by Nels L. Prak and Hugo Priemus. Delft, Netherlands: Delft University.

Konkoly, Antonia M. 2008. "Tenants Can Sue for Violation of Public Housing Demolition Law." *Housing Law Bulletin* 38 (June): 125.

Kotlowitz, Alex. 1992. *There Are No Children Here: The Story of Two Boys Growing Up in the Other America.* New York: Anchor Books.

Krislov, Marvin. 1988. "Ensuring Tenant Consultation before Public Housing Is Demolished or Sold." *Yale Law Journal* 97: 1745–64.

Ladd, Helen F., and Jens Ludwig. 1997. "Federal Housing Assistance, Residential Relocation, and Education Opportunities: Evidence from Baltimore." *State and Local Public Policy* 87 (2): 272–77.

Landis, John D., and Kirk McClure. 2010. "Rethinking Federal Housing Policy." *Journal of the American Planning Association* 76 (3): 319–48.

Levin, Julie E., and Murray S. Levin. 2007. "Public Housing Receiverships and the Kansas City Experience." *Housing Law Bulletin* 37 (February): 31–37.

Levy, Diane K., and Mark Woolley. 2007. "Relocation Is Not Enough: Employment Barriers among HOPE VI Families." June. Brief No. 6. Washington, D.C.: Metropolitan Housing and Communities Center, Urban Institute.

Lohr, Kathy. 2009. "Atlanta Housing Demolition Sparks Outcry." *National Public Radio*, January 27. http://www.npr.org/templates/story/story.php?storyId=87964901.

Lowenstein, Jeff K. 2008. "The Unwelcome Wagon." *Chicago Reporter*, February 6. http://www.chicagoreporter.com/index.php/c/Inside_Stories/d/The_Unwelcome_Wagon.

Macek, Steve. 2006. *Urban Nightmares: The Media, the Right, and the Moral Panic over the City.* Minneapolis: University of Minnesota Press.

Mahoney, Martha. 1990. "Law and Racial Geography: Public Housing and the Economy in New Orleans." *Stanford Law Review* 42: 1251–90.

Mandelker, Daniel R. 1973. *Housing Subsidies in the United States and England.* Indianapolis: Bobbs-Merrill.

Manjarrez, C. A., S. J. Popkin, and E. Guernsey. 2007. "Poor Health: Adding Insult to Injury for HOPE VI Families." June. Brief No. 5. Washington, D.C.: Metropolitan Housing and Communities Center, Urban Institute.

Manzo, Lynne C., Rachel Garshick Kleit, and Dawn M. Couch. 2005. "Social Sustainability in HOPE VI: The Immigrant Experience." Paper presented at the 35th Annual Meeting of the Urban Affairs Association.

———. 2008. "'Moving Three Times Is Like Having Your House on Fire Once': The Experience of Place and Impending Displacement among Public Housing Residents." *Urban Studies* 45 (9): 1855–78.

Marquis, Gerald P., and Soumen Ghosh. 2008. "Housing Opportunities for People Everywhere (HOPE VI): Who Gets Back In?" *Social Science Journal* 45: 401–18.

Massey, Dougles S., and Nancy A.Denton. 1993. *American Apartheid: Segregation and the Making of the Underclass.* Cambridge, Mass.: Harvard University Press.

Massey, Douglas S., and Shawn M. Kanaiaupuni. 1993. "Public Housing and the Concentration of Poverty." *Social Science Quarterly* 74 (1): 109–22.

McCarthy, Peggy. 1987. "Father Panik Village: High Hopes Are Now Despair." *New York Times*, August 2. http://www.nytimes.com/1987/08/02/nyregion/father-panik-village-high -hopes.html.

McCraven, Marilyn. 1996. "Going Out with a Bang." *Baltimore Sun*, June 28. http://articles.baltimoresun.com/1996-07-28/news/1996210098_1_lexington-terrace-demolition-terrace-residents.

McGhee, Fred L. 2004. "How HUD's HOPE VI Program Is Destroying a Historic Houston Neighborhood." Paper presented at the Urban Issues Program, GSN Forum, Austin: University of Texas at Austin.

McWilliams, Jeremiah. 2011. "Atlanta Housing Authority's Chief Negotiating Exit." *Atlanta Journal-Constitution*, October 3. http://www.ajc.com/news/atlanta/atlanta-housing-authoritys-chief-1193572.html.

Meehan, Eugene. 1979. *The Quality of Federal Policymaking: Programmed Failure in Public Housing.* Columbia: University of Missouri Press.

Mendenhall, Ruby, Stefanie DeLuca, and Greg Duncan. 2005. "Neighborhood Resources, Racial Segregation and Economic Mobility: Results from the Gautreaux Program." *Social Science Research* 35: 892–923.

Meyer, Stephen G. 2000. *As Long as They Don't Move Next Door: Segregation and Racial Conflict in American Neighborhoods.* Lanham, Md.: Rowman and Littlefield.

226   **REFERENCES**

Meyerson, Martin, and Edward C. Banfield. 1995. *Politics, Planning, and the Public Interest.* Glencoe, Ill.: Free Press.

Miller, Beth. 2007. "Cutbacks Cripple Public Housing." *News Journal,* April 11. http://www.delawareonline.com/apps/pbcs.dll/article?AID=/20070411/NEWS/704110359&.

Mitchell, J. Paul. 1985. *Federal Housing Policy and Programs: Past and Present.* New Brunswick, N.J.: Center for Urban Policy Research.

Mohl, Raymond A. 2000. "Planned Destruction: The Interstates and Central City Housing." In *From Tenements to the Taylor Homes: In Search of an Urban Housing Policy in Twentieth Century America,* edited by John F. Bauman, Roger Biles, and Kristin M. Szylvian, 226–45. University Park: Pennsylvania State University Press.

Montgomery, Roger, and Kate Bristol. 1987. *Pruitt-Igoe: An Annotated Bibliography.* Council of Planning Librarians Bibliography #205. Chicago: CPL.

Moore, Kesha S. 2009. "Gentrification in Black Face? The Return of the Black Middle Class to Urban Neighborhoods." *Urban Geography* 30 (2): 118–42.

National Commission on Severely Distressed Public Housing (NCSDPH). 1992. *The Final Report of the National Commission on Severely Distressed Public Housing.* A report to the Congress and the Secretary of Housing and Urban Development. Washington, D.C.: U.S. Government Printing Office.

National Housing Law Project (NHLP). 1990. *Public Housing in Peril: A Report on the Demolition and Sale of Public Housing Projects.* Berkeley, CA: National Housing Law Project.

———. 2002. *False HOPE: A Critical Assessment of the HOPE VI Public Housing Redevelopment Program.* Oakland, CA: National Housing Law Project.

"New Urbanists Urge Uncle Sam: 'Don't Abandon HOPE.'" 2003. *New Urban News,* March. http://www.newurgannews.com/Hope_VI_0303.html.

Newman, Harvey K. 2002. "The Atlanta Housing Authority's Olympic Legacy Program: Public Housing Projects to Mixed-Income Communities." Atlanta, GA: Research Atlanta.

Newman, Kathe. 2004. "Newark, Decline and Avoidance, Renaissance and Desire: From Disinvestment to Reinvestment." *Annals of the American Academy of Political and Social Sciences* 594 (July): 34–48.

Newman, Oscar. 1972. *Defensible Spaces: Crime Prevention through Urban Design.* New York: Macmillan.

Oakes, Amy, and Tom Pelton. 1999. "Blast to Wipe Out Episode in Public Housing History." *Baltimore Sun,* June 23. http://articles.baltimoresun.com/1999-06-23/news/9906230184_1_murphy-homes-demolition-public-housing.

Oakley, Deirdre, and Keri Burchfield. 2009. "Out of the Projects, Still in the Hood: The Spatial Constraints on Public-Housing Residents' Relocation in Chicago." *Journal of Urban Affairs* 31 (5): 589–614.

Oakley, Deirdre, Lesley Reid, and Erin Ruel. 2011. "Is the Grass Always Greener…? Destination Characteristics and Former Public Housing Residents' Views Six Months after Relocation." Atlanta: Georgia State Urban Health Initiative, Georgia State University.

Oakley, Dierdre, Erin Ruel, Lesley Reid, and Christina Sims. 2010. *Public Housing Relocation and Residential Segregation in Atlanta: Where Are Families Going?* Paper presented at the State of Black Atlanta Summit, Clark Atlanta University, Atlanta, GA.

Oakley, Deirdre, Erin Ruel, and G. Elton Wilson. N.d. "A Choice with No Options: Atlanta Public Housing Residents' Lived Experiences in the Face of Relocation." Department of Sociology, Georgia State University, Atlanta.

Okon, Bob. 2010a. "HAJ Defends Demolitions after HUD Attack." *Joliet Herald News*, January 27. http://www.suburbanchicagonews.com/heraldnews/news/2012752,4_1_J027_HAJ_S1_100127.article#.

———. 2010b. "HUD to City: Keep Public Housing." *Joliet Herald News*, January 31. http://www.suburbanchicagonews.com/heraldnews/news/2020685,4_1_JO31_HUD_S1-100131.article#.

Olivo, Antonio. 2006. "Stateway's Swan Song." *Chicago Tribune*, April 16. http://www.chicagotribune.com/news/opinion/chi-0604150268apr16.

Olivio, Russ. 2010. "HUD Balks at Housing Demolition." *Woonsocket Call*, July 13. http://www.woonsocketcall.com/content/view/165235/1/.

Oreopoulos, Philip. 2003. "The Long-Run Consequences of Living in a Poor Neighborhood." *Quarterly Journal of Economics* 118 (4): 1533–75.

Ouroussoff, Nicolai. 2006. "All Fall Down." *New York Times*, November 19.

Overton, Penelope. 2010. "Despite Need, Housing Authority Wants to Demolish 52 units in Waterbury." *Republican-American*, May 23. http://www.rep-am.com/articles/2010/5/03/23/news/local/484809.txt?taToken=95ae1f54f1ffa71dc2938b897451d3e5.

Parson, Don. 2005. *Making a Better World: Public Housing, the Red Scare, and the Direction of Modern Los Angeles*. Minneapolis: University of Minnesota Press.

Patillo, Mary. 2007. *Black on the Block: The Politics of Race and Class in the City*. Chicago: University of Chicago Press.

"Pelosi, Reid Ask Bush to Halt Demolition." 2007. *Times-Picayune*, December 15.

Pendall, Rolf. 2000. "Why Voucher and Certificate Users Live in Distressed Neighborhoods." *Housing Policy Debate* 11 (4): 881–910.

Petit, Becky. 2004. "Moving and Children's Social Connections: Neighborhood Context and the Consequences of Moving for Low-Income Families." *Sociological Forum* 19 (2): 285–311.

Pfeiffer, Deirdre. 2006. "Displacement through Discourse: Implementing and Contesting Public Housing Redevelopment in Cabrini Green." *Urban Anthropology* 35 (1): 39–74.

Polikoff, Alexander. 2009. "HOPE VI and the Deconcentration of Poverty." In *From Despair to Hope: HOPE VI and the New Promise of Public Housing in America's Cities*, edited by Henry Cisneros and Lora Engdahl. Washington, D.C.: Brookings Institution Press.

Popkin, Susan J. 2006. "The HOPE VI Program: What Has Happened to the Residents?" In *Where Are Poor People to Live? Transforming Public Housing Communities*, edited by Larry Bennett, Janet L. Smith, and Patricia A. Wright, 68–90. Armonk, N.Y.: M. E. Sharpe.

Popkin, Susan J., Larry F. Buron, Diane K. Levy, and Mary K. Cunningham. 2000. "The Gautreaux Legacy: What Might Mixed-Income and Dispersal Strategies Mean for the Poorest Public Housing Tenants?" *Housing Policy Debate* 11 (4): 911–42.

Popkin, Susan J., and Elizabeth Cove. 2007. "Safety Is the Most Important Thing: How HOPE VI Helped Families." Brief No. 2. Washington, D.C.: Metropolitan Housing and Communities Center, Urban Institute.

Popkin, Susan J., Victoria Gwiasda, Lynn M. Olson, Dennis P. Rosenbaum, and Larry Buron. 2000. *The Hidden War: Crime and the Tragedy of Public Housing in Chicago*. New Brunswick, N.J.: Rutgers University Press.

Popkin, Susan J., Bruce Katz, Mary K. Cunningham, Karen Brown, Jeremy Gustafson, and Margery A. Turner. 2004. "A Decade of Hope VI: Research Findings and Policy Challenges." Washington, D.C.: Urban Institute.

Popkin, Susan J., Michael J. Rich, Leah Hendey, Chris Hayes, and Joe Parilla. 2012. "Public Housing Transformation and Crime: Making the Case for Responsible Relocation." Urban Institute. http://www.urban.org/UploadedPDF/412523-public-housing-transformation.pdf.

Popkin, Susan J., James E. Rosenbaum, and Patricia M. Meaden. 1993. "Labor Market Experiences of Low-Income Black Women in Middle-Class Suburbs: Evidence from a Survey of Gautreaux Program Participants." *Journal of Policy Analysis and Management* 12 (3): 556–73.

Portes, Alejandro. 1994. "The Informal Economy and Its Paradoxes." In *The Handbook of Economic Sociology*, edited by Neil J.Smelser and Richard Swedberg, 426–49. Princeton: Princeton University Press.

Poverty and Race Research Action Council. 2008. "Statement of Fair Housing and Civil Rights Advocates on HOPE VI Reauthorization." *Poverty and Race* 17 (1): 7.

Powell, Julia Clayton. 1995. "Comment: *De facto* Demolition: The Hidden Deterioration of Public Housing." *Catholic University Law Review* 44 (Spring): 885–934.

Pratt, Timothy. 2008. "Demise of Vegas Public Housing 'Projects' Sought." *Las Vegas Sun*, July 1. http://www.lasvegassun.com/news/2008/jul/01/demise-vegas-public.

Pyles, Loretta. 2009. *Progressive Community Organizing: A Critical Approach for a Globalizing World.* New York: Routledge.

Rabushka, Alvin, and William G. Weissert. 1977. *Caseworkers or Police? How Tenants See Public Housing.* Stanford: Hoover Institution Press.

Radford, Gail. 2000. "The Federal Government and Housing during the Great Depression." In *From Tenements to the Taylor Homes: In Search of an Urban Housing Policy in Twentieth- Century America*, edited by John F. Bauman, Roger Biles, and Kristin M. Szylvian, 102–20. University Park: Pennsylvania State University Press.

Ratner, Lizzy. 2008. "New Orleans Redraws Its Color Line." *Nation*, September 15.

Reckdahl, Katy. 2008. "Critics Question Whether New New Orleans Public Housing Will Meet Needs." *Times-Picayune*, December 8. http://www.nola.com/news/index.ssf/2008/12/critics_question_whether_new_n.html.

———. 2009. "New Designs Hope to Avoid Past Problems in Public Housing Complexes." *Times-Picayune*, May 12. http://www.nola.com/news/index.ssf/2009/05/new_designs_hope_to_avoid_past.html.

———. 2011. "New C. J. Peete Complex Is Solid, Shiny—But Not as Social, Some Residents Say." *Times-Picayune*, August 21. http://www.nola.com/politics/index.ssf/2011/08/new_cj_peete_complex_is_solid.html.

Reed, Adolph, and Stephen Steinberg. 2006. "Liberal Bad Faith: In the Wake of Hurricane Katrina." *Black Commentator* no. 182, May. http://www.blackcommentator.com/182/182_cover_liberals_katrina.html.

Reed, Matthew Z. 2006. *Moving Out: Section 8 and Public Housing Relocation in Chicago.* PhD diss., Department of Sociology, Northwestern University.

Regan, Margaret. 2001. "*Don't Look at Me Different*: A New Book by Tucson's Teenagers Documents Life in the City's Projects." *Tucson Weekly.* January 11. http://www.tucsonweekly.com/tucson/dont-look-at-me-different/Content?oid=1067663.

Reichl, Alexander. 1999. "Learning from St. Thomas: Community, Capital, and the Redevelopment of Public Housing in New Orleans." *Journal of Urban Affairs* 21 (2): 169–88.

Rich, Michael J., Michael Leo Owens, Elizabeth Griffiths, Moshe Haspel, Kelly Hill, Adrienne Smith, and Katherine M. Stigers. 2010. "Evaluation of the McDaniel Glenn HOPE VI Revitalization: Final Report." Atlanta: Office of University-Community Partnerships, Emory University.

Robinson, Kelly. 2004. *Stella Wright Homes HOPE VI Project: Evaluation Interim Report.* Prepared for the Housing Authority of the City of Newark. Newark: Cornwall Center for Metropolitan Studies, Rutgers University—Newark.

Robinson, Ronald. 1994. "West Dallas versus the Lead Smelter." In *Unequal Protection: Environmental Justice and Communities of Color,* edited by Robert D. Bullard. San Francisco: Sierra Club Books.

Rogal, Brian J. and Beauty Turner. 2004. "Moving at Their Own Risk." *Chicago Reporter,* July. http://www.chicagoreporter.com/index.php/c/Cover_Stories/d/Moving_at_Their_Own_Risk.

Roisman, Florence W. 2001. "Opening the Suburbs to Racial Integration: Lessons for the 21st Century." *Western New England Law Review* 173: 173–221.

Roosevelt, Franklin Delano. 1935. "The Dedication of Techwood Homes." November 29. http://georgiainfo.galileo.usg.edu/FDRspeeches/FDRspeech35-2.htm.

Rubinowitz, Leonard S., and James E. Rosenbaum. 2000. *Crossing the Class and Color Lines: From Public Housing to White Suburbia.* Chicago: University of Chicago Press.

Salisbury, Harrison. 1958. *The Shook Up Generation.* New York: Harper.

Sanbonmatsu, Lisa, Jeffrey R. Kling, Greg J. Duncan, and Jeanne Brooks-Gunn. 2006. "Neighborhoods and Academic Achievement: Results From the Moving to Opportunity Experiment." *Journal of Human Resources* 41 (4): 649–91.

Schill, Michael H. 1993. "Distressed Public Housing: Where Do We Go from Here?" *University of Chicago Law Review* 60: 497–542.

———. 1997. "Chicago's Mixed-Income New Communities Strategy: The Future Face of Public Housing?" In *Affordable Housing and Urban Redevelopment in the United States,* in Willem van Vliet, 135–57. Urban Affairs Annual Reviews 46. Thousand Oaks, CA: Sage Publications.

Schneider, Craig, and Tammy Joyner. 2010. "Housing Crisis Reaches Full Boil in East Point; 62 Injured." *Atlanta Journal-Constitution,* August 12. http://www.ajc.com/news/atlanta/east-point-begins-taking-590299.html.

Schwartz, Alex, and Kian Tajbakhsh. 1997. "Mixed Income Housing: Unanswered Questions." *Cityscape: A Journal of Policy Development and Research* 3 (2): 71–92.

Seicshnaydre, Stacey E. 2007. "The More Things Change, the More They Stay the Same: In Search of a Just Public Housing Policy Post-Katrina." *Tulane Law Review* 81: 1263–75.

Seidel, Jon. 2010. "End Near for Ivanhoe 'Eyesore.'" *Post-Tribune,* April 6. http://www.post-trib.com/news/lake/2141915.new-givanhoe0406.article.

Silva, Cristina. 2008. "St. Pete: Housing Authority Will Pay $850,000 to Relocate Graham-Rogall Residents." *St. Petersburg Times,* April 24. http://blogs.tampabay.com/breakingnews /2008/04/st-pete-housing.html.

Simmons, Melody. 1993a. "Lexington Terrace Families Must Struggle Daily to Endure." *Baltimore Sun,* January 20. http://articles.baltimoresun.com/1993-01-20/news/1993020108_1_lexington-terrace-high-rise-building-public-housing.

———. 1993b. "Political Theater at High Rises." *Baltimore Sun,* January 26. http://articles.baltimoresun.com/1993-01-20/news/19903020108_1_lexington-terrace-high-rise-building-public-housing.

Skutch, Jan, 2010. "Hitch Village Demolition Begins." *Savannah Morning News,* April 2. http://savannahnow.com/news/2010-04-02/hitch-village-demolition-begins.

Smith, Janet. 2006a. "Public Housing Transformation." In *Where Are Poor People to Live? Transforming Public Housing Communities,* edited by Larry Bennett, Janet L. Smith, and Patricia A. Wright. Armonk, N.Y.: M. E. Sharpe.

———. 2006b. "The Chicago Housing Authority's Plan for Transformation." In *Where Are Poor People to Live? Transforming Public Housing Communities*, edited by Larry Bennett, Janet L. Smith, and Patricia A. Wright. Armonk, N.Y.: M. E. Sharpe.

Smith, Michael Peter, and Marlene Keller. 1983. "'Managed Growth' and the Politics of Uneven Development in New Orleans." In *Restructuring the City: The Political Economy of Urban Redevelopment*, edited by Susan S. Fainstein, Norman I. Fainstein, Richard Child Hill, Dennis Judd, and Michael Peter Smith. New York: Longman.

Smith, Neil. 2002. "New Globalism, New Urbanism: Gentrification as Global Urban Strategy." In *Spaces of Neoliberalism: Urban Restructuring in North America and Western Europe*, edited by Neil Brenner and Nik Theodore. Malden, MA: Blackwell

Smith, Robin E. 2002. *Housing Choice for HOPE VI Relocatees*. Washington, D.C.: Urban Institute.

Spence, Harry. 1993. "Rethinking the Social Role of Public Housing." *Housing Policy Debate* 4 (3): 355–68.

Springston. Jonathan. 2007. "Activists Mobilize to Save Atlanta Public Housing, Seek Legal Options." *Atlanta Progressive News*, April 11. http://www.atlanta progressivenews.come/news/0141.html.

Springston, Jonathan, and Matthew Cardinale. 2007. "Public Housing Evictions Starting Already, Residents Plead for Help." *Atlanta Progressive News*, April 17. http://www.atlantaprogressivenews.com/interspire/news/2007/04/17/exclusive-public-housing-evictions-starting-already-residents-plead-for-help.html.

Stegman, Michael A. 1991. *More Housing, More Fairly: Report of the Twentieth Century Fund Task Force on Affordable Housing*. New York: Twentieth Century Fund.

Stephens, Challen. 2009. "What's Right for Public Housing?" *Huntsville Times*, April 12. http://nl.newsbank.com/nl-search/we/Archives?p_action=print.

Stirgus, Eric. 2008. "Centennial Place's Renewed Purpose: A Decade Later, Proponents Hail Housing as Success." *Atlanta Journal-Constitution*, December 29. http://housingresearchorg.blogspot.com/2008/12/atlantas-centennial-place-has-renewed.html.

Stockard, James G., Jr. 1998. "Public Housing—The Next Sixty Years?" In *New Directions in Urban Public Housing*, edited by David P. Varady, Wolfgang F. E. Preiser, and Francis P. Russell, 237–64. New Brunswick, N.J.: Center for Urban Policy Research.

Struyk, Raymond J. 1980. *A New System for Public Housing: Salvaging a National Resource*. Washington, D.C.: Urban Institute Press.

Sullivan, Thomas P. 2004. *Independent Monitor's Report to the Chicago Housing Authority and the Central Advisory Council Regarding Phase II-2003 of the Plan for Transformation*. Chicago: Chicago Housing Authority.

Suresh, Geetha. 2000. *Spatial Analysis of Crime: Aggravated Assault, Homicide, and Rape Patterns in the City of Louisville*. PhD diss., University of Louisville.

Teitz, Michael B., and Karen Chapple. 1998. "The Causes of Inner-City Poverty: Eight Hypotheses in Search of Reality." *Cityscape* 3 (3): 33–70.

Tonrys, Michael. 1995. *Malign Neglect: Race, Crime, and Punishment in America*. New York: Oxford University Press.

Trudeau, Daniel. 2006. "The Persistence of Segregation in Buffalo, New York: *Comer vs. Cisneros* and Geographies of Relocation Decisions among Low-Income Black Households." *Urban Geography* 27 (1): 20–44.

Turbov, Mindy, and Valerie Piper. 2005. *HOPE VI and Mixed-finance Redevelopments: A Catalyst for Neighborhood Renewal.* Washington, D.C.: Brookings Institution.

Turner, Margery Austin. 1998. "Moving Out of Poverty: Expanding Mobility and Choice through Tenant-Based Housing Assistance." *Housing Policy Debate* 9 (2): 373–94.

———. 2009. "HOPE VI, Neighborhood Recovery, and the Health of Cities." In *From Despair to Hope: HOPE VI and the New Promise of Public Housing in America's Cities,* edited by Henry G. Cisneros and Lora Engdahl, 169–90. Washington, D.C.: Brookings Institution Press.

Turney, K., S. Clampet-Lundquist, K. Edin, J. R. Kling, and G. J. Duncan. 2006. "Neighborhood Effects on Barriers to Employment: Results from a Randomized Housing Mobility Experiment in Baltimore." Working Paper #511. Princeton: Industrial Relations Section. Princeton University.

Tuttle, Samantha M. 2008. "Tenants Force a Policy Change at HUD and Protect Subsidized Housing Stock in Doing So." *Clearinghouse Review: Journal of Poverty Law and Policy* 42 (3–4): 190–93. http://www.policyarchive.org/handle/10207/bitstreams/20611.pdf.

University Partnership for Community and Economic Development. N.d. *Belmont Heights Estates Economic Impact Analysis.* http://www.thafl.com/depts/CFAH/BHE_executive_summary.swf.

U.S. Department of Housing and Urban Development. 2002. *HOPE VI: Best Practices and Lessons Learned 1992–2002.* Submitted to the Committee on Appropriations, United States House of Representatives, Committee on Appropriations, United States Senate.

———. 2004. *Evaluation of the Welfare to Work Voucher Program: Report to Congress.* Washington, D.C.: U.S. Government Printing Office.

U.S. General Accounting Office. 1996. "HUD Takes Over the Housing Authority of New Orleans." GAO/RCED-96-67. May. Washington, D.C.: GAO.

———. 2002. *Public Housing: HOPE VI Leveraging Has Increased, But HUD Has Not Met Annual Reporting Requirement.* GAO-03-91. Washington, D.C.: GAO.

———. 2003. *Public Housing: HOPE VI Resident Issues and Changes in Neighborhoods Surrounding Grant Sites. Report to the Ranking Minority Member, Subcommittee on Housing and Transportation, Committee on Banking, Housing, and Urban Affairs, U.S. Senate.* GAO-04-109. Washington, D.C.: GAO.

Vale, Lawrence J. 1997. "Empathological Places: Residents' Ambivalence toward Remaining in Public Housing." *Journal of Planning Education and Research* 16: 159–75.

———. 2000. *From the Puritans to the Projects: Public Housing and Public Neighbors.* Cambridge: Harvard University Press.

———. 2002. *Reclaiming Public Housing: A Half Century of Struggle in Three Public Neighborhoods.* Cambridge: Harvard University Press.

Varady, David P., and Carole C. Walker. 2000. "Vouchering Out Distressed Subsidized Developments: Does Moving Lead to Improvements in Housing and Neighborhood Conditions?" *Housing Policy Debate* 11 (1): 115–62.

Venkatesh, Sudhir A. 2000. *American Project: The Rise and Fall of a Modern Ghetto.* Cambridge: Harvard University Press.

Venkatesh, Sudhir, and Isil Celimli. 2004. "Tearing Down the Community." *Shelterforce Online,* Issue #138, November/December. http://www.nhi.org/online/issues/138/chicago.html.

Vigdor, Jacob L. 2007. "The Katrina Effect: Was There a Bright Side to the Evacua-
    tion of Greater New Orleans?" *B.E. Journal of Economic Analysis & Policy* 7 (1):
    article 64. http://www.bepress.com/bejeap/vol7/iss1/art64
Vogt, Heidi. 2009. "What's Wrong with English Woods?" http://americancity.org/
    magazine/article/housing whats-wrong-with-english-woods-vogt/.
Wacquant, Loïc. 2008. *Urban Outcasts: A Comparative Sociology of Advanced
    Marginality.* Cambridge: Polity Press.
Washington, Tracie L., Brian D. Smedley, Beatrice Alvarez, and Jason Reece. N.d.
    "Housing in New Orleans: One Year after Katrina." New Orleans: National
    Association for the Advancement of Colored People Gulf Coast Advocacy Cen-
    ter, the Opportunity Agenda, and the Kirwan Institute for the Study of Race and
    Ethnicity.
Weaver, D. 2007. "Housing Officials Claim Surplus." http:////blog.nola.com/updates/
    2007/12/housing_officials_claim_surplu.html.
Weber, Rachel. 2002. "Extracting Value from the City: Neoliberalism and Urban Rede-
    velopment." In *Spaces of Neoliberalism: Urban Restructuring in North America
    and Western Europe,* edited by Neil Brenner and Nik Theodore, 172–93. Malden,
    MA: Blackwell.
Weisel, Deborah L., and Debbie Meagher. 1996. "HOPEVI Baseline Case Study: Earle
    Village, Charlotte, North Carolina." In *An Historical and Baseline Assessment of
    HOPE VI: Volume II Case Studies.* Washington, D.C.: U.S. Department of Hous-
    ing and Urban Development.
Weiss, Marc A. 1985. "The Origins and Legacy of Urban Renewal." In *Federal Hous-
    ing Policy and Programs: Past and Present,* edited by J. Paul Mitchell, 250–76. New
    Brunswick, N.J.: Center for Urban Policy Research.
Wexler, Harry J. 2001. "HOPE VI: Market Means/Public Ends—the Goals, Strategies,
    and Midterm Lessons of HUD's Urban Revitalization Demonstration Program."
    Journal of Affordable Housing 10 (3): 195–233.
Wilbert, Laurent. 2007. "Marchers Denied Entrance to Building." http://blog.nola.
    com/updates/2007/12/marchers_denied_entrance_to_bu.html.
Wilen, William P., and Rajesh D. Nayak. 2006. "Relocated Public Housing Residents
    Have Little Hope of Returning: Work Requirements for Mixed-Income Housing
    Developments. "In *Where Are Poor People to Live? Transforming Public Housing
    Communities,* edited by Larry Bennett, Janet L. Smith, and Patricia A. Wright,
    216–36. Armonk, N.Y.: M. E. Sharpe.
Williams, Rhonda Y. 2004. *The Politics of Public Housing: Black Women's Struggles
    against Urban Inequality.* Oxford: Oxford University Press.
Wilson, David. 2004. "Toward a Contingent Urban Neoliberalism." *Urban Geography*
    25 (8): 771–83.
Winslow, Samantha. 2010. "U.N. Report: Deep Concern over Housing for Amer-
    ica's Poor." March 11. http://news.medill.northwestern.edu/chicago/news.
    aspx?id=161594.
Wright, Gwendolyn. 1981. *Building the Dream: A Social History of Housing in America.*
    New York: Pantheon Books.
Wright, Patricia. 2006. "Community Resistance to CHA Transformation." In *Where
    Are Poor People to Live? Transforming Public Housing Communities,* edited by
    Larry Bennett, Janet L. Smith, and Patricia A. Wright. Armonk, N.Y.: M. E.
    Sharpe.
Wright, Patricia A., Yittayih Zelalem, Julie deGraaf, and Linda Roman. 1997. "The Plan
    to Voucher Out Public Housing: An Analysis of the Chicago Experience and
    a Case Study of the Proposal to Redevelop the Cabrini-Green Public Housing

Area." Publication #V-155. Chicago: Nathalie P. Voorhees Center for Neighborhood and Community Improvement, University of Illinois, Chicago.

Wyly, Elvin K., and Daniel J. Hammel. 1999. "Islands of Decay in Seas of Renewal: Housing Policy and the Resurgence of Gentrification." *Housing Policy Debate* 10 (4): 711–71.

Zhang, Yan, and Gretchen Weismann. 2006. "Public Housing's Cinderella: Policy Dynamics of HOPE VI in the Mid-1990s." In *Where Are Poor People To Live? Transforming Public Housing Communities*, edited by Larry Bennett, Janet L. Smith, and Patricia A. Wright, 41–67). Armonk, N.Y.: M. E. Sharpe.

Zielenbach, Sean. 2002. *The Economic Impact of HOPE VI on Neighborhoods*. Washington, D.C.: Housing Research Foundation.

———. 2003. "Assessing Economic Change in HOPE VI Neighborhoods." *Housing Policy Debate* 14 (4): 621–55.

Zielenbach, Sean, and Richard Voith. 2010. "HOPE VI and Neighborhood Economic Development: The Importance of Local Market Dynamics." *Cityscape: A Journal of Policy Development and Research* 12 (1): 99–131.

Index

ABLA, 1, 81
Achtenburg, Roberta, 61
Addison Terrace, 112
Alice Griffith, 128
Allegheny County, Pennsylvania, 61
Allen Parkway Village, 10, 56, 73, 161
Arapahoe Courts, 111, 164
Arroyo Vista, 59
Atlanta, 4, 6, 47–48, 66, 71, 76, 100–110, 118,
    128, 161, 163, 168, 170, 172, 181; Atlanta
    Housing Authority (AHA) of, 12, 17, 48,
    76, 101–9; and Atlanta model, 12, 103–5;
    Clark Howell Homes in, 100–104, 135,
    161; East Lake Meadows in, 101–2, 105–6;
    gangs and crime in, 101, 105; gentrification
    in, 104–6, 108; HOPE VI in, 102–3, 106;
    management of public housing in, 101–3,
    109; Mayor Bill Campbell, 102, 104; Mayor
    Maynard Jackson, 102, 104; McDaniel-Glen
    in, 106, 163; Olympic Games in, 102–4,
    106, 108–9; Resident Advisory Boards of,
    107–8; resident opposition to demolition in,
    105–9. See also *Atlanta Journal-Constitution;*
    Glover, Renee; Techwood Homes
Atlanta Journal-Constitution, 178

Bair, Edward, 158
Baker, Congressman Richard, 94
Baltimore, 10, 31, 38, 44, 61, 111, 118, 128, 133,
    139, 157–58, 170
Baron, Richard, 5, 40–41, 65–66, 188
Bauer, Catherine, 25, 33–34
Bedford Additions, 155, 187
Bernal Heights Dwellings, 115
black middle class, 16, 85, 164–66
Boles v. Kemp, 56
Boston, 15, 35, 37, 39, 129, 158, 160, 182, 186
Boston Housing Authority, 15
Boyd, Michelle, 85
Bronzeville, 16, 84–85, 161, 172
Brooke Amendment, 34
Brooks, David, 99
Burchell, Robert, 41
Bush, President George W., 69, 95
Byrd, Senator Harry, 28, 32

Cabrini-Green, 15, 73, 75, 77, 80–81, 86–88,
    162, 172, 175
Calthorpe, Peter, 5, 17
Carver Homes, 112
Centre on Housing Rights and Evictions
    (COHRE), 122
Charlotte, NC, 12–13, 133, 137, 160, 162–63,
    170, 172
Chicago, 1–2, 15–16, 31, 41, 47–48, 60, 70–71, 73,
    75–88, 108–10, 118, 128, 133–34, 138–39,
    141, 161–62, 172, 177, 187; Charles Swibel as
    chairman of Housing Authority of, 38;
    Chicago Daily News, 40; *Chicago Tribune,*
    138; community impacts of transforma-
    tion in, 82–86; gangs and crime in, 79–80,
    85–86; gentrification and revitalization in,
    83–85, 88, 108; high-rise public housing in,
    78, 80, 82, 88; HOPE VI in, 73, 80; Housing
    Authority of, 1, 12, 15, 36, 38, 59–60, 75–81,
    84–88, 134–36; Mayor Harold Washing-
    ton, 77; Mayor Richard M. Daley, 15, 108;
    mismanagement of public housing in, 75,
    77–81, 88, 109; mixed income development
    in, 77, 80, 82, 88; Plan For Transformation
    (PFT) of, 81–88, 99, 109; public housing
    tenant profile in, 77–78, 109; relocation
    outcomes in, 84–85; resident management
    of public housing in, 86–88; resident oppo-
    sition to demolition in, 86–88, 107, 109;
    siting of public housing in, 77–79, 82; State
    Street corridor in, 16, 78–79, 84, 88; viability
    tests in, 75, 79–82. *See also* ABLA; Cabrini
    Green; Henry Horner Homes; Robert Taylor
    Homes; State Street corridor; Stateway Gar-
    dens; Wentworth Homes; Yotaghan, Wardell
Choice Neighborhoods Initiative (CNI), 3,
    97, 187–88
Cisneros, HUD Secretary Henry, 5, 10, 61,
    65–66, 77, 181, 188, 190
Civil Right Act of 1964, 60, 90
Clampet-Lundquist, Susan, 147
Cleaborn Homes, 157
Clinton, President William J., 10–11, 13, 61, 181
Coalition to Protect Public Housing (CPPH),
    18, 86–88, 175

Coca Cola Company, 100, 104, 161
Columbia Villa, 146, 148–49
Comer v. Cisneros, 139
Commonwealth, 182, 186
concentrated poverty, 8, 12, 17, 45, 49, 72–74, 85, 90, 101, 104, 150–52, 157, 167, 184
Concerned Tenants Association of Father Panik Village v. Pierce, 55
Connie Chambers Homes, 10, 133, 168
crack cocaine, 8, 45, 49, 101
Cuomo, HUD Secretary Andrew, 43, 82, 188
Curley, Alexandra, 130
Curtis Park, 111, 164

deconcentration of poverty, 54, 64–65, 90, 142, 178, 180
de facto demolition, 10, 18, 48, 53–60, 80, 87, 102–3, 127, 133, 135, 141
demolition and disposition, 4, 50–51
Denton, Nancy, 109
Denver, 111, 118, 163–64
desegregation lawsuits, 60–61
Detroit, 7, 31, 71, 112–13, 118
discourse of disaster, 2, 8, 16–17, 20, 40–42, 45, 123
disparate racial impact, 8, 9, 22, 74, 110, 112–22, 164, 178, 188
dispersal, 17, 54, 60, 64, 97, 151, 180–82, 189
displacement, 16–21, 66, 100, 103, 112, 115–23, 128–32, 182; in black neighborhoods, 171–74; of crime, 85, 159; 147–48, 150–51, 178; direct, 114–22, 163–64, 170; disruptive impact of, 21, 129, 133–35; effects of, 158–60, 172 (*see also* neighborhood impacts); experience of, 124–27; indirect, 163–74, 188; and loss of community, 128–32. *See also* disparate racial impact; relocation
District of Columbia Housing Authority, 53–55. See also *Edwards v. District of Columbia;* Washington, D.C.
Donovan, HUD Secretary Shaun, 188
Duluth, MN, 124–28, 130–33, 138–40, 143–45; Housing Authority, 124–25, 127, 132–33, 137, 143–44; Hillside neighborhood of, 126, 140
Dunbar Manor, 112

Earle Village, 133, 137, 160, 162, 170, 172
Edwards v. District of Columbia, 53–55, 57
Ellen Wilson Dwellings, 161
El Paso, 113, 119
Emergency Relief and Reconstruction Act of 1932, 26
English Woods, 139
equivalent elimination, 28, 50

fair housing, 84, 107
fair share housing, 166
Feldman, Roberta, 44, 86
Fitzgerald, John, 158
Flint, MI, 132
Flores, Carol, 135
Fort Dupont, 53
Frank, Rep. Barney, 95
Fried, Marc, 129–30
Fullilove, Mindy, 130

Galvez, Martha, 139
gangs, 8, 49, 86, 101, 105, 157
Gans, Herbert, 129–30
Gautreaux, 5, 60, 77, 146, 152
gentrification, 14, 16, 52, 72–73, 76, 84–85, 104–6, 108, 132–33, 155, 157–67, 175, 182; black, 85, 164–66, 172–73; "third wave" 14, 181
Georgia Tech University, 100, 104, 161
Geronimus, Arline, 130
Glover, Renee, 12, 102–7, 109, 181, 184–85, 188
Gomez v. El Paso Housing Authority, 57
Great Depression, 6
Gutzman, Jon, 48

Hackworth, Jason, 14
Hammel, Daniel, 15, 158, 162
Harbor View, 124–28, 130–33, 137–40, 142–45
Hartford, CT, 71, 171
Hartman, Chester, 37
Hawkins v. Cisneros, 61
Henderson, Scott, 40–41
Henry Horner Homes, 80–81, 84, 87, 135, 187
Henry Horner Mothers Guild v. Chicago Housing Authority and the U.S. Department of Housing and Urban Development, 57–59
Hill district, Pittsburgh, 155–56
Holly Park, 157, 168, 170
HOPE VI, 3–4, 19, 22, 42, 56, 58–59, 62–64, 73, 77, 80, 85, 106, 116, 119, 123, 136, 138–39, 155, 177–79; displacement due to, 163, 166–74; in Duluth, 124–27, 131, 143–45; evolution of, 64–69, 180–84; leveraging private investment for, 15, 67–68, 162, 173; as "Negro removal," 121–22; and neighborhood spillover, 157–64; origins of, 11, 58, 61–66; and racial turnover, 168–73; and relocation of residents, 139–42, 151, 170; resident participation in, 136. *See also* Urban Revitalization Demonstration (URD)
Housing Act of 1937, 27, 32, 50, 53, 56

Housing Act of 1949, 29
Housing and Community Development Act
   of 1974, 49
Housing and Urban Development (HUD),
   U.S. Department of, 10, 49, 57–58, 60–61,
   64, 69; approval of demolition by, 4, 22, 50,
   53–55, 59, 70, 81, 91, 94–97, 102, 104, 120,
   180, 186–87; and emphasis on leveraging
   investment, 15, 67, 162, 173; impaction rules
   of, 63, 179–80; and New Urbanism, 66, 186;
   and oversight of public housing authorities,
   56, 58, 66, 75, 77, 81, 91, 93; political position of, 65, 181; public housing program
   operation of, 38–39, 185; Reinvention Blueprint of, 65; takeover of CHA by, 77, 81, 87;
   takeover of HANO by, 91; and "Troubled
   Agency" list, 52, 64, 76, 81
Housing Authority of Kansas City
   (HAKC), 56–57
Housing Authority of New Orleans (HANO),
   58, 60, 76, 89–97
Housing Authority of the City of Los Angeles,
   (HACLA), 14, 18, 81
Housing Choice Vouchers, 14, 84, 86, 106, 135,
   141–42. *See also* Section 8; vouchers
Houston, 10, 56, 73, 161
Hunt, Bradford, 35, 47, 80
Huntsville, AL, 139
Hurricane Katrina, 18, 58, 60, 73, 76, 91,
   93–99, 108–9
Hyra, Derek, 85

Iberville, 26, 89, 91, 94, 97, 186
Ida Barbour Homes, 168, 170

Jackson, HUD Secretary Alphonso, 94, 96, 98

Kansas City, MO, 52, 56, 168
Katz, Bruce, 15
Keating, Larry, 135
Keene, Danya, 130
Keynesianism, 6, 9
King, Martin Luther, 109
King, Myrna, 88
Kleit, Rachel, 139
Knoxville, TN, 118–19, 162

Lafayette Courts, 157
Lafitte, 26, 89, 91, 94–96
Lake Parc Place, 77, 80
Lamarr Terrace, 157
Lane, Vincent, 77, 79–81
Las Vegas, 4
Lexington Terrace, 38, 128, 133

Lonsdale Homes, 111
Los Angeles, 119
Los Angeles Times, 30
Louisville, KY, 137, 157, 161, 172
Low income housing tax credit (LIHTC), 4,
   82, 177

MacArthur Foundation, 82
Major Reconstruction of Obsolete Public
   Housing (MROP), 63–65
Manchester Homes, 160, 172
Martin Luther King Towers, 160
Massey, Douglas, 109
McCoy, Mary Patillo, 85
McKay, Claude, 155
Meehan, Eugene, 46–47
Memphis, 4, 48, 71, 76, 112, 118, 142, 157,
   172, 183
Memphis Daily News, 41
Miami, 72, 112, 128
Milwaukee, 72, 160, 171
Minneapolis, 112, 128, 134–35, 139, 177
Minneapolis Public Housing Authority,
   177–78
Mission Main, 15, 160
mixed income developments, 10, 58, 77, 80, 82,
   88, 102, 125, 156–57, 164, 185, 188
mobility programs, 60, 77, 152
Modern Housing movement, 25–27, 35
modernist architecture, 5–6, 10, 33–34
Moving to Opportunity program (MTO),
   61–62, 77, 146, 152, 182–83, 189
Museum of Public Housing, 1–2

National Apartment Owners Association, 28
National Association of Home Builders
   (NAHB), 28
National Association of Real Estate Boards
   (NAREB), 28, 30
National Commission on Severely Distressed
   Public Housing (NCSDPH), 11, 22, 58,
   62–66, 77, 120, 179–81, 183–85, 187
National Housing Law Project (NHLP) 51–52,
   54, 58, 114
National Register of Historic Places, 100
"negro removal," 112, 121–22
neighborhood impacts, 20, 22, 82–86, 105,
   156–57, 159–74, 185, 188; on crime, 20,
   159, 175, 185; on property values, 20, 105,
   158–62; 164, 175, 183; of spillover investment, 15, 20, 157–64, 175, 181–82
neoliberalism, 5, 9–19, 178
Newark, 55–56, 139
Newark Housing Authority, 55–56

New Deal, 4–7, 23, 27; architecture and design of, 5, 26, 47; social welfare policy of, 5–6

Newman, Harvey, 162

New Orleans, 15, 18, 26, 48, 58, 73, 76, 89–99, 108–10, 112, 127, 161–62, 186; "big four" housing developments in, 94–99; C. J. Peete in, 89–90, 94–96, 99; design of public housing in, 89, 96–97; Desire neighborhood and housing projects in, 91, 93, 97, 99; D. W. Cooper in, 89–90, 94–96; Fischer Projects in, 91, 99; gentrification and revitalization in, 91–93, 97, 108; HOPE VI in, 93–94, 97; and Hurricane Katrina, 91, 93–99, 108–9; management of public housing in, 91–93, 109; Mayor Ray Nagin, 94, 96; resident opposition to demolition in, 76, 94–98, 109; and St. Bernard Parish, 89–90, 94–96. *See also* Housing Authority of New Orleans (HANO); Hurricane Katrina; Iberville; Lafitte

New Urbanism, 5, 66, 125, 156, 186, 188

New York City, 35, 47–48, 69, 71–72, 133

New York City Housing Authority (NYCHA), 13, 37, 42, 81, 133

Nixon, President Richard, 49

Oakland Housing Authority, 69

Obama, President Barak, 95, 187–88

Omaha, NE, 61, 112

one for one replacement, 3, 50, 57–59, 63, 65–66, 69, 93, 125, 187

"one strike and you're out," 13

"opportunity neighborhoods," 84, 123, 141

Outhwaite Homes, 26

Park Duvalle, 137, 157

Pelosi, Rep. Nancy, 95

Pfeiffer, Deirdre, 16

phased redevelopment, 84, 125, 176, 187

Philadelphia, 31, 47, 71, 118, 139, 160, 168, 170

Phoenix, 48, 72

Piper, Valerie, 159

Pittsburgh, 112, 128, 155–56, 160, 171–72, 187

Pittsburgh Housing Authority, 129, 155

Polikoff, Alexander, 5, 17

Ponce de Leon Courts, 167–68, 170

Popkin, Susan, 184

Portland, OR, 47, 74, 130, 139, 146, 148

Poverty and Race Research Action Council, 189

privatization, 12–15, 103, 178

progressive movement, 25–27, 35

Pruitt-Igoe, 34, 40–41, 49, 51

public housing authority (PHA), 11–13, 30–31, 36, 43, 52; de facto demolition by, 54, 58–59, 120; demolition by, 4, 48–51, 54, 58–59, 65, 68, 120, 180, 186; fiscal responsibilities of, 33–34, 37; management by, 39, 46; one for one replacement by, 50, 125; sale of public housing by, 14, 68; tenant selection by, 35–37, 47, 136

public housing: changing demographics of, 7–8, 36–37, 77–78, 90, 109, 113; as communism/socialism, 28–29, 40; concentration of, 17, 30–32, 77–79, 82, 90, 163; cost containment in, 32–35, 37, 68, 88, 185; design of, 5, 10, 26, 32–34, 47, 82, 89, 96–97, 100; high-rise developments of, 33–34, 40, 43, 78, 80, 82, 88, 183; income eligibility for, 35–36, 38, 77, 90; integration of, 37, 90; legislative battles over, 27–29; media coverage of, 40–41, 45; origins of, 6, 25–29; over-representation of blacks in, 7, 36, 40, 72, 74, 90, 98, 109, 111–12, 114, 118; resident management and activism in, 39, 43–45, 86–88, 184; resident opposition to demolition of, 17–19, 76, 86–88, 94–98, 105–9, 127–28, 190; sale of, 14, 68–69, 71–72; segregation within, 36, 60, 111; social welfare orientation of, 13, 36–38, 40, 77; siting difficulties of, 31–32, 78, 139; stigmatization of, 16, 157; success of, 24, 42–43, 47; tenant selection for, 13, 35–38, 47, 90, 100; waiting lists for, 24, 45, 47, 90, 177–78, 188

Public Works Administration (PWA), 26–27

Quality Housing and Work Responsibility Act (QHWRA), 68

racial segregation, 8, 46, 60, 73, 90–91, 113, 141

racial turnover, 16, 166, 168–73

Reagan, President Ronald, 9, 14, 50

real estate lobby, 28–29

Reichl, Alexander, 91

Reid, Sen. Harry, 95

relocation, 17–20, 84–86, 135–42; community and place attachment effects on, 127, 129–31, 142, 145, 148–49, 152; individual outcomes of, 19–20, 106, 121, 123–24, 145–54, 175–77; reactions to, 142–45; resegregation resulting from, 21, 84, 97, 106, 127, 139–42, 170, 175, 183; and social capital, 123, 129–31, 142, 145, 148–49, 152; and social support networks, 21, 121, 130, 147–48, 150, 152–53, 176, 190. *See also* displacement

Residents of Public Housing in Richmond Against Mass Evictions (RePHRAME), 18
return of residents to redevelopment site, 19–20, 106–7, 127, 136–38, 176
Richmond, VA, 18, 112, 139
Ripley Arnold Homes, 69
Robert Taylor Homes, 16, 40, 44, 75, 78, 80–81, 84–85, 87, 172
Rockford, IL, 59
Roosevelt, President Franklin D., 6–7, 26–27
"root shock", 130

Salt Lake City, 69–70
San Antonio, 118–19
San Diego Housing Commission, 14, 69
San Francisco, 113, 115, 128
San Francisco Human Rights Commission, 187
Schmoke, Kurt, 39
Schuylkill Falls, 168, 170
Scott Homes, 112
Scudder Homes, 56
Seattle, 128, 130, 148, 157, 168, 170
Section 8, 49, 59–61, 77, 93, 98, 106, 126, 131, 135, 139–40, 147, 178. See also Housing Choice Vouchers; vouchers
Section 18, 50, 53–57, 59–60
severely distressed public housing, 2, 11, 63–64, 120
Shuldiner, Joseph, 81, 87
slum clearance, 25–29, 32, 40, 50, 100, 121. See also "negro removal"; urban renewal
Smith, Neil, 14
Springview Apartments, 118–19
Stall, Susan, 44, 86
Stateway Gardens, 16, 79, 84, 138
St. Clair Village, 112, 129
Stockard, James, 42
St. Paul, MN, 47–48, 69, 139
St. Paul Housing Authority, 48
St. Petersburgh, FL, 69, 71–72
St. Thomas, 15, 73, 89–94, 97, 99, 161–62
Sullivan, Thomas, 84
Sumner Field, 128
superblocks, 10, 32, 130

Tampa, 72, 74, 158, 168, 170
Techwood Homes, 6, 26, 66, 100–104, 106, 108, 135, 161–62, 168, 170, 172
tenant screening, 12–13, 136–38, 176
Thatcher, Prime Minister Margaret, 9, 14
Theron B. Watkins, 56
Thompson v. HUD, 61`
Tinsley v. Kemp, 56–57

tracking studies, 128, 141–42, 145–49, 153
"troubled" PHAs, 52, 56, 64, 76, 81
Truman, President Harry S., 29
Tucson, 10, 20, 72, 133, 168
Turbov, Mindy, 159
Turner, Margery Austin, 155, 157

United Nations Human Rights Commission, 88, 122
United States Chamber of Commerce, 28
United States General Accounting Office (GAO), 76, 159
United States Housing Authority (USHA), 32–33, 47
United States Savings & Loan League, 28
University of Illinois-Chicago, 84
Urban Institute, 34, 140, 146–47, 160
urban renewal, 9, 29, 31, 37, 50, 100, 112, 121, 123, 129, 151, 155, 175–76. See also "negro removal"; slum clearance
Urban Revitalization Demonstration (URD), 58, 62, 65–66. See also HOPE VI
U.S. v. Certain Lands in the City of Louisville, 27

Vale, Larry, 35, 37
Velez v. Chester Housing Authority, 57–58
Venkatesh, Sudhir, 44
viability test, 66, 70, 75, 79–82
Vine Hill Homes, 168
Vitter, Sen. David, 95
vouchers, 4, 65, 67, 84, 93, 95, 97, 106, 138, 178. See also Housing Choice Vouchers; Section 8

Wagner, Sen. Robert F., 27–28
Walker v. HUD, 61
Washington, D.C., 7, 31, 53, 76, 112, 118, 139, 158, 161. See also District of Columbia Housing Authority
Waters, Rep. Maxine, 95
Wayne Minor, 52
Wentworth Homes, 16, 44, 86
Williams, Rhonda, 38, 44
Wilson, August, 155–56
Windsor Terrace, 160
Wood, Edith Elmer, 36
Woonsocket, R.I., 69–70
Works Progress Administration (WPA), 6
worst case housing needs, 177
Wyly, Elvin, 15, 158, 162

Yotaghan, Wardell, 86, 88, 123, 175

Zielenbach, Sean, 159